_2⁰⁰_

SIMPLY SENSATIONAL

presented by
TWIGS, The Auxiliary of
The Children's Medical Center
Dayton, Ohio

Proceeds from the sale of "Simply Sensational" will benefit The Children's Medical Center of Dayton, Ohio.

For additional copies, use the order forms at the back of the book or write:

Simply Sensational
The Children's Medical Center
One Children's Plaza
Dayton, Ohio 45404-1815

Price $14.95 plus $2.50 shipping and handling. Ohio residents add $.97 sales tax.

The Children's Medical Center
TWIGS
Dayton, Ohio

First Printing   November 1986   20,000

Library of Congress Catalog Card Number 86-51278

ISBN Number 0-9605370-2-3.

Printed By
Wimmer Brothers
Memphis, TN

CHAIRMEN

Mary Glesige   Gail Moore

Editor
Marianne Patton
Co-Editors
Dianne Ryan
JoAnn Graf

Typing/Proofreading Chairman
Pat Miles
Typing Co-Chairman
Anita Drummond

Finance Chairman
Linda von Mohr

Recording Secretary
Lynn Carr

Recipe Chairmen
Kathy McAlpine
Kathy O'Bryan

Publicity/Promotions
Ann Kingston
Dianne van Ruiten

Retail Marketing Chairman
Joanie Braisted
Retail Marketing Co-Chairman
Kathy McAlpine

Wholesale Marketing Chairman
Arlene Augusta

Cover Design By
Jayne McDougall
McDougall Marketing Services

Design and Layout
Judy Hayes

Wine Selections
Karen Davis
Arrow Wine

Recipe Testing Chairmen

Carol Barthel
Sandy Clark
Linda Lee
Bonnie Leuber
Annette Jordan
Ginny Ostberg

Karen Miltko
Bonnie Hoying
Paula Thalman
Linda Wegley
Lois Thomas
Mary Seaman

C. Paul Bissonnette
Vice President – Chief Development Officer
The Children's Medical Center

Dedication

The compilation of a cookbook requires the use of many talents, hours of work, and unending encouragement. Thanks to the many TWIGS in the Dayton area, who gave of their time and skills so generously, we were able to produce a quality cookbook. Our appreciation goes to every person who volunteered to help in creating "Simply Sensational". Last, but not forgotten, are the many husbands and families who became taste testers, cooks, and babysitters during our endeavor. We could not have done it without their unselfish support.

Forward

"Simply Sensational" is presented to you through the dedication and hard work of the Auxiliary of The Children's Medical Center of Dayton, Ohio. Our organization, known as TWIGS, has been actively involved in service projects and fund raising since our formation in 1965, for the express purpose of providing our community with the best pediatric facility possible.

These Terrific Women in Giving (TWIGS) are comprised of approximately 1100 members from the Miami Valley. Three years of planning, preparation, and thousands of hours have gone into the completion of "Simply Sensational".

From casual dining to elegant presentations, and from children's parties to wine complimented entrees and helpful hints, we're sure you will find our cookbook a special addition to your collection.

Over 3500 recipes were submitted for consideration. Each one was triple tested for quality and accuracy before the final selections were made. From beginning to end, you are sure to find recipes that will suit your culinary abilities from the easiest to the more challenging...recipes to help you present a simple elegance so much a part of today's life style. Written in clear and concise form, each section will be found easy to follow and suitable for all cooking talents.

Keeping in mind the many children we are supporting through our cookbook endeavor, we invite you to relax and enjoy the delights that "Simply Sensational" will bring you.

Table of Contents

APPETIZERS

APPETIZERS

Berry Tea

Very Refreshing!

2	quarts strongly brewed tea, cooled	1	(6-ounce) can frozen pink lemonade, thawed
1	(10-ounce) package frozen strawberries, thawed	¼	cup sugar

1. Mix ingredients together in large pitcher. Add ice cubes according to preference.

May only be prepared ahead 2 to 3 hours.

Bocci Ball

Great for brunch. A nice change from screwdrivers!

32	ounces orange juice	8	ounces club soda
10	ounces Amaretto		

1. Mix orange juice and Amaretto. Stir in club soda. Pour over ice in old fashioned cocktail glasses.

FOR A SINGLE SERVING

1	ounce Amaretto	enough club soda to fill
3	ounces orange juice	old fashioned glass

 APPETIZERS

Cape Codder

YIELDS: 1 serving

Serve over a tall glass of cracked ice.

1 cup cranberry juice	1 ounce vodka
2 teaspoons lime juice, freshly squeezed	(optional)

1. Combine ingredients and pour over ice.

Cool Breeze

YIELDS: 12 (6-ounce) drinks

1 dozen ice cubes	24 ounces orange juice
12 ounces light rum	24 ounces pineapple juice
6 ounces apricot brandy	1 ounce grenadine
3 ounces triple sec	

1. Blend the first four ingredients in a blender.

2. In a pitcher, combine orange and pineapple juice. Add blended mixture and grenadine. Stir. Serve immediately.

Molly Hogans

YIELDS: 12 servings

1 (6-ounce) can orange juice concentrate	½ cup sugar
1 (6-ounce) can lemonade concentrate	3 eggs
1 (6-ounce) can water	1 teaspoon vanilla
	1 pint gin
	7-Up or Sprite

1. Mix all ingredients in blender except gin and 7-Up. Add gin and blend. (Blender will be very full.)

2. Mix one shot or more of Molly Hogan mixture over ice in tall glass. Add 7-Up or Sprite to fill glass.

May be made ahead a few days. Add gin and 7-Up before serving.

Roseanna Banana Kabana

YIELDS: 1 (12-ounce) serving

Guests are sure to enjoy the name as well as the fun of this tasty dessert/drink.

½ medium ripe banana	1¼ ounces cream of coconut
1¼ cups crushed ice	1 ounce half and half
1½ ounces Kahlua	

1. Place banana and ice in electric blender. Add remaining ingredients and blend on slow speed 10 to 20 seconds or until rich and creamy.

2. May substitute a scoop of chocolate chip ice cream for half and half for a thicker, richer drink.

 APPETIZERS

Chocolate Mint Patty

YIELDS: 4 servings

Great for a refreshing dessert drink.

¼ cup white
Creme de Menthe
¼ cup Creme de Cocoa
1 quart chocolate
ice cream

mint sprigs, chocolate
curls, or crushed
peppermint candy

1. Measure liqueurs into blender. Add ice cream, a spoonful at a time, blending smooth after each addition.

2. Pour into glasses and serve immediately. Garnish with mint sprigs, chocolate curls, or crushed peppermint candy.

Strawberry Cream Daiquiri

YIELDS: 5 cups

Pretty to serve as a dessert too!

10 ounces frozen
strawberries
2 ounces frozen limeade
concentrate
4 ounces frozen lemonade
concentrate

1½ ounces grenadine
syrup
5 ounces rum
1 pint vanilla ice cream
fresh strawberries

1. Combine strawberries, limeade, lemonade, grenadine, and rum in blender. Gradually add ice cream. Blend until smooth and thick. Serve garnished with a fresh strawberry perched on rim of glass.

Also good with raspberries. Freeze leftovers.

Tropical Smash

YIELDS: 20 servings

Imagine yourself in the Bahamas and enjoy!

1 (46-ounce) can pineapple juice	1 (12-ounce) can cream of coconut
1 (12-ounce) can frozen lemonade concentrate	2 cups light rum or vodka 7-Up

1. In a large freezer container, mix pineapple juice, lemonade, and cream of coconut. Add rum.

2. Cover and store in freezer, stirring occasionally, until it reaches "slush" consistency.

3. Serve ½ glass of slush with up to ½ glass 7-Up. Stir to mix. May also be served straight from the freezer.

Apricot Mist Punch

YIELDS: 7 quarts

Enjoyable with or without alcohol added.

46 ounces apricot nectar	4 ounces lemon juice
46 ounces pineapple juice	3 quarts Vernor's ginger ale
18 ounces frozen limeade concentrate	1 fifth vodka or gin (optional)

1. Combine all juices and pour over ice ring in a punch bowl. Add ginger ale and vodka or gin just before serving. Any leftover may be frozen.

Juices may be mixed one day ahead. Ice ring can be made with lemonade.

# APPETIZERS

Christmas Red Punch

An ice ring with orange slices is an attractive addition.

2   (6-ounce) cans frozen
    lemonade, prepared
    according to directions
1   quart cranberry juice
1   quart ginger ale

1   (6-ounce) can frozen
    orange juice, undiluted
    orange slices to float

1.   Combine all ingredients and stir well.

Gala Champagne Punch

YIELDS: 6-8 servings

Traditionally served at showers and weddings.

1   bottle champagne
1   liter ginger ale
1   bottle Sauterne wine

ice or ice ring
whole strawberries

1.   Combine the above ingredients in a punch bowl. Strawberries may be used in the ice ring or as a garnish.

Golden Gin Punch

YIELDS: 3 quarts

Garnish with orange slices and maraschino cherries for an elegant look.

1   cup gin
1   cup Galliano
1   (6-ounce) can lemonade
    concentrate

1   (32-ounce) club soda,
    chilled
1   (32-ounce) ginger ale,
    chilled

1.   Combine first 3 ingredients. Chill. When ready to serve, combine chilled mixture, club soda, and ginger ale in punch bowl with an ice ring.

Watermelon Wine Cooler

YIELDS: 15 servings

Consider this for your summertime – funtime entertaining!

1 oval watermelon	1 pint raspberries - fresh
1 bottle berry wine	is best or 1 (10-ounce)
1 quart club soda	package frozen, thawed,
⅓ fifth gin	and undrained
	lemon or lime slices

1. Slice off top section of watermelon, making an oval opening. Scoop out fruit using a melon baller or spoon. Cut into balls or chunks. Chill watermelon shell.

2. In a large pitcher or container, combine wine, club soda, and gin. Gently stir in lemon or lime slices, raspberries, and watermelon. Chill 4 to 6 hours. Pour into watermelon shell. Serve.

Must be made 4 to 6 hours ahead.

White Grape Punch

YIELDS: 15 servings

A non-alcoholic, fun punch.

2 quarts white grape juice, chilled	1 quart ginger ale or 7-Up
½ (6-ounce) can frozen lemonade concentrate	1 quart pineapple sherbert
2 cups water	

1. Combine grape juice, lemonade, water, and ginger ale in punch bowl. Float 1 quart pineapple sherbert on top. Serve immediately.

# APPETIZERS

Apple Wine

YIELDS: 48 ounces

A warming beverage that will add to the enjoyment of a crisp autumn day.

3 cups apple juice	2 tablespoons fresh lemon
¼ cup sugar	juice
3 inch cinnamon stick	lemon peel
6 cloves	1 bottle Rhine wine

1. Combine apple juice, sugar, and spices in pan. Bring to a boil. Simmer 15 minutes.

2. Strain out spices. Add lemon juice, peel, and wine. Heat, do not boil. Serve hot.

Store any leftover in refrigerator and reheat before serving. Great with cheese crackers or anything salty and crunchy.

Cider Punch

YIELDS: 18 (4-ounce) servings

Both children and adults will enjoy this fall treat.

1 gallon apple cider	2 teaspoons ground cinnamon
1 (6-ounce) frozen lemonade concentrate	¼ teaspoon ground nutmeg orange slices or
1 (6-ounce) frozen orange juice concentrate	cinnamon sticks
½ cup brown sugar, packed	1 tablespoon allspice
1 tablespoon ground cloves	4 oranges (optional) whole cloves (optional)

1. Simmer ingredients in a large pan over medium heat. Garnish cups with orange slice or cinnamon stick.

2. To keep punch warm, and as a lovely garnish, stud 4 oranges all over with whole cloves. Bake in a preheated 350 degree oven for 45 minutes. Float in punch bowl.

May be prepared one day ahead.

Creamy Buttered Rum

YIELDS: 24 servings

A nice addition to your tree-trimming party.

1 cup butter or margarine, softened	1 teaspoon ground cinnamon
½ cup brown sugar, packed	1 pint vanilla ice cream, softened
½ cup powdered sugar, sifted	rum or brandy (optional)
1 teaspoon ground nutmeg	boiling water
	whipped cream
	cinnamon sticks

1. Cream together butter, brown sugar, powdered sugar, nutmeg, and cinnamon with electric mixer.

2. Blend with softened ice cream. Turn into a 4 cup freezer container. Seal and freeze overnight. Will not freeze solid.

3. To serve, spoon 2 to 4 tablespoons ice cream mixture into each cup. Add 3 tablespoons rum and ½ cup boiling water to each cup. Stir well. Garnish with whipped cream and a cinnamon stick.

Must be made ahead one day and frozen.

Hot Buttered Pineapple

YIELDS: 18 servings

Try this served with appetizers before your holiday meal.

1 (46-ounce) can unsweetened pineapple juice	1 teaspoon ground nutmeg
	1 bottle dry white wine
1 (6-ounce) can frozen limeade concentrate	cinnamon sticks
	pats of butter

1. Place pineapple juice, limeade, and nutmeg in large saucepan. Bring just to boil. Reduce heat immediately and add wine. Heat through, but do not boil. Pour into cups. Add a cinnamon stick to each and float a small pat of butter on top of each cup.

Make ahead 2 to 3 hours. Add wine just before guests arrive.

Caviar Supreme

For an incredible taste and elegant appetizer.

1½ packages unflavored gelatin	¼ cup cold water

1. Soften gelatin in ¼ cup cold water and set cup in warm water to liquify.

FIRST LAYER

4 hard cooked eggs, finely chopped	2 green onions, finely chopped
½ cup Hellmann's mayonnaise	¾ teaspoon salt
¼ cup parsley, finely chopped	⅛ teaspoon Tabasco sauce

1. Combine all ingredients. Mix thoroughly. Set aside.

SECOND LAYER

1 medium avocado, pureed	2 tablespoons lemon juice
1 medium avocado, chopped	2 tablespoons Hellmann's mayonnaise
2 green onions, finely chopped	½ teaspoon salt

1. Mix all ingredients. Set aside.

THIRD LAYER

1 cup sour cream	¼ cup red or green onion, minced

1. Mix all ingredients. Set aside.

continued

Caviar Supreme *continued*

FOURTH LAYER
1   (3½-ounce) jar red
     or black caviar

1. Divide the gelatin into thirds, mixing one part through each of the first 3 layer mixtures.

2. Grease bottom and sides of an 8 inch springform pan. Or line bottom and sides of a 1 quart souffle dish with smooth foil, extending 4 inches above the rim. Spray lightly with Pam. Spread egg mixture into prepared dish. Smooth top. Wipe side of dish clean above layer. Gently spread avocado mixture over egg layer. Smooth top and wipe foil clean above layer. Spread sour cream mixture over avocado layer and smooth top. Cover tightly with plastic wrap for 24 hours, refrigerate.

3. To serve, lift out of dish by foil "handles" and transfer with large spatula onto serving platter. Spread caviar over top. Serve with party pumpernickle slices.

Must be prepared 1 day ahead.

Helpful Hints: Heat lemons well before using; there will be twice the amount of juice.

Cheese Stuffed Baguettes

YIELDS: 25 slices

Eye catching.

1   (20-inch) loaf French Baguette or 2 mini Baquettes (the thinner the better)
½   cup Hellmann's mayonnaise
½   cup fresh parsley, finely chopped

2   (8-ounce) packages cream cheese, softened
1   package Italian salad dressing mix
1   jar pimentos, drained and chopped

1. Cut loaf of bread into 4 equal parts to make it easier to work with. Hollow out loaf so that walls are about 1 inch thick.

2. Spread interior walls with ¼ cup of mayonnaise. Sprinkle in parsley to coat walls.

3. Combine all remaining ingredients. Divide into 4 parts and pack into bread. Try not to disturb the parsley spread. Cover lightly and refrigerate 4-5 hours. Then slice into ¾ inch slices.

Note: Parsley should form a little ring within the loaf.

May be prepared 1 day ahead. Also freezes well up to 1 month.

Helpful Hints: The usual proportions for salad dressing is 1 part vinegar or lemon juice to 2-3 parts oil, depending on taste.

Chicken Bites with International Sauce

YIELDS: 20 servings

Pop'em in your mouth and enjoy!

4	whole chicken breasts	2	bay leaves
2	cups water	2	teaspoons Accent
2	onions, sliced	1½	teaspoons salt
2	celery tops		

1. Put chicken breasts in a kettle with a tight fitting lid. Add water and remaining ingredients. Cover. Bring to a boil. Reduce heat and simmer until tender.

2. Remove skin from chicken and discard. Remove meat from bones in large pieces. Refrigerate. When cool, cut chicken into bite size pieces.

SAUCE

1	cup sour cream	¼	teaspoon Tabasco sauce
½	cup mayonnaise	1	teaspoon curry powder
¼	cup chili sauce	2	tablespoons chutney, finely minced
2	tablespoons horseradish, drained	4	tablespoons capers
1	tablespoon Worcestershire sauce	2	tablespoons parsley, chopped
2	tablespoons lemon juice		

1. Combine all ingredients and pour over chicken pieces. Refrigerate several hours. To serve, place in serving dish and sprinkle with additional parsley and capers.

Salmon Souffle' Roll

YIELDS: 20-24 slices

An elegant appetizer to premier at your most impressive dinner party.

SPONGE ROLL

⅓ cup butter or margarine	6 egg yolks
⅔ cup all purpose flour	6 egg whites
1¾ cups milk	dash salt

1. Line a 17 x 12 x 2 inch baking pan with foil; butter and flour the foil.

2. In saucepan, melt the ⅓ cup butter or margarine; blend in ⅓ cup of flour. Add milk, all at once, cook and stir until thickened and bubbly. Remove from heat. Beat in egg yolks, one at a time, beating well after each; set aside. In large mixing bowl, beat egg whites until stiff peaks form. Fold ¼ of egg whites into sauce. Sift ½ of remaining flour and salt over mixture; fold in. Fold in ½ remaining egg whites. Repeat with remaining flour and egg whites.

3. Spread batter evenly in prepared pan. Bake in a preheated 350 degree oven for 25-30 minutes. Turn out onto lightly floured kitchen towel. Starting at narrow end, immediately roll up jelly roll style. Cool.

SALMON SANDWICH ROLL (FILLING)

1 (15½-ounce) can salmon, drained, flaked and bones removed	1 tablespoon fresh parsley, snipped
2 (8-ounce) packages Neufchatel cheese, softened	1½ teaspoons fresh dill, snipped, (or ½ teaspoon dried dill weed)
2 tablespoons lemon juice	⅓ cup walnuts, finely chopped

1. In mixing bowl, combine salmon, 6 ounces of the Neufchatel cheese, the lemon juice, parsley, and dill. Beat with spoon until smooth. Stir in walnuts.

2. Unroll sponge roll. Spread salmon mixture over roll. Quarter roll lengthwise. Starting at narrow end, roll up one quarter, jelly roll style. Place roll at one end of the second quarter and roll up. Repeat with remaining quarters to make an ever widening pin wheel. Place roll, cut side down, on a serving platter.

continued

Salmon Souffle' Roll *continued*

FROSTING

remaining Neufchatel cheese	walnut halves (optional)
	pimento (optional)
1/3 cup mayonnaise	lemon slices (optional)
milk	

1. In bowl, beat cheese with mayonnaise until fluffy. Add milk, if necessary, to make of spreading consistency.

2. Frost top and sides of roll with cheese and mayonnaise mixture. Cover loosely and chill thoroughly.

3. At serving time, arrange walnut halves and fresh dill on sides of salmon roll. Garnish top with pimento and lemon slices. Cut into small wedges to serve.

Prosciutto Sandwich Rounds

YIELDS: 10 sandwiches

Prosciutto is a tasty meat most often found in the deli section.

1/4	pound prosciutto, cut into thin strips		salt to taste
		1	package party pumpernickel
1/2	cup unsalted butter, cold		pepper, coarsely ground
2	teaspoons lemon juice		parsley, finely chopped (optional)

1. Combine the prosciutto, butter, and lemon juice in a blender or a food processor fitted with the metal blade. Process using on/off motion, scraping down the sides of the work bowl until the prosciutto is finely chopped and evenly incorporated into the butter. Add salt to taste and process just until it is incorporated.

2. Using a round biscuit cutter, cut each slice of pumpernickel into a 2 inch round.

3. Spread one round of the bread with about 1 tablespoon of the prosciutto mixture and smooth to the edge of the bread. Sprinkle with pepper. Top with a second round of bread and press gently. Garnish the sides with parsley, if desired.

May be prepared early in the day.

Sensational Snow Peas

YIELDS: 100 snow peas

A pastry tube eases the preparation of the great number of snow peas you'll need to stuff—for these will disappear fast.

100 snow peas

1. Place snow peas in large bowl. Cover with boiling water. Let stand 1 minute. Drain peas and immediately place in ice water. Drain well. Split peas open on seam.

FILLING

2 (8-ounce) packages cream cheese, softened	1 teaspoon dry mustard
¼ cup Parmesan cheese, grated	1 teaspoon Worcestershire sauce
3 tablespoons catsup	½ teaspoon salt
1½ teaspoons dried dill weed	½ teaspoon white pepper, freshly ground

1. Combine all ingredients and mix well.

2. Using pastry tube with ¼ to ⅛ inch writing tip, pipe filling into center of each pea pod. Chill until ready to serve.

Filling may be prepared up to 1 week ahead. Stuff peas 1 day ahead and refrigerate.

Helpful Hints: Leave the juice in the jar after pickles are all gone. Place small pieces of carrots, celery, cauliflower, broccoli or other veggies in jar to marinate.

Un-Mexican Haystack

YIELDS: 16-20

A surprise of ham and chopped walnuts make this a uniquely attractive presentation.

2 **(8-ounce) packages cream cheese, softened**	1 **dash Tabasco sauce salt and pepper to taste**
3 **tablespoons mayonnaise**	2 **cups ham, shredded**
8 **green onions, chopped**	12 **medium size flour tortillas**
1 **green pepper, chopped**	½ **cup walnuts, chopped**
1 **tablespoon Worcestershire sauce**	**fresh parsley, chopped**
1 **teaspoon garlic powder**	

1. In a large mixing bowl or food processor, combine cream cheese, mayonnaise, onions, green pepper, Worcestershire sauce, garlic powder, Tabasco sauce, salt, and pepper. Mix well. Stir in ham.

2. Place a tortilla on a large round plate. Spread a thin layer of ham mixture over tortilla. Repeat layers, ending with ham mixture on top of entire stack. Sprinkle chopped nuts and chopped parsley on the top layer of the stack.

3. Cover and refrigerate at least 1 hour.

4. Cut into wedges or small cubes and serve with a decorative toothpick inserted in each piece.

May be prepared one day ahead and refrigerated.

Vegetable Pizza

YIELDS: 36-40 pieces

This zany and unique pizza is a fresh idea to add to your favorite appetizers.

2 packages crescent
   rolls
1 cup Miracle Whip
1 (8-ounce) package cream
   cheese, softened
1 teaspoon parsley,
   finely chopped
½ teaspoon garlic salt
1 teaspoon Accent
1 tablespoon onion,
   finely chopped

1 teaspoon Lawry's
   seasoned salt
2 cups Cheddar or Mozzarella
   cheese, shredded
2 cups fresh vegetables,
   chopped (onions, green
   peppers, carrots,
   radishes, broccoli,
   olives)

1. Pat rolls flat on slightly greased cookie sheet or pizza pan. Bake in a preheated 350 degree oven for 8-10 minutes until golden brown.

2. Combine Miracle Whip, cream cheese, and seasonings in a small bowl and blend until creamy.

3. Spread this mixture on cooled crust. Sprinkle shredded cheese over this. Arrange vegetables on the top. Chill. Cut into bite size pieces.

May be prepared early in the day and refrigerated.

Bagel Chips

YIELDS: 2 dozen

Watch these chips disappear quickly. These are very much like the ones sold in gourmet shops.

1 package frozen bagels (6), plain	6 tablespoons oil garlic salt

1. Slice partially frozen bagels in rings about ¼ inch thick. Brush lightly with oil and sprinkle with garlic salt. Place on ungreased baking sheet.

2. Bake in a preheated 400 degree oven for approximately 10 minutes or until lightly browned; turning after the first 5 minutes. Cool on paper towels.

3. Store in an airtight container. Serve with Sundried Tomato Cheese Spread.

Herb Crunch

YIELDS: 4-6 cups

Great for TV snacks or at a party. Men love this!

1 (16-ounce) box oyster crackers	1 teaspoon dill weed
½ teaspoon lemon pepper	1 package Hidden Valley Ranch dressing mix
½ teaspoon garlic salt	½ cup oil

1. Toss all ingredients together.

2. Spread on cookie sheet and bake in a preheated 250 degree oven for 15-20 minutes.

May be prepared ahead 1 week and stored in airtight container.

Herb Nuts

YIELDS: 4 cups

A good snack variation.

3   tablespoons butter, melted
3   tablespoons Worcestershire sauce
1   teaspoon salt
1   teaspoon cinnamon

¼   teaspoon garlic powder
¼   teaspoon cayenne pepper
    dash Tabasco sauce
1   pound pecan halves

1. Mix all ingredients until pecans are coated. Place nuts on cookie sheet. Bake in a preheated 300 degree oven for 20-25 minutes, stirring frequently.

Spiced Mixed Nuts

YIELDS: 3½ cups

Watch these disappear by the handful.

1   egg white, slightly beaten
1   teaspoon water
1   (8-ounce) jar or 1¾ cups dry roasted peanuts
½   cup unblanched whole almonds

½   cup walnut halves
¾   cup sugar
1   tablespoon pumpkin pie spice
¾   teaspoon salt

1. Combine egg white and water. Add nuts; toss to coat.

2. Combine sugar, spice, and salt. Add to nuts; toss to coat well.

3. Place in single layer on lightly greased baking sheet. Bake in a preheated 300 degree oven for 20-25 minutes. Remove and cool on wax paper. Break up large clusters.

May be prepared 1 week in advance.

Bacon and Tomato Spread

YIELDS: 1¼ cups

This is best in summer when tomatoes are fresh.

1 (8-ounce) package cream cheese, softened
½ teaspoon celery salt
6 slices bacon, cooked and crumbled

1 large, fresh tomato, peeled, seeded, drained, finely chopped
¼ cup green pepper, chopped parsley to garnish

1. Combine cream cheese and celery salt. Stir in bacon, tomato, and green pepper. Cover and chill.

2. Serve in large hollowed out tomato. Spread on toast points or melba rounds. Garnish with parsley.

Black Pepper Dip

YIELDS: 2½ cups

A great dip for veggies that is different.

¼ cup water
1½ teaspoons lemon juice
2 dashes Tabasco sauce
½ teaspoon Worcestershire sauce
½ teaspoon A-1 steak sauce
1 teaspoon dry mustard
1 teaspoon sugar

1 teaspoon salt
1 teaspoon garlic, dried and granulated
¼ cup Parmesan cheese
4 tablespoons black pepper, freshly crushed
2 cups Hellmann's mayonnaise

1. Mix all ingredients. Cover and refrigerate.

May be prepared ahead.

Caponata

YIELDS: 3½ cups

A Mideastern dip that utilizes an eggplant as its shell.

1	large eggplant	1	tablespoon red wine vinegar
1	tablespoon lemon juice	2	large tomatoes, peeled, seeded, and chopped
¼	cup olive or vegetable oil	2	teaspoons sugar
1	green pepper, seeded and diced	½	teaspoon basil
2	celery stalks, diced	½	teaspoon salt
1	medium onion, diced	¼	teaspoon cayenne pepper
1	carrot, finely chopped	2	tablespoons parsley, chopped
1	clove garlic, crushed		Pita bread
2	tablespoons tomato paste		

1. Cut eggplant in half lengthwise. Use a spoon to scoop out pulp, leaving a ½ inch thick shell. Reserve pulp. Use hollowed shell for container. Brush inside of eggplant shell with lemon juice.

2. In a large skillet, heat oil. Add eggplant and saute until soft, 3 to 4 minutes. Add remaining ingredients. Cook over medium heat, stirring occasionally, for about 15 to 20 minutes, until vegetables are all tender. Mixture should be thick but not dry. Spoon mixture into eggplant shell. Serve warm or cold with small wedges of Pita bread.

Carrot Dip

YIELDS: 2½ cups

You start with carrots as a base but add a variety of vegetables to dip in and indulge.

1   (8-ounce) package cream
    cheese, softened
1   carrot, shredded
2   tablespoons onion,
    finely minced

½   cup pecans, chopped
1   teaspoon prepared mustard
⅓   cup mayonnaise

1.   Blend together the first five ingredients with a fork. Add mayonnaise, a little at a time, to smooth. Serve with crackers or fresh vegetables.

May be prepared 2 days ahead.

Creamy Fruit Spread

YIELDS: 3½ cups

A nice choice to serve at a wine tasting.

2   (8-ounce) packages cream
    cheese, softened
¼   cup butter, softened
1   cup powdered sugar,
    sifted
2   tablespoons orange juice

1   tablespoon orange rind,
    grated
½   teaspoon vanilla
1   cup walnuts or pecans,
    finely chopped
1   orange rind, finely grated

1.   Beat first six ingredients until smooth. Chill for three hours or longer.

2.   Form into a ball. Garnish with nuts and orange rind. Serve with apple and pear slices, ginger snaps, vanilla wafers, or muffins.

Must be prepared early in the day.

Curried Egg Mold

YIELDS: 5 cups

2	envelopes unflavored gelatin
½	cup cold water
2	chicken bouillon cubes
1	cup boiling water
1	tablespoon curry
2	tablespoons lemon juice
1¼	cups mayonnaise

2	tablespoons Worcestershire sauce
1	tablespoon Tabasco sauce
2	teaspoons pepper (or less)
8	hard boiled eggs, finely chopped

1. Dissolve gelatin in ½ cup cold water.

2. Dissolve bouillon cubes in 1 cup boiling water. Add gelatin to bouillon. Allow mixture to cool. Add remaining ingredients to cooled bouillon mixture. Place this mixture in blender and blend until smooth.

3. Pour into oiled 5 cup mold and chill. Remove from mold and serve with crackers.

Curry and Chutney Cheese Spread

YIELDS: 10 servings

A unique spread best served on wheat or rye crackers.

6	ounces cream cheese
8	ounces sharp Cheddar cheese spread
3	tablespoons sherry
½	teaspoon curry

¼	teaspoon salt
	MSG to taste
10	ounces chutney
¼	cup scallions, minced
1	cup green onions, chopped

1. Mix all ingredients except chutney, scallions and green onions with an electric beater. Spread in a shallow dish and chill until firm.

2. Before serving spread chopped chutney over cheese mixture and cover with green onions.

May be prepared 1 to 2 days ahead.

Deviled Pate'

YIELDS: 2 cups

Using prepared spreads saves preparation time.

1 (4½-ounce) can deviled ham	1 (8-ounce) package cream cheese, softened
4½ ounces liverwurst (Braunschweiger)	few dashes Tabasco sauce

1. Mix all ingredients together. Refrigerate overnight for flavors to blend. Serve with crackers.

Moroccan Dip

YIELDS: 1½ cups

This unusual Mideastern spread is easily made in the blender.

1 (15-ounce) can garbanzo beans, drained	1 teaspoon Worcestershire sauce
2 tablespoons vegetable oil	2 tablespoons sesame seeds, untoasted
1 tablespoon lemon juice	2 tablespoons parsley, chopped
2 tablespoons onion, chopped	Pita bread
½ teaspoon salt	black olives for garnish

1. In blender, combine beans, oil, lemon juice, and onion. Process until smooth. Add salt, Worcestershire sauce, and sesame seeds. Process briefly.

2. Spoon into serving dish. Garnish with parsley and slices of black olives. Serve with wedges of Pita bread.

May be made 2 to 3 days ahead.

 APPETIZERS

Open House Cheese Spread

YIELDS: 2½ cups

Surround with grape clusters and serve with crisp crackers.

- 2 (8-ounce) packages cream cheese, softened
- 3 tablespoons brandy
- ⅓ cup chutney, finely chopped
- ¼ cup green onions, finely chopped
- ¼ cup toasted almonds, chopped
- ¼ teaspoon curry powder
- 1 cup green grapes, halved and seeded
  green onion tops to garnish
  grape clusters

1. In large bowl, mix the first six ingredients until well blended. Chill. When firm, mound in oval shape on a serving tray. Cheese may be refrigerated for up to two days at this point.

2. Cover surface with grape halves, cut side down, to resemble a pineapple. Insert green onion tops at top of cheese mound.

Cheese may be prepared up to 2 days ahead.

Luscious Fruit Dip

YIELDS: 6 cups

A wonderful touch with the abundance of fresh fruits so easily found in summer or at holiday time.

- 1 (8-ounce package) cream cheese
- 1 cup Cool Whip
- ¾ cup brown sugar
- ⅓ cup Kahlua or Amaretto
- 1 cup sour cream
- ½ cup unsalted peanuts, chopped (optional)

1. Soften cream cheese. Blend in all ingredients. Serve as a dip for fresh fruit.

May be prepared ahead 1 to 2 days.

Peanut Butter Dip

YIELDS: 1 cup

A delight for your peanut butter lover.

1 mango, hollowed out	¼ cup lemon juice
½ cup crunchy peanut butter	2 tablespoons catsup
3 tablespoons brown sugar	1 teaspoon soy sauce
½ teaspoon Tabasco sauce	

1. Combine all ingredients. Serve in a hollowed out mango cup with crudites.

May be prepared up to 1 week ahead.

Rumaki Pate'

YIELDS: 1½ cups

Serve in a crockery dish alongside a basket of your favorite crackers.

4 slices bacon, diced	1 tablespoon white vinegar
½ pound chicken livers	½ teaspoon Dijon mustard
1 green onion, chopped	3 tablespoons butter, melted
1 tablespoon soy sauce	1 (6-ounce) can water chestnuts, drained and finely chopped
⅛ teaspoon garlic salt	

1. In medium skillet, cook bacon until most of fat is removed, but bacon is still soft.

2. Pat chicken livers dry with paper towel. Add livers and onions to bacon. Saute over low heat until livers are lightly browned. Drain on paper towels.

3. In blender, combine cooked bacon, sauteed livers and onions, soy sauce, garlic salt, vinegar, mustard, and butter. Blend 3-10 seconds until well mixed, but not entirely smooth. Spoon into small crock or bowl. Stir in water chestnuts. Refrigerate until well chilled. Serve with crackers.

Must be prepared a few hours ahead to chill.

Salsa Sensational

YIELDS: 3 cups

1 (8-ounce) can pitted
  ripe olives, chopped
3-4 small or average
  tomatoes, chopped
1 bunch green onions,
  slice the tender area
  as thin as possible

1 can green chilies,
  chopped
1 cup red wine vinegar
  and oil salad dressing
  (Marzetti's or Good
  Seasons)

1. Mix all ingredients and marinate several hours or overnight to blend flavors. Serve with Doritos or Fritos.

Variation: Use 1 cup salad olives rather than black olives and add 3 small canned banana peppers, chopped.

Must be prepared ahead to marinate.

Pepperoni Dip

YIELDS: 1 pint

1 pint sour cream
½ pound pepperoni,
  finely chopped

1 round loaf of bread
  or crackers

1. Mix sour cream and pepperoni well. Store covered in refrigerator for two days before serving. This allows the sour cream to absorb the flavor and the pepperoni to soften.

2. Serve in a hollowed out loaf of bread with pieces of bread for dunking or with crackers.

Must be prepared 2 days ahead.

Savory Shrimp Mold

YIELDS: 4-5 cups

This makes a pretty presentation at any party.

1	can tomato soup	1	cup celery, diced
1	envelope Knox gelatin	½	cup onion, diced
¼	cup cold water	1	pound shrimp, cooked
1	(8-ounce) package cream		and diced
	cheese, softened	1	cup mayonnaise

1. Heat soup to boiling.

2. Dissolve gelatin in cold water. Add soup to gelatin mixture. Add softened cream cheese and blend. Add remaining ingredients. Pour into greased 4-5 cup mold and chill overnight. Serve with crackers.

Must be prepared ahead 1 day.

Snappy Cheese-Pepper Pie

YIELDS: 12-15 servings

An appetizer to get those taste buds flowing!

1	(8-ounce) jar Vlasic hot or banana pepper rings, sliced and well drained	1	(8-ounce) package mild Cheddar cheese, shredded
		4	tablespoons milk
1	(8-ounce) package Monterey Jack cheese, shredded	4	tablespoons flour
		3	eggs

1. Place peppers in bottom of a pie plate. Sprinkle cheeses over peppers.

2. Combine milk, flour, and eggs and pour over cheese. Bake in a preheated 350 degree oven for 30 minutes. Serve with crackers.

May be prepared early in the day.

 APPETIZERS

Spicy Italian Gouda Spread

YIELDS: 1¼ cups

Serve with crispy crackers, crunchy fall apples, and your favorite carafe of wine.

1 (8-ounce) Gouda cheese, softened, and in wax shell	½ cup sour cream 1 tablespoon Italian salad dressing mix

1. Cut circle from top of Gouda, reserving any cheese cut off. Hollow out cheese, leaving ¼ inch shell of cheese on all sides; set aside.

2. In small mixing bowl, combine cheese from inside of shell and from top with sour cream and dry salad dressing mix. Beat with electric mixer until well blended and fairly smooth.

3. Spoon cheese mixture into cheese shell. Cover and chill.

May be prepared 3 days ahead. Store in airtight container.

Sundried Tomato Spread

YIELDS: 1½ cups

Different!

1 (8-ounce) package cream cheese, softened 4 green onions, chopped	½ cup Genovesi dried tomatoes, chopped

1. Place cream cheese, onions, and tomatoes in a food processor and process with on/off turns, scraping down side of the work bowl as necessary until smooth and well blended.

Serving suggestions: Serve as an appetizer spread surrounded by crackers, bread, English muffins, or crudities. Use as a stuffing for celery, artichoke bottoms, and other vegetables.

Tabouli

YIELDS: 6 cups

Appealing served with large Fritos or Tostado chips.

3 cups boiling water
1½ cups Bulgur wheat, washed and drained (purchase in health food store)
1 medium onion, chopped
2 large tomatoes, diced
1 large green pepper, chopped
½ cup olive oil
½ cup white wine vinegar
1 teaspoon salt
½ teaspoon sugar
2 tablespoons lemon juice
½ cup fresh parsley, finely chopped
½ teaspoon garlic powder
½ teaspoon dried basil
½ teaspoon dried tarragon
3 tablespoons fresh mint, finely chopped, or
3 teaspoons dried mint, crumbled

1. Pour water over wheat in large bowl and let stand for 2-3 hours or until water is absorbed. Mix onion, tomatoes, peppers, and parsley into the wheat.

2. Mix remaining nine ingredients in jar and shake well. Pour over wheat mixture and toss. Cover and refrigerate 4-6 hours or overnight to allow flavors to blend. Keeps well for 2-3 days.

 **APPETIZERS**

Taste of Autumn

YIELDS: 1²/₃ cups

A nice kick-off to the football season.

- 1 (8-ounce) package cream cheese, softened
- ½ cup Miracle Whip salad dressing
- 1 teaspoon lemon juice
- ½ cup (2-ounces) Cheddar cheese, shredded
- ¼ cup celery, finely chopped
- ½ cup apples, unpeeled and finely chopped

1. Combine cream cheese, salad dressing, and lemon juice; mixing until well blended. Add cheese, celery, and apples. Mix well. Chill and serve with apple wedges, crackers, and party rye bread.

Make ahead only 2 hours or apples will turn brown.

Sausage Philly

YIELDS: 20 balls

Make plenty of these. They'll go fast!

- ¾ pound Jimmy Dean sausage cooked, crumbled, and drained
- 1 (8-ounce) package cream cheese, softened
- 1 tablespoon stuffed green olives, drained and chopped
- 1 tablespoon green onions, finely chopped
- ½ cup Parmesan cheese
- ½ teaspoon salt

1. Mix sausage with cream cheese. Add chopped olives, onions, and salt. Form into small balls and roll in Parmesan cheese. Serve cold or at room temperature on toothpicks.

May be prepared 2 days ahead and refrigerated.

Bacon Pinwheels

An easy appetizer that disappears fast.

2	(8-ounce) tubes crescent rolls	1	pound bacon
1	(8-ounce) carton sour cream	⅛	teaspoon garlic salt

1. Unroll crescent rolls into 2-piece rectangles. Pinch perforated sections together. Flatten slightly with rolling pin. Spread sour cream on rectangular sections. Fry bacon and crumble over sour cream. Sprinkle sparingly with garlic salt.

2. Roll up each rectangle and slice into 6 sections. Place on ungreased cookie sheet and bake in a preheated 350 degree oven for 9-11 minutes until golden. Serve at once.

May be frozen and reheated.

Bacon Wrap-Ups

Quick, easy and tasty!

Wrap a half slice of bacon around any of the following, securing with a toothpick. Broil until bacon is crisp or bake in a preheated 350 degree oven until crisp.

pineapple chunks	artichoke hearts
canned peach chunks	stuffed olives
cooked chicken livers	pitted prunes or dates
Brazil nuts	pickle chunks
raw scallops	pickled onions
raw or canned oysters	cooked shrimp
luncheon meat cubes	watermelon rind
Feta cheese	canned mushrooms
Vienna sausages	hot dog chunks
water chestnuts	

VARIATIONS

1. Marinate water chestnuts in soy sauce 30 minutes. Roll each chestnut in sugar, then wrap in bacon, and secure with toothpick. Place on broiler rack, sprinkle with brown sugar. Bake in a preheated 400 degree oven for 20 minutes. Drain on paper towel. Best made early in the day and reheated same night in a preheated 350 degree oven for 6-7 minutes.

2. Marinate water chestnuts in ½ cup liquid from can and ½ cup white vinegar for 8 hours or overnight. Precook bacon half done. Roll chestnuts and bacon in brown sugar. Roll bacon around chestnuts. Secure with toothpick. Bake in casserole dish in a preheated 400 degree oven until bacon is done.

3. Wrap half strip of bacon around water chestnuts. Mix ½ cup ketchup and ¼ cup brown sugar. Pour over water chestnuts and bake in a preheated 350 degree oven for 30 minutes.

Bambini

½	pound frozen puff pastry, thawed
20	slices pepperoni (about ½ of a 3½-ounce package)
½	cup Mozzarella cheese, grated
1	cup Ricotta cheese
¼	cup Parmesan cheese, freshly grated
1	egg yolk, beaten

1. Roll the puff pastry to ⅛ inch thickness. Cut circles ¼ to ½ inch larger than the pepperoni slices. Center a slice of pepperoni on a circle.

2. Combine Mozzarella, Ricotta, and Parmesan cheeses. Top each pepperoni circle with about 1 level tablespoon of cheese mixture.

3. Paint the edges of the dough with egg yolk. Top with another circle of dough, stretching slightly. Press edges with the tines of a fork to seal. Refrigerate circles as you go. Place on an ungreased cookie sheet.

4. Bake in a preheated 350 degree oven for 7 minutes or until golden and puffed. Serve warm.

To store, freeze the unbaked rounds on a cookie sheet. When frozen, package in layers and wrap in freezer wrap. Place frozen puffs on ungreased sheet and bake.

Helpful Hints: If you drop a part of egg yolk into the whites, moisten a cloth with cold water, touch to the yolk and it will adhere to the cloth.

Bread Pot Fondue

YIELDS: 12-15 servings

Slice this serving bowl later for great cheese sandwiches.

1 round firm loaf of bread (1½ pounds, 8-10 inches in diameter)	½ cup green onion, chopped
2 cups sharp Cheddar cheese, shredded	1 (3-ounce) can whole mild or hot green chilies, drained and chopped
2 (3-ounce) packages cream cheese, softened	1 teaspoon Worcestershire sauce
1½ cups sour cream	2 tablespoons vegetable oil
1 cup cooked ham, diced (optional)	1 tablespoon butter, melted assorted raw vegetables

1. Slice off top of bread, reserve top. Hollow out inside with small paring knife, leaving ½ inch thick shell. Cut removed bread into 1 inch cubes; reserve for toasting.

2. Combine cheeses and sour cream in bowl. Stir in ham, green onion, chilies, and Worcestershire sauce. Spoon mixture into bread shell; replace top of bread. Tightly wrap loaf with several layers of aluminum foil; set on cookie sheet. Bake in a preheated 350 degree oven for 1 hour and 10 minutes, or until cheese is heated through.

3. Meanwhile, stir together bread cubes, oil, and melted butter. Arrange on cookie sheet. Bake in a preheated 350 degree oven for 10-15 minutes, stirring occasionally.

4. Remove bread from oven when done. Unwrap and stir cheese filling. Place on platter with bread cubes and raw vegetables. Purchase extra bread for additional bread cubes.

Cheezy Tortilla Crisps

YIELDS: 6-8 servings

Use lo-cal cheese and you have a terrific diet-time munchie.

6	(8-inch) flour tortillas	2	small tomatoes, chopped
2	cups Monterey Jack cheese, grated	⅓	cup ripe olives, chopped
1	(4-ounce) can green chilies, chopped	¼	cup green onions, chopped taco sauce (optional)

1. Place tortillas on two large baking sheets. Sprinkle each with cheese, just to cover tortilla. It's best not to overload with cheese. Layer chilies, tomatoes, olives, and onion on each.

2. Bake in a preheated 400 degree oven for 5 minutes until cheese melts and tortillas are crisp. Cut in wedges and serve with taco sauce.

Cherry Tomato Canape

YIELDS: 24 servings

1	cup Swiss cheese, grated	⅛	teaspoon cayenne pepper
⅔	cup mayonnaise	½	pound bacon, cooked and crumbled
½	cup green onion, finely minced	1	pint cherry tomatoes, sliced
6	tablespoons green pepper, finely minced	1	loaf party rye or pumpernickle
⅛	teaspoon garlic powder		
¼	teaspoon seasoned salt		

1. Combine first 7 ingredients. Set aside.

2. Toast bread on one side. Spread other side with additional mayonnaise. Top with tomato slice and cheese mixture. Sprinkle with bacon. Bake in a preheated 350 degree oven for 5 minutes, until bubbly and brown.

Cherry Almond Roundups

YIELDS: 36 meatballs

1 pound fresh ground pork	1 egg, beaten
¼ cup cracker crumbs	½ cup almonds, finely ground
2 tablespoons onion, finely diced	1 teaspoon parsley flakes
2 tablespoons lemon juice	¼ teaspoon pepper
½ teaspoon salt	

1. In a mixing bowl, combine all ingredients. Shape into 1 inch balls and cook in skillet until brown and cooked through; drain.

SAUCE

1 (12-ounce) jar cherry preserves	1 tablespoon light corn syrup
2 tablespoons wine vinegar	¼ teaspoon nutmeg
¼ teaspoon cinnamon	¼ teaspoon salt
¼ teaspoon cloves	3 tablespoons slivered almonds, toasted

1. In a small saucepan, mix all ingredients together. Bring to a boil and simmer 2 minutes. Add toasted slivered almonds. Pour cherry sauce over meatballs and simmer 5 minutes. Serve hot.

Tarragon Mushrooms

1 pound fresh mushrooms	1½ teaspoons tarragon leaves, crumbled
1½ cups dairy sour cream	1½ teaspoons salt
2 tablespoons fresh lemon juice	¼ teaspoon ground white pepper
1 tablespoon onion, finely grated	

1. Rinse, pat dry, and halve fresh mushrooms.

2. Combine remaining ingredients. Add mixture to the mushrooms and toss to coat. Cover and refrigerate at least 1 hour.

Must be prepared ahead to marinate.

Chicken Pillows

For best flavor be sure to marinate the chicken overnight.

2 whole chicken breasts, boned and skinned	½ teaspoon salt
	⅛ teaspoon pepper
3 tablespoons lemon juice	1 tablespoon oregano
2 tablespoons vegetable oil	½ pound phyllo dough (pastry)
¼ teaspoon garlic powder	½ cup butter, melted

1. Cut chicken into 1 inch cubes. Combine lemon juice, oil, garlic powder, salt, pepper, and oregano in a small bowl. Add chicken pieces and coat with marinade. Cover and refrigerate overnight.

2. Cut phyllo dough in half lengthwise, forming 2 long strips. Fold each in half lengthwise to form rectangles, and brush with melted butter.

3. Using 2 pieces of chicken, place on one end of phyllo and roll to midpoint, fold in each side and continue rolling to form a neat package. Brush tops with melted butter. Place seam side down on cookie sheet or shallow tray.

4. Bake in a preheated 375 degree oven for 20 minutes, or until golden brown.

Must start preparation 1 day ahead. Freezes well.

Helpful Hints: When marinating meats, place meat and marinade in zip lock bag, press out air and seal. Marinade stays close to meat and you don't have a dirty dish or pan.

Chicken Pop'ems

YIELDS: 60 pieces

Better than your favorite carry-out and worth the effort. Your kids will enjoy these as a tasty finger food dinner.

4	chicken breasts, boned, split, and skin removed	½	teaspoon seasoned salt
1	cup round buttery crackers, finely crushed (about 24)	1	teaspoon dried thyme leaves
		1	teaspoon dried basil leaves
½	cup Parmesan cheese, grated	¼	teaspoon pepper
¼	cup walnuts, finely chopped	½	cup butter or margarine, melted

1. Cover 2 baking sheets with aluminum foil. Cut chicken into 1 inch pieces. Mix cracker crumbs, cheese, walnuts, seasoned salt, thyme, basil, and pepper.

2. Dip chicken pieces into melted butter, then into crumb mixture. Place chicken pieces about ½ inch apart on baking sheets.

3. Bake, uncovered, in a preheated 400 degree oven for 20 to 25 minutes or until golden brown.

Bleu Cheese Nibbles

YIELDS: 40 pieces

Devilishly good!

1	(8-ounce) package refrigerator biscuits, cut into quarters	¼	cup Bleu cheese, crumbled
¼	cup butter	1	teaspoon Worcestershire sauce

1. Arrange biscuits in a cake pan so they touch each other.

2. In a small saucepan melt butter and cheese, add Worcestershire sauce. Pour cheese mixture over biscuits.

3. Bake in a preheated 400 degree oven for 12-15 minutes or until golden. Serve hot.

Chinese Sausage Bites

YIELDS: 30 meatballs

Let these meatballs heat in their wonderful oriental sauce to pick up their appealing flavor.

1 pound bulk pork sausage	6 tablespoons brown sugar, packed
1 egg, slightly beaten	2 tablespoons vinegar
½ cup bread crumbs	2 tablespoons soy sauce
¾ cup chili sauce	
¼ teaspoon garlic salt	

1. Mix the sausage, egg, and crumbs. Shape into balls, using approximately 1 teaspoon of mix for each.

2. Cook until evenly browned and cooked through. Can be done in skillet or microwave. Drain. Set aside.

3. In a saucepan, mix the last 5 ingredients. Cook slowly for 20 minutes, stirring occasionally. To serve, place meatballs in a serving dish and cover with sauce. Serve warm.

Meatballs can be made in advance and frozen. Sauce can be made 1 to 2 weeks in advance and kept in the refrigerator.

Crispy Cheese Squares

YIELDS: 6 dozen

These cheese stacks utilize a blend of several savory seasonings.

2	(5-ounce) jars Old English Cheese (Kraft)	¾	tablespoon Worcestershire sauce
1	cup butter, softened	½	tablespoon Beau Monde
½	tablespoon Tabasco sauce	1	tablespoon dill weed
½	tablespoon onion powder	2	loaves Pepperidge Farm thin sliced bread

1. Mix first seven ingredients to make a cheese spread.

2. Remove crusts from bread. Spread cheese mixture on three slices of bread and stack them one on top of the other. Cut the stack into thirds, then each third into halves. To freeze, place cheese squares on cookie sheet in freezer until frozen. Then place in freezer bag.

3. Bake in a preheated 400 degree oven for 10 minutes. If frozen, bake 15 minutes at 400 degrees.

May be prepared ahead 1 to 2 days and refrigerated or freeze as long as 1 month.

Curry Rum Chicken Skewers

YIELDS: 24

2   whole chicken breasts, boned and skinned
2   teaspoons unsalted butter
1   tablespoon curry powder
1/3   cup rum
2   tablespoons molasses

1/3   cup pineapple juice
3   tablespoons lime juice
1   tablespoon salt
1   (20-ounce) can pineapple chunks or fresh pineapple, cut into chunks

1. Cut chicken into ½ inch cubes.

2. Heat butter in saucepan until it foams. Stir in curry, rum, and molasses. Using a long kitchen match, carefully ignite the rum and shake until flame subsides. Stir in pineapple juice, lime juice, and salt. Cool.

3. Toss marinade with chicken and pineapple. Marinate for 1 hour or more.

4. Preheat broiler. Arrange 2 pieces of chicken and 2 pieces of pineapple alternately on bamboo cocktail skewers. Place on baking sheet lined with foil. Broil 4 inches from heat about 3 minutes. Turn once. Serve hot.

May be made ahead.

French Cheese Loaf

YIELDS: 12 servings

1   loaf French bread
½   cup mayonnaise
½   cup black olives, chopped
½   cup mushrooms, chopped

4   cups Mozzarella cheese, grated
¼   teaspoon garlic powder
1   medium onion, chopped

1. Cut bread in half lengthwise.

2. Mix remaining ingredients. Spread on loaves of bread.

3. Bake in a preheated 350 degree oven for 15-20 minutes. Use foil lined cookie sheets for easier clean up.

Dilly Cheese Puffs

YIELDS: 72 pieces

Here is a tasty appetizer that can be made ahead and stored in the freezer for up to 6 months.

1 loaf French bread, unsliced	½ cup butter
2 (3-ounce) packages cream cheese	2 egg whites, stiffly beaten
1 cup (4-ounces) Cheddar cheese, grated	2 teaspoons dried dill weed
	1 teaspoon Worcestershire sauce
	1 tablespoon onion, grated

1. Remove crust from French bread. Cut bread into 1 inch squares.

2. Melt cream cheese, Cheddar cheese, and butter in a double boiler until creamy. Fold in beaten egg whites. Add remaining ingredients.

3. Dip cubes in hot cheese mixture, using a long kitchen or fondue fork. Place on cookie sheet.

4. Can be frozen at this point and stored in plastic in the freezer for up to 6 months.

5. Bake in a preheated 450 degree oven for 8 minutes. If frozen, bake an additional 3-5 minutes.

Ham and Cheese Onyums

YIELDS: 25 squares

Onyum-yummy good!

1	(13¾-ounce) package hot roll mix	½	teaspoon curry powder
4	tablespoons freeze dried chives	½	teaspoon garlic powder
1	cup Hellmann's mayonnaise	1	(2.8-ounce) can french fried onion rings (Durkee)
1	pound Swiss cheese, shredded	5	ounces ground ham

1. Make hot roll mix as on the package, add 2 tablespoons of the chives to the dough. Cover and let rise until double, about 30 minutes. Put dough in a greased 9 x 13 inch pan.

2. In a small bowl, mix the mayonnaise with the rest of the ingredients, except onion rings and the remaining chives. Spread over the dough.

3. Bake in a preheated 375 degree oven for 20 minutes.

4. Crumble onion rings, finely; mix with chives; sprinkle on top. Bake 5 minutes more. Cut into squares.

To freeze, assemble dish up to adding onion topping. Bake for 50 minutes from freezer. Add onion and chive mixture and bake 5 minutes more.

 APPETIZERS

Ham and Cheese Toasties

YIELDS: 3 dozen

Yummy as an appetizer or a snappy luncheon sandwich.

2	tablespoons orange marmalade	½	(8-ounce) package Swiss cheese, sliced
½	teaspoon dry mustard	2	tablespoons margarine or butter
1	(8-ounce) package cooked ham, sliced	¼	cup milk
1	(8-ounce) loaf party rye bread, sliced	1	egg

1. In cup, stir marmalade and mustard until well mixed; set aside. Cut ham slices to fit on half of the bread slices; cut cheese slices to arrange on top of ham; top with a dollop of marmalade mixture and another bread slice.

2. Melt margarine in a 15½ x 10½ inch jelly roll pan. In pie plate with fork, beat milk and egg until well mixed. Dip sandwiches, one at a time, into egg mixture to coat on all sides. Place sandwiches, in one layer, in jelly roll pan.

3. Bake in a preheated 450 degree oven until golden brown on both sides, about 20 minutes. Cut each sandwich in half. Serve hot.

Marinara Mushrooms

YIELDS: 24

24	medium mushrooms, wiped clean, stems removed and chopped olive oil	½	cup black olives, chopped
		¾	cup Marinara sauce (homemade or commercial)
1	cup seasoned bread crumbs	6	tablespoons Parmesan cheese, freshly grated

1. Roll each mushroom cap in small amount of olive oil and place on baking sheet or dish.

2. Combine remaining ingredients including stems. Stuff into mushrooms. Bake in a preheated 350 degree oven 10 minutes, just to heat through.

Mexicali Tartlets

Ole'! To this pick-me-up appetizer!

FILLING

1 cup sour cream	1 cup tortilla chips, coarsely crumbled
2 tablespoons taco sauce	
2 ounces black olives, chopped	

1. Mix all ingredients together in a small bowl. Set aside.

SHELLS

1 pound ground round, very lean	1 cup (4-ounces) Cheddar cheese, shredded
2 tablespoons taco sauce	

1. Mix beef, taco sauce, and ½ cup Cheddar cheese with hands.

2. Place meat on bottom and sides of 1½ inch miniature muffin cups, forming a shell.

3. Place a spoonful of filling into each shell, mounding slightly. Sprinkle Cheddar cheese over tops.

4. Bake in a preheated 425 degree oven for 6-8 minutes. With the tip of a knife, remove tartlets from the pan. Serve immediately.

5. To freeze, place on baking sheet and flash freeze. Place in plastic container or freezer bag. To serve, place frozen tartlets on baking sheet or in muffin cups and reheat at 375 degrees for 10 minutes.

Variation: For a main dish, substitute a 9 inch pie plate for muffin tin. Bake in a preheated 375 degree oven for 35 minutes. Makes 6 main dish servings.

Mexican Pinas

YIELDS: 24 pieces

Making this appetizer early in the day will help the flavor grow even yummier by serving time.

- ½ cup butter
- ⅛ teaspoon garlic salt
- 1 (4-ounce) can green chilies, chopped and well drained
- 1 (8-ounce) package Cheddar cheese, shredded
- 1 cup Hellmann's mayonnaise
- 1 loaf cocktail rye bread

1. Mix butter, garlic salt, and chilies. Spread on bread slices.

2. Mix Cheddar cheese and mayonnaise together. Spread over mixture on bread slices. Place bread slices on cookie sheet. Toast under broiler about 3 minutes or until cheese melts.

Variation: Eliminate the green chilies. To the cheese mixture add 1 cup black olives, chopped, and/or 1 cup green onions, chopped.

Reuben Roll-Ups

YIELDS: 24

An appetizer that will remind you of your favorite deli.

- 1 package refrigerator crescent rolls
- 1 (8-ounce) can sauerkraut, well drained
- 1 tablespoon Thousand Island dressing
- 8 thin slices cooked corned beef
- 2 slices Swiss cheese, cut in ½ inch strips

1. Unroll crescent rolls; separate into triangles. Combine sauerkraut with salad dressing. Place sliced corned beef across wide end of triangle. Spread 2 tablespoons of sauerkraut on corned beef; top with 2 strips of cheese. Roll up, beginning at wide end of triangle.

2. Bake on an ungreased baking sheet in a preheated 350 degree oven for 10-15 minutes or until golden brown. Remove from oven and slice each into thirds. Place on heating tray or eat immediately.

Roquefort Strudel

YIELDS: 12-14 servings

An elegant hors d'oeuvre that can also serve well as a dessert with a stemmed crystal of Bordeaux.

1 (8-ounce) package cream cheese, softened	dash of cayenne pepper
3 tablespoons butter, softened	10 sheets of phyllo dough
¼ pound Roquefort cheese, crumbled	½ cup unsalted butter, melted and clarified
2 egg yolks	½ cup bread crumbs

1. Cream together the cream cheese and the butter. Beat in the crumbled Roquefort and the egg yolks until the mixture resembles a smooth batter. Season with cayenne pepper. Chill for one hour. Remove phyllo dough from the refrigerator and allow to stand for one hour.

2. Spread a towel over your working space. Place a sheet of phyllo in the center of it. Brush the sheet with a light coating of butter and sprinkle it with some bread crumbs. Place another sheet of phyllo over the first and repeat this procedure until 5 sheets have been used.

3. Spread half the cheese mixture in an even mound along the longest side of the pastry nearest you. Fold in the flaps of dough at the sides of the filling. Lift up the end of the towel and roll the pastry over the filling and continue to roll until the filling is completely enclosed.

4. Transfer the strudel to a lightly greased baking sheet and brush the top with melted butter. Repeat this with the ingredients remaining to form a second strudel. May be refrigerated or frozen at this point. To bake, bring to room temperature and bake in a preheated 375 degree oven for 30 to 35 minutes or until golden brown. Allow to cool slightly before cutting into two inch slices with a serrated knife. Serve warm.

May be made ahead up to 2 days and refrigerated.

Sausage Stuffed Mushrooms

YIELDS: 24 mushrooms

Make ahead and reheat in the microwave.

24 medium mushrooms	2 tablespoons parsley
2 tablespoons butter or margarine	1 tablespoon lime juice
¼ cup onion, chopped	¼ teaspoon garlic powder
2 tablespoons dry white wine	1 teaspoon oregano
¼ cup dry bread crumbs	⅛ teaspoon pepper
¼ cup fully cooked, spicy, pork sausage, crumbled	½ cup (2-ounces) Cheddar cheese, finely shredded

1. Cut stems from mushrooms and chop. Measure enough for ¼ cup.

2. Melt butter in 10 inch skillet until butter begins to bubble. Cook mushroom caps top side down until light brown; remove caps with slotted spoon.

3. Cook onion in same skillet until tender. Stir in wine. Simmer, uncovered, 2 minutes. Stir in ¼ cup chopped mushroom stems and remaining ingredients, except cheese, and cool slightly.

4. Shape stuffing into 24 small balls and place one in each mushroom cap. Sprinkle with cheese. Broil on cookie sheet for about 3 minutes.

Seafood Dip in a Shell

1	pint sour cream	½	package dry onion soup mix
1	tablespoon horseradish, drained	1	(7-ounce) can shrimp, drained
1	tablespoon lemon juice	1	(7-ounce) can crabmeat, drained
½	teaspoon salt	1	round loaf French bread, whole
¼	teaspoon curry powder		
¼	teaspoon dry mustard		

1. In a bowl, combine sour cream and next 6 ingredients; mix well. Fold in seafood and chill.

2. Cut off the top of the loaf of bread and hollow out the loaf. Bake in a preheated 250 degree oven for 20 minutes or until lightly toasted.

3. Place chilled seafood mixture in hollow loaf and put top on for lid. Serve with fresh vegetables for dipping and later eat the bread and container itself.

Dip may be prepared a day in advance.

 APPETIZERS

Seaside Oysters

YIELDS: 6 servings

Bake in shells for individual servings, if desired.

½	pound mushrooms, thinly sliced	3	tablespoons parsley, chopped
6	tablespoons butter	¼	teaspoon salt
3	tablespoons flour	⅛	teaspoon cayenne pepper
1-2	dozen fresh oysters	⅛	teaspoon garlic powder
⅓	cup dry sherry	½	cup bread crumbs
3	tablespoons green onion, sliced		

1. Saute mushrooms in 2 tablespoons butter. Set aside.

2. Melt remaining butter. Stir in flour, cook slightly. Combine all ingredients except bread crumbs. Place in buttered 1½ quart casserole. Top with crumbs.

3. Bake in a preheated 350 degree oven for 15 minutes. Add optional toppings.

Optional Toppings: bacon, cooked and crumbled; Parmesan cheese

Spacheezies

YIELDS: 48 pieces

1	cup flour	½	pound Monterey Jack cheese, shredded
½	teaspoon salt		
1	teaspoon baking powder	½	pound Cheddar cheese, shredded
1	cup milk		
2	eggs, beaten	1	(10-ounce) package frozen spinach, drained
¼	cup margarine, melted		

1. Combine flour, salt, and baking powder. Add milk and beaten eggs. Combine melted margarine, cheeses, and spinach. Stir everything together and pour into a greased 9 x 13 inch baking dish.

2. Bake in a preheated 375 degree oven for 30-35 minutes. Cut into squares and serve.

May prepare ahead and freeze. Reheat and serve.

"Sticky Fingers" Riblets

YIELDS: 30-35 pieces

A throw away baking dish and your favorite butcher are the key to this appetizer's easy success.

3   pounds pork spareribs

MARINADE

¼ cup prepared mustard	3 tablespoons cider vinegar
¼ cup light molasses or brown sugar, packed	2 tablespoons Worcestershire sauce
¼ cup soy sauce	2 teaspoons Tabasco sauce

1. Use a throw-away baking dish, as these can be quite messy to clean up.

2. Have butcher cut the rack of ribs in half, down the middle to form little riblets. Then cut between bones to separate each one.

3. In a shallow baking dish, spread the ribs in a single layer. Mix all of the marinade ingredients together. Pour over the spareribs and chill covered, for 3 or more hours.

4. Bake in a preheated 300 degree oven for 1½ hours or until tender. Baste frequently with the sauce and turn once after the top has become brown and crusted.

Zingy Viennas

YIELDS: 8 servings

1 large can Vienna sausages, cut in bite size pieces	½ teaspoon oregano
	1 tablespoon fresh lemon juice
2 tablespoons butter	

1. Melt butter in fry pan. Add sausages and fry until lightly browned. Add oregano and continue to brown. Just before removing from heat, add lemon juice and stir. Serve with toothpicks.

Tamale Bites

YIELDS: 65 meatballs

A nice variation from the traditional Swedish meatballs.

2 cups baked corn bread, crumbled	1½ pounds ground beef
1 (10-ounce) can enchilada sauce, mild	1 (8-ounce) can tomato sauce
½ teaspoon salt	½ cup Monterey Jack cheese with jalapenos, shredded

1. Combine corn bread crumbs, ½ cup enchilada sauce, and salt. Add ground beef; mix well.

2. Shape into 1 inch balls. Place in shallow baking pan. Bake, uncovered, in a preheated 350 degree oven for 18-20 minutes or until done. Drain.

3. Meanwhile, in a small saucepan, heat together tomato sauce and remaining enchilada sauce. Place cooked meatballs in chafing dish; pour sauce over and top with cheese. Keep warm over low heat. Serve with toothpicks.

May be prepared up to 2 weeks in advance to point of adding cheese.

Chafing Dish Crab

YIELDS: 12 servings or 3 cups

2 (8-ounce) packages cream cheese, softened	½ teaspoon salt
1 teaspoon prepared mustard	¼ teaspoon garlic salt
4 tablespoons Sauterne wine	½ teaspoon onion juice
4 teaspoons powdered sugar	1 pound frozen (thawed) or fresh crabmeat in chunks

1. Combine all ingredients except crabmeat. Stir until well blended. Mix in crabmeat and heat through. Serve in chafing dish with crackers.

Creamy Parmesan Fondue

YIELDS: 10 servings

A wonderful dipper for bread cubes or any number of fresh vegetables.

1½ cups milk	½ teaspoon garlic salt
2 (8-ounce) packages cream cheese, softened	¾ cup Parmesan cheese, grated

1. With electric mixer, add milk to cream cheese. Blend well. Heat slowly in saucepan; add ½ teaspoon salt and garlic salt. Slowly add Parmesan cheese and blend until smooth.

2. Pour into fondue pot; heat. Serve French bread cubes, carrot sticks, green peppers, or mushrooms as dippers.

May be prepared 2 days ahead.

Gail's Hot Crab Dip

YIELDS: 25 servings

This is a wonderful seafood dip with just the right amount of Cheddar cheese zip.

1 (8-ounce) package cream cheese	2 (16-ounce) cans crabmeat
1 can tomato soup	dash of Worcestershire sauce
1 pound Cheddar cheese, shredded	dash of Tabasco sauce

1. Melt cream cheese in double boiler. Add soup, cheese, crabmeat, Worcestershire sauce, and Tabasco sauce.

2. Serve in chafing dish with small slices of pumpernickle bread or crackers.

May be prepared several days ahead.

Hott Metts

A take me out to the ball game treat!

1   package Kielbasa, sliced into
     bite-size pieces

1. Fry pieces in Pam sprayed frypan.

SAUCE

1 cup beer	¼ cup vinegar
¾ cup brown sugar, packed	¼ cup mustard
4 teaspoons cornstarch	4 teaspoons horseradish

1. Combine beer, brown sugar, and cornstarch together. Blend in vinegar, mustard, and horseradish. Cook until thick and bubbly. Pour sauce into fondue or chafing dish. Add Kielbasa. Use toothpicks to lift out of chafing dish.

This can be made 2 to 3 days ahead and rewarmed to serve.

Indy 500 Mushroom Dip

The race is on for this appetizer!

1 pound fresh mushrooms	3 teaspoons flour
6 tablespoons butter	1 cup sour cream
1 medium onion, minced	½ teaspoon Worcestershire
salt and pepper	sauce
to taste	

1. Wash and slice mushrooms. Saute in butter with onions over low heat, 5-8 minutes. Season with salt and pepper to taste; sprinkle flour over mushroom mixture. Stir gently and cook 3 minutes. Add sour cream and Worcestershire sauce. Heat until mixture thickens. This takes only a short time—watch carefully not to overcook. Serve in chafing dish with crackers.

This may be prepared a day or two before a party and reheated in a double boiler over very low heat. Does not do well rewarmed in microwave, becomes too soupy.

Seacoast Shrimp Dip

YIELDS: 2 cups

A New England pleasure that goes well with bread sticks or fresh vegetables.

1 **can cream of shrimp soup**	½ **(7-ounce) bag frozen shrimp or ¼ pound fresh shrimp, cooked and drained**
½ **pound Baby Swiss cheese, shredded**	

1. Combine soup and cheese in a chafing dish or fondue pot. Heat and stir until melted. Add shrimp (small size shrimp work well).

2. Serve with bread sticks, garlic rounds, or cubes of crusty bread. Also good with cold vegetables.

This may be easily doubled to fill a large chafing dish.

Steak Bites

YIELDS: 50 pieces

Presented in a chafing dish this makes a truly elegant appetizer. Watch your male guests be impressed!

2 **pounds round or sirloin steak, ½ inch thick**	2 **ounces whiskey**
½ **cup soy sauce**	2 **garlic cloves, minced**
½ **cup cooking oil**	1 **teaspoon pepper**
2 **tablespoons dry mustard**	1 **teaspoon Tabasco sauce**
2 **tablespoons sugar**	

1. Cut steak into bite size pieces.

2. Combine remaining ingredients; pour over steak. Let stand for 5 hours at room temperature, stirring occasionally.

3. Bring to a boil, over low heat, just before serving. Serve in a chafing dish.

Teriyaki Roll-Ups

YIELDS: 50 servings

½ pound flank steak
(it slices easier if
partially frozen)
½ cup onions, chopped
1 garlic clove, crushed
3-4 tablespoons soy sauce

1 tablespoon salad oil
2 tablespoons brown sugar
½ tablespoon black pepper,
crushed
2 tablespoons dry sherry
2 (8½-ounce) cans water
chestnuts, drained

1. Wipe steak with damp paper towel. Trim off excess fat. Cut steak in half lengthwise; cut into strips, no more than ¼ inch thick.

2. In a small bowl, mix the rest of the ingredients, except the water chestnuts, for marinade.

3. Wrap each chestnut in a steak slice and fasten with wooden pick. Dip in marinade.

4. Arrange in shallow glass baking dish. Pour rest of marinade over steak, covering well. Let stand covered in refrigerator about 2 hours. Turn after 1 hour to marinate other side.

5. Place on ungreased rack in broiler pan. Broil 2-3 minutes on each side. Do not overcook. Arrange on warm platter or keep warm in chafing dish.

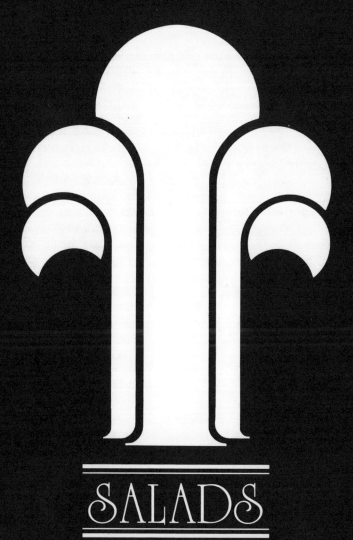

SALADS

SALADS

Asparagus Tomato Salad

YIELDS: 4 servings

For an elegant presentation, arrange individual servings on pretty glass salad plates.

¾ pound asparagus	½ teaspoon paprika
½ cup salad oil	½ teaspoon dry mustard
2 tablespoons vinegar	dash cayenne
2 tablespoons lemon juice	2 medium tomatoes
2 teaspoons sugar	lettuce leaves
½ teaspoon salt	

1. Cook asparagus in small amount of boiling, salted water. Cover pan and cook for about 5 minutes, until crisp tender. Drain.

2. Combine remaining ingredients except tomatoes and lettuce.

3. Arrange asparagus in shallow dish and cover with dressing. Cover and refrigerate overnight.

4. To serve, drain and arrange on lettuce leaves. Top with tomato slices and spoon dressing over each salad.

Easy. Must be prepared 24 hours ahead.

 SALADS

Bay Artichoke Salad

DRESSING

¾ cup oil
¼ cup white wine vinegar
1 teaspoon sugar

½ teaspoon salt
½ teaspoon paprika
dash pepper

SALAD

1 (9-ounce) package frozen artichoke hearts, cooked and drained
1 (8-ounce) package frozen green beans, cooked and drained

3 cups salad greens, torn into bite size pieces
¼ cup onion, thinly sliced
8 to 10 cherry tomatoes, halved
½ cup (2-ounces) Bleu cheese, crumbled

1. In medium bowl, combine dressing ingredients. Add artichoke hearts and beans. Toss lightly and refrigerate until chilled, about 3 hours.

2. In large salad bowl, toss dressing mixture with salad greens, onion, tomatoes, and cheese. Serve immediately.

Must be prepared a few hours ahead to chill.

Classic Bleu Cheese Dressing

This may also be used as a dip for vegetables.

¾ cup Hellmann's mayonnaise
¾ cup sour cream
1 tablespoon wine vinegar few grinds black pepper
1 teaspoon garlic, minced

2 tablespoons onion, finely chopped
1 tablespoon lemon juice
½ cup (2-ounces) Bleu cheese, crumbled
2 tablespoons parsley, chopped

1. Combine mayonnaise and sour cream and mix well. Add remaining ingredients and stir well. Chill for 3 hours or longer.

Must prepare ahead.

Bleu Cheese Slaw

YIELDS: 4-6 servings

Quite different from traditional cole slaw. Not sweet at all!

6 cups cabbage, shredded	2 tablespoons green onion, chopped
2 tablespoons pimento, chopped	

DRESSING

½ cup sour cream	½ teaspoon sugar
2 tablespoons mayonnaise	1 cup (4-ounces) Bleu cheese, crumbled
1 tablespoon lemon juice	

1. Combine cabbage, pimento, and onion tops. Chill thoroughly.

2. Mix together dressing ingredients; chill. Pour over cabbage and toss. If desired, garnish with slices of hard cooked egg.

Creamy Bacon Dressing

YIELDS: 1 cup

Goes well with spinach or lettuce salads.

2 tablespoons vinegar	4 slices crisp bacon, crumbled
¾ cup Hellmann's mayonnaise	1 tablespoon light Karo syrup or honey
⅛ teaspoon salt	
2 tablespoons onion, chopped	

1. Stir all ingredients together. Keep refrigerated in covered container.

SALADS

Corn Salad

A great summer salad idea.

1   (12-ounce) can whole
    yellow corn, drained
1   (12-ounce) can whole
    white corn, drained
½   cup onions, finely
    chopped
½   cup celery, finely
    chopped
½   cup green pepper, finely
    chopped

1   (2-ounce) jar pimentos,
    chopped and drained
½   cup sugar
½   cup white wine vinegar
⅛   teaspoon garlic powder

1. Combine corn, onions, celery, green pepper, and pimentos. Mix well and set aside.

2. Combine sugar, vinegar, and garlic powder. Pour over vegetables, tossing gently. Cover and chill 8 hours or overnight.

Must be prepared ahead.

Creamy Peppercorn Salad Dressing

Pepper lover's dream!

1½ cups sour cream
½   cup Hellmann's
    mayonnaise

1   tablespoon whole
    peppercorns
1½ teaspoons salt

1. Mix sour cream and mayonnaise together in a bowl with a lid.

2. Grind peppercorns coarsely. Add salt. Combine with sour cream mixture. Mix well. Store covered in refrigerator until ready to use. Will keep in refrigerator for one week.

Note: Add milk or cream to thin, if necessary. May be prepared up to 5 days ahead.

Creamy Pea Salad

YIELDS: 4 servings

Best when made and served on the same day.

DRESSING

⅓ cup sour cream	1 teaspoon sugar
2 tablespoons red wine vinegar	½ teaspoon salt
	⅛ teaspoon garlic powder

1. Combine all ingredients in small bowl.

SALAD

1 (10-ounce) package tiny green peas, thawed and drained	3 strips bacon, cooked and crumbled
1 (8-ounce) can water chestnuts, drained and sliced	1 (2-ounce) jar red pimentos, drained and chopped
3 tablespoons green onion, chopped	

1. In large bowl combine above and add dressing. Toss lightly to coat. Serve in lettuce lined bowl.

French Celery Seed Dressing

YIELDS: 4 cups

This recipe fills three cruet bottles. Keep one and use two for gifts!

1½ cups sugar	1 tablespoon dry mustard
½ cup vinegar	1 teaspoon salt
2 cups Mazola oil, divided	1 (14-ounce) bottle catsup
	1 tablespoon celery seed

1. Beat sugar, vinegar, 1 cup oil, mustard, and salt until thick.

2. Add second cup of Mazola, catsup, and celery seed. Mix and pour into bottles or container.

Cucumber Cooler

CREAM MIXTURE

¼ cup whipping cream	¼ cup sour cream

1. To make matured cream mixture, combine whipping cream and sour cream in mixing bowl and whisk lightly. Cover bowl loosely with plastic wrap. Let set at room temperature overnight. Chill at least 4 hours. This mixture will keep in refrigerator 2-3 weeks.

5 tablespoons matured cream mixture	dash pepper
1 tablespoon fresh lemon juice	½ teaspoon any herb combination—parsley, tarragon, chervil, chives
¼ teaspon salt	sliced cucumbers

1. Combine matured cream mixture, lemon juice, salt, pepper, and herbs. Serve over sliced cucumbers.

Cream mixture must be prepared 1 day ahead.

Greek Salad Dressing

YIELDS: 1¼ cups

This dressing stores well in the refrigerator for three weeks.

¾ cup oil	⅜ cup wine vinegar
1 teaspoon oregano	2 teaspoons sugar
½ teaspoon salt	1 clove garlic, crushed

1. Combine all ingredients. Remove garlic clove after 6 to 8 hours.

Serve with greens, shredded red cabbage, cala mata olives, and Feta cheese.

Must be prepared ahead several hours.

Dilled Relish Tray

YIELDS: 8 servings

Great to take to a covered dish dinner.

MARINADE
1¾ cups sugar	2 cups white vinegar
4 teaspoons salt	1 cup water
2 teaspoons dill weed	

1. Combine all ingredients in a medium saucepan. Heat to boiling.

VEGETABLES
2 large Bermuda onions	2 cans (3 or 4 ounces)
4 medium cucumbers	mushroom caps

1. Peel and thinly slice onions. Separate into rings and place in large bowl.

2. Pare or score cucumbers with a fork. Slice thin and place in medium size bowl.

3. Drain mushrooms and place in a small bowl.

4. Pour heated marinade over individual vegetables. Cover and chill several hours or overnight. When ready to serve, remove vegetables from marinade with slotted spoon. Spoon into a sectioned relish tray.

This recipe may easily be cut in half. May be made ahead 3 or 4 days.

Frenchy Cauliflower Salad Bowl

YIELDS: 8-10 servings

A zip of Bleu cheese will highlight this crispy garden combo.

1 small head cauliflower, broken into florets	⅔ cup French salad dressing
½ large Bermuda onion, sliced and separated into rings	4 cups lettuce or mixed greens, torn in bite size pieces
½ cup green olives with pimentos, sliced	½ cup (2-ounces) Bleu cheese, crumbled
	1 cup croutons

1. Slice cauliflowerets into a large salad bowl. Add onion rings and olives. Pour ⅔ cup French dressing over all and toss to coat vegetables. Cover and refrigerate for 30 minutes.

2. Just before serving add lettuce, Bleu cheese, and croutons. Toss lightly. Pass extra French dressing, if desired.

Fresh Mushroom Salad

YIELDS: 8 servings

This colorful salad makes a sensational brunch addition.

1 cup salad oil	4 teaspoons lemon juice
2 teaspoons salt	2 pounds fresh mushrooms, sliced
2½ teaspoons dried basil	
2½ teaspoons Dijon mustard	1 cup green onions, thinly sliced, including some green
½ teaspoon pepper	
½ teaspoon paprika	
5 tablespoons white vinegar	1 pint cherry tomatoes

1. In a large bowl combine first 8 ingredients. Whisk until well blended. Mix in mushrooms and onions. Cover and marinate at room temperature for 1 hour. Stir occasionally. Just before serving mix in tomatoes.

Prepare at least 1 hour ahead to marinate.

Fresh Asparagus with Creamy Vinaigrette

YIELDS: 4 servings

32	asparagus spears
2	tablespoons shallots, minced
2	tablespoons Dijon mustard
1	tablespoon sour cream
1	tablespoon red wine vinegar

	salt and freshly ground pepper
½	cup peanut oil
	Boston lettuce leaves
	lemon wedges

1. Remove and discard lower tough ends of asparagus spears. Steam stalks over simmering water until barely tender. Drain and refresh under cold water. Chill.

2. Combine next four ingredients with salt and pepper to taste in blender. With blender running slowly, add oil until blended and thickened.

3. Line plates with lettuce leaves. Arrange asparagus spears over lettuce and drizzle with vinaigrette. Garnish with lemon wedge.

Gazpacho Salad

YIELDS: 8 servings

Very festive!

4-5	tomatoes, chopped
2	cucumbers, diced
2	green peppers, chopped
2	bunches radishes, sliced
1	large sweet red onion, sliced
12 to 14	black olives
2	cloves garlic, minced

¼	cup olive oil
⅓	cup white wine vinegar
1	teaspoon salt
¼	teaspoon Tabasco sauce
1	tablespoon parsley, minced
2	tablespoons chives, minced
⅛	teaspoon pepper

1. Alternate layers of tomatoes, cucumbers, peppers, radishes, onions, and olives.

2. Combine remaining ingredients. Pour over vegetables. Cover and refrigerate for several hours. Serve in clear glass bowl or trifle dish.

Must be prepared ahead.

 SALADS

Garden Platter Salad with Dutch Onion Rings

YIELDS: 8 servings

A lovely platter for a summer barbeque.

DUTCH ONION RINGS
2   medium white
     sweet onions
¼   cup sour cream

¼   teaspoon salt
½   teaspoon celery seed
1   teaspoon lemon juice

1. Slice onions ¼ inch thick. Separate into rings. Place in bowl and cover with boiling water. Let stand 2 minutes and drain. Chill.

2. Combine sour cream with salt, celery seed, and lemon juice. Just before serving, toss sour cream mixture with onions.

SALAD
2-3 large fresh tomatoes,
     sliced
1   small cucumber, sliced
     Italian salad dressing

¼   teaspoon salt
¼   teaspoon pepper
¼   to ½ teaspoon dill weed
1   teaspoon parsley, snipped

1. At serving time, mound onions in center of platter. Border with overlapping tomato and cucumber slices. Drizzle with Italian salad dressing. Sprinkle with salt, pepper, dill weed, and parsley.

Lemon and Oil Dressing

YIELDS: 1⅓ cups

1   cup olive oil
5   tablespoons lemon juice
2   teaspoons onion juice

2   tablespoons sugar
½   teaspoon salt
     dash of pepper

1. In a blender, mix together half of the olive oil and all of the remaining ingredients. Add the remaining olive oil and whirl together until smooth.

Marinated Cauliflower

YIELDS: 8 servings

Chill before serving and add a cheerful garnish of tomato wedges.

1 large head cauliflower
1 package garlic salad dressing mix (Good Seasons preferred)
2 tablespoons cider vinegar
2 tablespoons water
⅔ cup salad oil
½ cup sour cream

2 scallions, chopped
½ cup (2-ounces) Bleu cheese, crumbled
2 tablespoons slivered almonds
2 tablespoons bacon, crumbled

1. Steam cauliflower for 10-15 minutes. May leave cauliflower whole or break into florets. Cool.

2. Combine salad dressing mix with vinegar, water, and salad oil. Add remaining ingredients to dressing. Mix well. Pour over cooled cauliflower.

Easy. May be prepared ahead.

Pea and Cashew Salad

YIELDS: 8-10 servings

A salad with a nutty kind of crunch.

2 (10-ounce) packages frozen peas
½ cup onion, chopped
1 cup celery, chopped

¼ cup mayonnaise
salt and pepper to taste
1 cup salted cashews

1. Thaw and drain peas. Mix with onion and celery. Fold in mayonnaise, salt, and pepper. Refrigerate. Just before serving, mix in cashews.

Easy. Prepare early in the day.

Patio Salad

YIELDS: 12 servings

A pretty combination of garden fresh vegetables

MARINADE
1 cup olive oil	1½ teaspoons sugar
⅔ cup vinegar	2-3 cloves garlic, minced
2½ teaspoons salt	1 teaspoon oregano
1½ teaspoons pepper	

1. Mix all ingredients. Shake well and set aside.

SALAD
Use a total of 2½ to 3 quarts of at least 6 of these:

cauliflower, broken into florets	broccoli, broken into florets
carrots, 3 inch sticks	canned water chestnuts, sliced
fresh mushrooms	canned artichoke hearts
cherry tomatoes	
green onions, ¾ inch slices	

1. Wash vegetables. Cut into bite size pieces. Place all vegetables in a large container. Pour marinade over all. Cover and refrigerate for 24 hours or overnight. Stir often.

Must prepare 1 day ahead.

Pea Pod Salad

YIELDS: 6-8 servings

Cool, green, and crisp. Chilled plates are a must!

DRESSING
1/3 cup vegetable oil	1/2 teaspoon salt
2 tablespoons lemon juice	1 teaspoon sugar
1 tablespoon white wine vinegar	1 clove garlic, minced

1. Combine all ingredients and mix well.

SALAD
12-16 ounces pea pods, cooked tender crisp and chilled	1 (5-ounce) can water chestnuts, sliced and drained
1 cup cherry tomatoes, halved	7 green onions, chopped

1. Place vegetables in salad bowl and toss with dressing just before serving.

Prepare early in the day and toss with dressing before serving.

Roman Cups

These individual antipasto salads taste of Italy. Choose a variety of colorful relishes to tuck into crisp green pepper Roman Cups. Helps you out of the relish tray rut.

To prepare cups, slice tops off fresh green peppers; scoop out. (Cut sliver off bottoms of tipsy ones.) Stuff with marinated artichoke hearts, stuffed green olives and ripe olives, pickles, tomato wedges, and celery and carrot sticks. Drizzle with Italian dressing. Serve with cornucopias of salami slices twisted around cheese sticks.

 SALADS

Sensational Broccoli Crunch

YIELDS: 8 servings

Simply sensational!

SALAD

2 heads broccoli, cut into florets	1 cup Cheddar cheese, shredded
½ pound bacon, cooked and crumbled (reserve 4 tablespoons for garnish)	1 small red onion, cut into thin rings

DRESSING

1 cup mayonnaise	⅓ cup sugar
2 tablespoons red wine vinegar	

1. Combine salad ingredients. Store in refrigerator.

2. Combine dressing ingredients. Store in refrigerator.

3. Just before serving toss salad with dressing. Garnish with crumbled bacon.

Variation: Do not add Cheddar cheese. Add 3 ounces salted sunflower seeds.

Easy. Make ahead early in the day.

A Classic Caesar Salad

YIELDS: 6-8 servings

2	cloves garlic, peeled and pressed	1	small head romaine	
¾	cup olive oil	1	teaspoon salt	
2	cups bread cubes		black pepper	
	Parmesan cheese, grated	1	egg	
1	small head lettuce		juice of 1 lemon	
1	large bunch watercress	6	filets of anchovies, finely cut	

1. Combine oil and garlic. Refrigerate overnight.

2. To prepare croutons, spread bread cubes on a baking sheet. Toss with 3 table-spoons of the garlic oil. Bake in a preheated 225 degree oven for 2 hours. Sprinkle with Parmesan cheese.

3. Break washed, drained, and chilled lettuces.

4. Combine prepared garlic oil, salt, and pepper. Scatter over greens and toss gently.

5. Boil egg one minute; break over salad, squeeze lemon juice over egg. Sprinkle anchovy bits on top salad and gently toss to completely coat lettuce.

GARNISH

	Parmesan cheese, grated	4	whole anchovy filets
1	small can black olives, drained and finely chopped		

1. To garnish salad, sprinkle with Parmesan cheese. Make an X on top cheese with black olives and spread anchovy filets on top of salad.

Belgium Salad

YIELDS: 8 servings

    1   (10-ounce) package
         frozen Brussels sprouts

1. Cook Brussels sprouts in boiling salted water until just tender, about 5 minutes. Drain.

MARINADE
½   cup salad oil
¼   cup vinegar
¼   cup Italian salad
    dressing
1   teaspoon dried parsley
    flakes

½   teaspoon salt
¼   teaspoon dried basil
⅛   teaspoon pepper
1   clove garlic, crushed

1. In a screw-top jar, combine marinade ingredients. Cover and shake well.

2. Cut Brussels sprouts in half, lengthwise, and add to marinade. Chill all day or overnight.

SALAD
1   head lettuce, torn
    into bite size pieces
½   medium red onion,
    sliced and separated
    into rings

6   slices bacon, crisp
    cooked, drained, and
    crumbled

1. In salad bowl, arrange lettuce, onions, and bacon.

2. Drain Brussels sprouts, reserving marinade. Add Brussels sprouts to salad, toss gently. Use as much marinade as needed to coat the greens.

Berry Patch Salad

YIELDS: 6-8 servings

This salad is very attractive, layered in a trifle dish or clear glass bowl.

CELERY SEED DRESSING

½ to ¾ cup sugar	½ cup oil
1 teaspoon salt	¼ cup white vinegar
1 teaspoon mustard	1 teaspoon celery seeds

1. Combine all ingredients, except for celery seeds, in a saucepan. Heat at low temperature. Stir to blend until sugar dissolves. Add celery seeds. Chill until thickened. Shake well before serving. Dressing keeps well in refrigerator for 2 to 3 weeks.

SALAD

1 medium red onion, sliced into rings	1 small head lettuce
	1 quart fresh strawberries

1. Put onions in colander and pour a saucepan of boiling water over them (this softens and sweetens them). Drain. Break lettuce into bite size pieces, add sliced strawberries. Mix lightly. Add onion rings. Just before serving, add dressing, to taste, and toss.

Greens may be a mixture of several kinds of lettuce and spinach or all spinach.

Steak House Salad Dressing

YIELDS: 2 cups

A local steak house favorite!

1 cup oil	1 tablespoon salt
¾ cup cider vinegar	4 cloves garlic, mashed
⅓ cup sugar	

1. Place all ingredients in blender. Blend for 5 minutes. Do not store in refrigerator or it will get very thick.

 SALADS

Bibb Toss and Dressing

YIELDS: 4 servings

Easy, elegant, and best with bibb lettuce. Dressing may be prepared one week ahead.

DRESSING

3	tablespoons olive oil	½	teaspoon salt
3	tablespoons vegetable oil	¼	teaspoon pepper
2	tablespoons cider vinegar	1	tablespoon sugar
1	tablespoon lemon juice		

1. Combine all ingredients in a jar and shake well.

SALAD

2	heads bibb lettuce, torn	¼	cup pecan halves

1. Pour dressing over lettuce and pecan halves. Serve immediately.

Cauliflower and Bacon Salad

YIELDS: 12 servings

Easy, excellent, and different!

1	head lettuce, torn into bite size pieces	½	pound bacon, cooked and crumbled
1	head cauliflower, cut into florets	1	cup Hellmann's mayonnaise
1	small red onion, sliced into thin rings	⅓	cup Parmesan cheese
		3	tablespoons sugar

1. In a large bowl, layer lettuce, cauliflower, onion, and bacon.

2. Combine remaining ingredients and spread over salad. Cover and refrigerate until ready to serve (up to 14 hours). Toss before serving.

Dennis' Salad

Making this dressing a day ahead of serving will greatly enhance its flavor.

DRESSING

1	cup Hellmann's mayonnaise
½	cup salad oil
1-2	cloves garlic*
½	teaspoon dried oregano
2-3	stalks celery, cut into large chunks

2	green onions (include tops), chopped*
1	teaspoon anchovy paste*
1	tablespoon lemon juice* few grinds pepper

*These ingredients may be varied to individual taste.

1. In a blender, combine the salad dressing ingredients and blend until creamy and evenly pale green in color. Chill overnight.

SALAD

1   large head romaine
      lettuce
      seasoned croutons

Parmesan cheese,
freshly grated

1. Wash and tear lettuce; blot with paper toweling to remove excess water. Chill.

2. At serving time, toss lettuce with dressing. Add croutons and sprinkle liberally with grated cheese. Toss again and serve.

 SALADS

Dinner Party Salad

YIELDS: 6-8 servings

A nice introduction to an elegant entree such as Black Tie Standing Rib Roast.

DRESSING

½	cup olive oil		½	teaspoon salt
2	tablespoons lemon juice		¼	teaspoon dry mustard
1	teaspoon white wine vinegar		2	cloves garlic, minced
1	teaspoon dill weed		½	pound small shrimp, cooked

1. Blend dressing ingredients well in a glass jar or with a wire whisk. Marinate shrimp in dressing 4 to 6 hours.

SALAD

4	cups romaine lettuce		¾	cup Monterey Jack cheese, cubed
4	cups Boston or bibb lettuce		½	cucumber, thinly sliced

1. Just before serving, toss dressing and shrimp with remaining salad ingredients.

Must begin preparing early in the day.

Make-Ahead Spinach Salad

YIELDS: 6 servings

6	cups spinach, lettuce and romaine, torn into bite size pieces, discard stems		¼	cup green onion, thinly sliced
			2	hard cooked eggs, sliced
½	medium cucumber, thinly sliced		¾	to 1 cup thick Bleu cheese dressing
⅓	cup radishes, thinly sliced		5	slices bacon, fried and crumbled
			½	cup salted Spanish peanuts

1. Wash greens and dry well. Arrange greens in a shallow salad bowl. Layer with cucumbers, radishes, onions, and eggs. Spread dressing over the top. Cover and chill overnight. Just before serving, sprinkle with bacon and peanuts. Toss and serve.

Must be made 1 day ahead.

Parmesan Salad

YIELDS: 8-12 servings

Blend this dressing early in the day to compliment the colorful blend of vegetables.

DRESSING

⅔ cup olive oil	⅛ teaspoon pepper
⅓ cup red wine vinegar	½ teaspoon oregano
½ teaspoon salt	1-2 cloves garlic, crushed

1. Blend all ingredients and let set at room temperature at least 4-5 hours before serving.

SALAD

1 head lettuce, washed, drained, and well chilled	½ cup ripe olives, sliced (optional)
3 green onions, sliced	1 large tomato
1 bunch broccoli	½ cup Parmesan cheese, freshly grated

1. Several hours before serving tear lettuce into bite size pieces; add green onion.

2. Cut broccoli florets into bite size pieces. Peel and slice the large broccoli stems. Add to salad. Add olives; cover and chill until serving time.

3. At serving time, cut tomato into wedges and add to salad. Sprinkle with Parmesan cheese. Shake salad dressing and toss salad with desired amount of dressing.

Helpful Hints: Always tear lettuce for tossed salads. Cutting it will cause lettuce to turn brown and gives salad a bitter taste.

Spinach with Honey Mustard Dressing

YIELDS: 4 servings

DRESSING

2	tablespoons salad oil
2	tablespoons cider vinegar
2	tablespoons honey
2	tablespoons Dijon mustard
1	clove garlic, crushed and minced
½	teaspoon pepper, freshly ground
2	tablespoons sesame seeds, toasted

1. Shake all ingredients in a glass jar and refrigerate 24 hours for flavors to blend.

SALAD

2	bunches spinach, washed, dried, stemmed, and crisped
4	green onions (tops only), chopped
1	large orange, peeled, cut in half, and thinly sliced
4	slices crisp bacon, crumbled

1. Just before serving, toss salad ingredients with dressing (use all or as much as suits your taste). Place salad on plates and garnish with crumbled bacon.

Chicken Taco Salad

YIELDS: 4-6 servings

The beauty of this dish is in the layering, so use a clear glass bowl or trifle dish. Easily doubled.

DRESSING

1	medium avocado
1	tablespoon lemon juice
½	cup sour cream
¼	cup vegetable oil
1	clove garlic, minced
½	teaspoon sugar
½	teaspoon chili powder
¼	teaspoon salt
¼	teaspoon hot pepper sauce

1. Mix dressing ingredients until smooth. This may be done in a blender. Chill.

SALAD

½	medium head lettuce, shredded
2	cups cooked chicken, cubed
1	tomato, seeded and chopped
½	cup ripe olives, sliced
¼	cup scallions, sliced
8	slices bacon, fried and crumbled
¾	cup Cheddar cheese, grated
1	cup corn chips, crushed

1. Layer salad ingredients beginning with lettuce and ending with cheese, in 2 quart glass dish.

2. Spread chilled dressing over top and sprinkle with crushed corn chips.

Variation: Use two 6½-ounce cans of tuna, drained, in place of the chicken.

Must be made ahead.

Cobb Salad

YIELDS: 6 servings

The hallmark of this salad is the way the ingredients are arranged in symmetrical bands over the greens—a beautiful luncheon presentation!

5	cups mixed salad greens, torn in bite size pieces	½	cup Bleu cheese, crumbled
2	medium tomatoes, peeled, seeded, and diced	1	medium avocado, peeled and diced
2	whole chicken breasts, poached, chilled, and diced	4-5	green onions, chopped your favorite salad dressing
3	hard boiled eggs, chopped		
8	slices bacon, fried, and crumbled		

1. Place salad greens in a large shallow salad bowl.

2. Arrange the tomatoes in a band over the greens down the center of the bowl from edge to edge.

3. Arrange the chicken in two bands, one on each side of the tomatoes. Continue arranging bands of the ingredients on each side working out from the middle.

4. Serve each person a portion of the salad and pass the dressing on the side.

Helpful Hints: To keep a vegetable salad from becoming soggy when it has to stand for a few hours, place a saucer upside down on the bottom of the bowl before filling it with salad. The moisture will run underneath and the salad will remain fresh and crisp.

Crabmeat Salad on Fried Noodles

Yields: 8 servings

For ease in preparation, make the noodles a day ahead.

2	(6-ounce) packages frozen crabmeat, thawed and drained	1	tablespoon lemon juice
		⅛	teaspoon curry powder
		1	teaspoon soy sauce
1	(10-ounce) package frozen peas, thawed	⅛	teaspoon garlic salt
		1½	cups fettuccini, broken in 3-4 inch pieces
1	cup celery, chopped		peanut oil
1	small onion, minced		fresh parsley, chopped
¾	cup mayonnaise		

1. Combine first 4 ingredients; toss well.

2. Combine next 5 ingredients, mixing well. Pour dressing over crab mixture and toss lightly. Chill.

3. Cook fettuccini according to package directions; drain. Rinse with cold water and drain. Pat almost dry with paper towels or run through salad spinner.

4. Heat oil to 350 degrees in large skillet. Drop several noodles into hot oil, and stir to separate (oil will splatter if enough water was not drained from noodles). Fry about one minute or until lightly browned. Drain on paper towels. Repeat procedure with the remaining noodles.

5. Serve crabmeat mixture over fried noodles. Sprinkle with chopped parsley.

 SALADS

Curried Chicken Salad

YIELDS: 4 servings

Dry Chenin Blanc goes well with this salad.

2	whole chicken breasts, split, boned, cubed		salt and pepper to taste
1	tart green apple, cubed and unpeeled	1	teaspoon lemon juice
		⅔	cup Hellmann's mayonnaise
3	green onions, tops only, chopped	2	teaspoons curry powder
		2	large ripe avocados
2	stalks celery, chopped		lemon wedges
¼	cup slivered almonds, toasted		

1. Poach chicken breasts lightly in simmering water just until done. Cool, skin, and cube.

2. Combine all ingredients and chill. Serve mounded on avocado halves or in lettuce cups. Garnish with lemon wedges.

Lemonade Fruit Dressing

YIELDS: 1½ cups

Sweet and very tangy!

1	egg	1	cup Cool Whip or ½ cup whipping cream, whipped
3	tablespoons sugar		
3	ounces frozen lemonade concentrate		

1. Beat egg in saucepan until lemon colored. Stir in sugar and lemonade concentrate. Cook until thickened. Cool and add Cool Whip or whipped cream. Place in a glass container, cover, and refrigerate.

Serve a dollop over any kind of fresh fruit. In winter use canned pineapple, oranges, grapes, and bananas. This dressing is also good over gingerbread.

Will store in refrigerator about 1 week.

Exotic Chicken Salad

YIELDS: 6 servings

Perfect for that special luncheon.

SALAD

3 cups cooked chicken, cut in chunks	1 cup fresh pineapple chunks or (9-ounce) can
1 cup celery	1 cup slivered almonds (reserve ¼ cup for garnish)
1 cup orange sections	

DRESSING

2 tablespoons salad oil	2 tablespoons vinegar
½ cup Hellmann's mayonnaise or sour cream	½ teaspoon salt dash of marjoram
2 tablespoons orange juice	

1. Combine all salad ingredients in bowl.

2. Mix all dressing ingredients. Toss salad and dressing. Garnish with almonds.

Victoria House Dressing

YIELDS: 1½ cups

1 egg	¼ teaspoon prepared mustard
1 ounce Bleu cheese juice of ½ lemon	1 clove garlic, peeled
½ teaspoon salt	½ cup olive oil
	½ cup sour cream

1. Bring all ingredients to room temperature. Place the first six ingredients in blender. Blend at low speed.

2. Very slowly add the oil while blender is running. Add the sour cream and mix until blended. The dressing will be slightly thickened.

Japanese Salad

YIELDS: 8 servings

An Oriental flair with easy to find ingredients.

DRESSING

4	tablespoons sugar	½	teaspoon pepper
2	teaspoons salt	4	tablespoons white vinegar
3	teaspoons Accent	½	cup salad oil

1. Shake all ingredients together and refrigerate or make just before serving.

SALAD

2	whole chicken breasts	1	small can chow mein noodles
1	head lettuce, shredded		
3	green onions, chopped	1	small package slivered almonds
¼	cup poppy seeds		

1. Boil chicken breasts until tender and tear into slivers. Add lettuce and green onions.

2. Add poppy seeds, chow mein noodles, and almonds just before serving. Toss with dressing and serve immediately.

Mandarin Shrimp Salad

YIELDS: 6 servings

A pleasant blend of tropical fruit, fresh seafood, and garden greens.

3	cups iceberg lettuce, torn	1	medium onion, thinly sliced
1	cup romaine, torn	2	tablespoons vinegar
9	ounces fresh baby shrimp, cooked	¼	cup vegetable oil
1	(11-ounce) can mandarin oranges, drained	2	teaspoons sesame seeds
		2	teaspoons soy sauce
1	cup slivered almonds, toasted	2	teaspoons lemon juice
		2	teaspoons dry sherry

1. Toast almonds by placing them on a baking sheet and bake in a preheated 350 degree oven until lightly browned. Watch closely.

2. Combine first six ingredients in a large bowl.

3. Combine remaining ingredients and mix well. Pour over salad mixture just before serving; toss gently to coat. Serve immediately.

Reuben Salad

YIELDS: 6 servings

A great salad for a casual luncheon on the patio or even a summer supper!

8	cups leaf lettuce, torn	1	cup Swiss cheese, cubed
1	cup cooked corned beef, cut in thin strips	1	cup rye croutons
1	(8-ounce) can sauerkraut, rinsed, drained, chilled	¾	cup Thousand Island dressing
		½	teaspoon caraway seed

1. In a large salad bowl, combine lettuce, corned beef, sauerkraut, cheese, and rye croutons.

2. Combine salad dressing and caraway seed, pour over salad and toss.

Melon Melee

- ¼ pound prosciutto ham, cut into 2 inch strips
- ¼ pound sliced, smoked turkey or chicken, cut into 2 inch strips
- ½ large honeydew or cantalope melon, scooped into balls
- 1 cup cherry tomatoes, sliced in half
- 1 tablespoon fresh basil
- 4 cups assorted lettuce such as romaine, chicory, endive, torn

1. Place all ingredients in bowl. Just before serving add enough Melon Vinaigrette to coat and then toss.

MELON VINAIGRETTE

- 1 small clove garlic, crushed
- ½ teaspoon coarse salt
- ¼ teaspoon Dijon mustard
- ⅓ cup olive oil
  juice of ½ lime
- 2-4 tablespoons Midori melon liqueur

1. Mash garlic and salt together in food processor. Add remaining ingredients and mix well.

Note: Midori liqueur may be bought in small bottles at wine and beverage stores.

Genovesi Pasta Salad

YIELDS: 8 servings

1 cup small tomato pasta shells
1 cup small spinach pasta shells
2 teaspoons salt
2 cups zucchini, cubed
⅓ cup vinegar
1 teaspoon prepared mustard
1 small clove garlic, crushed

1 tablespoon Worcestershire sauce
1 cup vegetable oil
pinch freshly ground black pepper
1 cup Genovesi dried tomatoes, drained and cut into strips
8 ounces Feta or Goat cheese, cubed

1. Cook tomato and spinach pasta in a large pot of boiling water seasoned with ½ teaspoon salt until tender, 8 to 10 minutes. Rinse, drain, and set aside. Blanch zucchini in boiling water seasoned with ½ teaspoon salt until crisp tender, 2 to 4 minutes. Rinse in cold water, drain, and set aside.

2. In small mixing bowl, combine remaining teaspoon salt, vinegar, mustard, garlic, Worcestershire, and oil, season with pepper and beat with a wire whisk until mustard is incorporated. Taste and correct seasoning, if necessary.

3. In a large mixing bowl, combine cooked pasta with one cup of the vinaigrette and toss. Allow pasta to rest and absorb the vinaigrette for about 30 minutes.

4. Just before serving time, add remaining vinaigrette, zucchini, tomatoes, and cheese and toss well. Season to taste.

GARNISH

1 pound fresh spinach leaves, washed and dried

2 tablespoons fresh parsley, chopped
2 tablespoons fresh cilantro, chopped

1. To serve, arrange a bed of fresh spinach leaves on individual plates, mound pasta salad on top, and garnish with chopped parsley and cilantro.

German Pasta Salad

YIELDS: 4-6 servings

A great main dish salad.

12	ounces Kielbasa (Polish sausage)	3	tablespoons sugar
½	cup water	2	tablespoons flour
1½	cups shell or rotini pasta, uncooked	½	teaspoon salt
6	slices bacon	⅛	teaspoon pepper
3	tablespoons bacon drippings	¾	cup water
1	cup fresh mushrooms, sliced	¼	cup tarragon vinegar
		2	tablespoons parsley

1. Simmer sliced sausage, covered in ½ cup water, for 20 minutes.

2. Cook pasta according to package directions. Drain.

3. Cook bacon and crumble. Saute mushrooms in 3 tablespoons bacon drippings for 2 minutes. Stir in sugar, flour, salt, and pepper. Add ¾ cup water and vinegar. Cook and stir until thick. Add sausage, pasta, bacon, and parsley. Toss well and serve immediately.

Sumptuous Shrimp Salad

YIELDS: 6-8 servings

Toss and enjoy!

1	cup rice, cooked and chilled	3	tablespoons French dressing
1	pound shrimp, cooked	1	tablespoon black olives, chopped
¾	teaspoon salt	1	cup raw cauliflower, cut in small florets
1	tablespoon lemon juice	⅓	cup mayonnaise
1	tablespoon green onion, minced		

1. Combine all ingredients. Serve on a bed of spinach or romaine leaves.

Manhattan Deli Salad

YIELDS: 8-10 servings

- 12 ounces spiral pasta
- 1¼ cups pitted ripe olives, sliced
- 1 cup red or green pepper, chopped
- ¼ pound hard salami, cut into thin strips
- ¼ pound Provolone cheese, cut into thin strips
- 1 small red onion, sliced into rings
- ¼ to ½ cup Parmesan cheese, grated
- ¼ cup parsley, finely chopped
- ¾ cup Wishbone Italian dressing

1. Cook pasta according to package directions.

2. Combine olives, pepper, salami, Provolone cheese, onion, Parmesan cheese, parsley, and dressing in a large bowl. Add pasta and toss well. Serve at room temperature or chilled.

Variation: 12 ounces cheese filled tortellini may be used in place of spiral pasta.

May be prepared ahead 2 to 3 days.

Watercress Dressing

YIELDS: ¾ cup

Bright green color. An excellent delicate flavor.

- ½ cup olive oil
- 2 tablespoons cider vinegar
- ½ bunch watercress, coarse stems removed, washed and dried
- ½ clove garlic
- ⅛ teaspoon salt

1. Whirl together all ingredients in a blender until thoroughly mixed and light. The specks of watercress will coat the lettuce and flavor it.

Enough for 2 heads of Boston lettuce. Top with slivered, blanched almonds.

 **SALADS**

Sunshine Pasta Salad

SALAD

1	(20-ounce) can pineapple chunks	1	cup celery, sliced
4	cups corkscrew pasta, cooked	½	cup fresh parsley, chopped
2	cups fresh broccoli florets	⅓	cup green onion, chopped
1	cup frozen peas, thawed	⅓	cup red bell pepper, diced

1. Drain pineapple, reserving 2 tablespoons of juice.

2. Combine all ingredients in large bowl.

DRESSING

2	tablespoons pineapple juice	2	tablespoons lemon juice
1	clove garlic, crushed	2	tablespoons Dijon mustard
¾	cup olive oil	2	teaspoons dried basil
⅓	cup white vinegar		salt to taste

1. Combine all ingredients and shake well.

2. Toss prepared salad mixture with dressing and let marinate 1 hour before serving.

Must be made ahead.

Vinaigrette Tortellini Salad

YIELDS: 6-8 servings

A tasty pasta salad that serves well as a side dish or a first course.

MARINADE
- ¼ cup rosé or tarragon vinegar
- 1 tablespoon Worcestershire sauce
- 1½ tablespoons Dijon mustard
- ½ to 1 teaspoon coarsely ground pepper
- 1 small clove garlic, minced
- 1 tablespoon sugar
- 1 teaspoon salt
- dash of Tabasco sauce

1. Combine marinade ingredients. Blend well.

SALAD
- 7 ounces tortellini
- ¼ cup olive oil
- ¼ cup vegetable oil
- ½ cup celery, diced
- ½ cup scallions, chopped
- ½ cup cucumber, diced
- ½ cup Cheddar cheese, diced
- ¼ cup parsley, chopped
- ⅓ cup pimento, chopped

1. Cook tortellini until al denté. Drain and rinse in cold water. Place tortellini in medium bowl and add oils. Toss well. Add remaining ingredients to tortellini and mix. Pour marinade over mixture and toss well. Cover and refrigerate for 8-12 hours. Serve cold or at room temperature.

Must be prepared at least 8 to 12 hours before serving.

Bavarian Potato Salad

YIELDS: 12 servings

A hint of bacon and a touch of cream all add to the wonderful blending of this old world recipe.

5 eggs, hard boiled	⅔ cup water
3 pounds red potatoes	1 cup cider vinegar
1 medium onion, diced	⅔ cup sugar
½ cup celery, diced	2 tablespoons plus
1 teaspoon salt	2 teaspoons cornstarch
⅛ teaspoon pepper	⅛ cup coffee cream
3 strips bacon, reserve drippings	

1. Peel and slice eggs, reserving 1 egg for garnish.

2. Boil potatoes. When cool enough to handle, peel and slice. To potatoes add onion, celery, and eggs. Add salt and pepper.

3. Fry bacon, then crumble, and set aside. To bacon drippings add water, vinegar, and sugar. Bring to a boil, stirring.

4. Dissolve cornstarch in 3 tablespoons water and add to mixture. Stir constantly and bring to a boil until thickened. Remove from heat; slowly add cream. Pour sauce over warm potato mixture and add crumbled bacon. Stir to mix and garnish with egg slices. Serve at room temperature or chilled.

May be prepared 1 day ahead.

Helpful Hints: Potato Salad tip—Potatoes have a better flavor if cooked in the skins or baked. Cut up potatoes while warm, not cold.

Bleu Cheese and Bacon Potatoes

YIELDS: 8 servings

The man in your life will love these!

20 small new red potatoes	¼ cup whipping cream
½ pound bacon, fried, drained, and crumbled	(lightly whipped)
1 cup mayonnaise	¼ cup Bleu cheese, crumbled
	parsley, finely chopped

1. Boil potatoes until just tender.

2. Combine mayonnaise, lightly whipped cream, and Bleu cheese. Fold dressing into whole or sliced potatoes. Garnish with crumbled bacon and parsley.

Greek Potato Salad

YIELDS: 12 servings

Delicious served either hot or cold.

8-10 Idaho potatoes	1 green pepper, chopped
1 cup Marzetti's Italian dressing, divided	½ cup celery, chopped
2 ripe tomatoes, chopped	1 can pitted ripe olives, chopped
1 large sweet onion, chopped	1 tablespoon oregano
	1 tablespoon parsley flakes

1. Bake whole potatoes until jackets are crisp. While hot, cut into bite size pieces with jackets.

2. Pour ½ cup dressing over potatoes and set aside.

3. Chop the tomatoes, onion, green pepper, celery, and olives and add to the potatoes. Toss in the remaining ½ cup dressing, oregano, and parsley.

Note: Salad is always best served the same day, but will keep well in the refrigerator for 2-3 days.

Creamy Coconut Mold

YIELDS: 12 servings

If prepared in a ring mold, fill the center with fresh fruit for a spectacular look.

1½ cups cold water
2 envelopes unflavored
    gelatin
1 (24-ounce) carton
    cottage cheese
1 (14-ounce) can Eagle
    Brand sweetened
    condensed milk

1 (3-ounce) package cream
    cheese, softened
1 cup coconut, shredded
1 cup nuts, chopped
½ teaspoon almond extract
3 cups fresh fruit, cut
    into bite size pieces

1. Lightly oil 1½ quart mold. (A ring mold works best.)

2. In small saucepan, sprinkle gelatin over water to soften. Stir over low heat until gelatin dissolves. Set aside.

3. In large bowl, combine cottage cheese, sweetened condensed milk, cream cheese, coconut, nuts, and extract. Mix well. Stir in gelatin. Refrigerate until slightly thickened, about 10 minutes. Stir and pour mixture into mold. Refrigerate 3 hours or until firm.

4. To unmold, gently run knife around edge. Turn onto serving plate. Serve with fruit in the center and around edges as garnish.

Must be prepared ahead.

Frozen Lime Mint Salad

YIELDS: 16 servings

Cheerfully cool, light, and refreshing.

1   (8¼-ounce) can
    crushed pineapple,
    undrained
1   (20-ounce) can crushed
    pineapple, undrained
1   (3-ounce) package lime
    Jello

1   (7-ounce) jar marshmallow
    cream
1   cup butter mints,
    coarsely chopped
1   (8-ounce) carton Cool
    Whip, thawed

1. In a large bowl combine both cans of pineapple, dry Jello, marshmallow cream, and mints. Fold in Cool Whip.

2. Spoon mixture into 16 muffin liners in muffin tin. Cover and freeze 6 hours or overnight. Peel off paper and serve on lettuce. Garnish with mint sprigs. Serve immediately.

Must be prepared in advance.

White French Dressing

YIELDS: 1½ cups

1   cup vegetable oil
2   tablespoons white
    wine vinegar
6   tablespoons sour cream
¼   cup orange juice
2   tablespoons lemon juice

¼   cup powdered sugar, sifted
¼   teaspoon salt
¾   teaspoon dry mustard
¾   teaspoon Worcestershire
    sauce
1   small clove garlic, minced

1. Process all ingredients in electric blender on medium speed for 2 minutes or until thickened. Refrigerate in a covered container.

Lemon Blueberry Mold

YIELDS: 8 servings

A pretty, easy-to-make gelatin mold.

FIRST LAYER

1   small package lemon   1   (20-ounce) can blueberries
    Jello

1. Drain blueberries. Measure juice, adding enough water to make 1¾ cups. Heat to boiling. Add Jello. Dissolve and cool until consistency of unbeaten egg white.

2. Fold in drained blueberries. Pour in 1½ quart mold and chill.

SECOND LAYER

1   small package lemon   1   cup whipping cream
     Jello   1½   tablespoons powdered sugar
1¾   cups boiling water   1   teaspoon vanilla
2   (3-ounce) packages cream
     cheese, softened

1. Dissolve Jello in water and cool until consistency of an unbeaten egg white.

2. Beat softened cream cheese and whipping cream until stiff. Add powdered sugar and vanilla. Beat into partially thickened Jello. Pour over first layer. Chill until set. Garnish with lettuce.

Easy. Must be prepared ahead.

Raspberry Mold

YIELDS: 6-8 servings

1 (10-ounce) package frozen raspberries, thawed or 2 cups fresh
1 (6-ounce) package raspberry Jello
2 cups boiling water

2 cups vanilla ice cream
1 (6-ounce) can frozen pink lemonade concentrate
¼ cup pecans, chopped

1. Drain raspberries and reserve juice.

2. Dissolve gelatin in boiling water. Add ice cream, a small amount at a time, until melted. Add lemonade and then the reserved raspberry juice. Chill until partially set.

3. Fold in drained raspberries and pecans. Pour into a lightly oiled mold or individual goblets. Unmold before serving and garnish with raspberries and mint leaves.

Must be prepared ahead.

Helpful Hints: Grease mold with a vegetable spray or mayonnaise to aid in unmolding of gelatin salad.

Sherried Grape Mold

YIELDS: 6-8 servings

Perfect for a New Year's buffet.

¾ cup sugar
2 envelopes unflavored gelatin
1 cup water
2 cups white wine

⅔ cup sweet sherry
3 cups seedless green or red grapes (about 1 pound)
¾ cup sour cream

1. Combine sugar, gelatin, and water in a saucepan. Cook over low heat, stirring constantly until sugar and gelatin are dissolved. Add wine and sherry.

2. Rinse and drain grapes. Place half of them in a 6 cup mold. Pour half the gelatin mixture over the grapes.

3. Pour remaining gelatin mixture in a bowl. Place both containers in refrigerator to chill.

4. Once the mixture in the bowl is slightly thickened, remove it from the refrigerator. Add sour cream and whip until fluffy. Fold in remaining grapes. Pour into mold. Chill until firm. When ready to serve, quickly dip the mold in hot water and invert onto platter. Remove mold. Garnish with grape clusters.

Must be prepared ahead.

Strawberry Surprise

YIELDS: 12-16 servings

A delicious gelatin with a surprise pretzel base!

FIRST LAYER
2   cups fresh pretzels, crushed

¼   cup sugar
¾   cup margarine, melted

1. Combine above ingredients and press in a 9 x 13 inch pan. Bake in a preheated 325 degree oven for 10 minutes. Cool.

SECOND LAYER
1   package Dream Whip
1   (8-ounce) package cream cheese, softened

¾   cup sugar

1. Prepare Dream Whip according to directions. Blend with cream cheese and sugar. Spread over cooled first layer. Refrigerate until third layer is ready.

THIRD LAYER
1   large package strawberry Jello
2   cups pineapple juice

2   (10-ounce) packages frozen strawberries

1. Heat pineapple juice almost to boiling point. Mix juice, gelatin, and strawberries together and let set in bowl about 15 minutes. Gently spoon mixture over second layer. Refrigerate until third layer is firm. Cut into squares to serve.

Easy. May be prepared 1 to 2 days ahead.

Tangy Fruit Mold

YIELDS: 8 servings

Serve individually in parfait glasses for an elegant touch.

3 cups water
1 (6-ounce) package
  peach gelatin
1 (8-ounce) carton
  plain yogurt
1 (3-ounce) package
  cream cheese, softened
  and cubed

1 (6-ounce) can frozen
  lemonade concentrate,
  thawed
  strawberries, raspberries,
  blueberries, grapes, or
  peach slices

1. Heat water to boiling in small saucepan. Dissolve gelatin in boiling water.

2. Pour 2¼ cups hot gelatin into blender container. Set aside remaining 1¼ cups gelatin. Add yogurt, cream cheese, and lemonade concentrate to gelatin in blender. Blend until smooth. Pour into 10 inch glass pie plate or quiche pan. Refrigerate until firm. Arrange fruit over top.

3. Refrigerate reserved gelatin until thick enough to coat a spoon. Spoon thickened gelatin evenly over fruit to glaze. Cover. Refrigerate overnight or until set. (May use 8 parfait glasses in place of pie plate.)

Must be prepared ahead.

Banana-Peanut Salad

YIELDS: 4 servings

A very fresh tasting salad!

2	oranges	1	tablespoon cornstarch
1	lemon	4	bananas, sliced
½	cup sugar	½	cup dry roasted peanuts

1. Squeeze juice from oranges and lemon (any pulp is okay). In a small saucepan, mix juices with sugar and cornstarch. Heat to boiling and stir until thickened to a sauce. Remove and cool. (If sauce is made ahead, store in refrigerator in covered container.)

2. To serve, slice bananas and add peanuts; gently stir sauce through to coat fruit. Serve immediately or chill in refrigerator until ready to use.

Glazed Fresh Fruit

YIELDS: 4 servings

A terrific fruit accompaniment without sugar.

1	tablespoon cornstarch	1	cup orange sections
¼	teaspoon ground ginger	2	cups strawberries, halved
1	cup orange juice	1	cup apples, chopped

1. Stir together cornstarch and ginger in small saucepan. Gradually stir in orange juice until smooth. Bring to a boil over medium heat, stirring constantly. Boil 1 minute. Allow to cool to room temperature.

2. Toss fruit together in large bowl and chill. Just before serving pour juice mixture over fruit. Toss gently and coat well.

47 calories per ½ cup serving.

Black Fruit Salad

YIELDS: 4 servings

For a variation use a combination of green grapes, kiwis, and green apples.

1 cup black cherries, pitted	juice of 1 lemon
½ cup blueberries	1 cup sour cream
1 cup black grapes	fresh mint sprigs
⅓ cup light brown sugar, packed	

1. Combine fruits and sprinkle with brown sugar and lemon juice. Let stand for 2 hours, tossing several times.

2. Lift out fruit with slotted spoon and divide equally among 4 balloon wine glasses.

3. Stir sour cream into collected juices in bowl. Serve fruits topped with a dollop of sour cream sauce and a sprig of fresh mint.

If you double the fruit recipe, the sauce does not need to be doubled.

Must be prepared ahead.

Helpful Hints: Freeze citrus rinds before grating. This makes the job easier.

Carry-In Fruit Salad

YIELDS: 20 servings

A colorful symphony of early summer fruits.

1 **pound blueberries**	1 **fresh pineapple**
1 **quart strawberries, sliced**	1 **small package Jello instant vanilla pudding**
1 **pound white grapes, sliced or whole**	1 **can peach pie filling**
1 **pound purple grapes, sliced or whole**	

1. Prepare all fruits as noted above.

2. Peel pineapple, cut in quarters, remove core, and cut into cubes. Save any juice that accumulates.

3. Mix together pudding and pie filling. Pour over fruit and mix. Let stand 24 hours. If mixture is too thick, thin with pineapple juice.

Note: The fruit is easily halved. Save the rest of the dressing for use as a fruit dip.

May be prepared 1 day ahead.

Kiwi Fruit Compote

YIELDS: 6 servings

A good choice for a brunch fruit salad.

2 **kiwi, pared, sliced, and halved**	1 **cup red grapes, halved and sliced**
1 **red apple, cored and thinly sliced**	1 **banana, peeled and sliced**
2 **tablespoons Grand Marnier or Triple Sec**	

1. Gently toss together all ingredients. Serve on Boston lettuce leaves.

Creamy Fruit Salad

YIELDS: 8 servings

1 (15-ounce) can pineapple chunks	2 bananas, sliced
2 tablespoons lemon juice	2 apples, cubed
1 cup sugar	½ pound seedless grapes, halved
1 tablespoon flour	½ cup whipping cream, whipped
2 egg yolks	
2 oranges, sectioned	

1. Drain pineapple, reserving juice, and set aside. Add enough water to pineapple juice to make 1 cup. Combine with next four ingredients in a heavy saucepan and mix well. Cook over medium heat, stirring constantly, until dressing is smooth and thickened. Remove from heat and cool completely.

2. Combine pineapple and remaining fruit in a large bowl.

3. Add whipped cream to dressing mixture and fold into fruit. Chill well.

Must be prepared early in the day.

Raspberries and Bananas

YIELDS: 4 servings

2 (10-ounce) packages frozen sweetened raspberries	2 tablespoons unblanched almonds, sliced fresh mint leaves (optional)
4 ripe bananas	
3 teaspoons lemon juice	

1. Thaw and drain raspberries, reserve ¼ cup syrup. Peel bananas; cut diagonally into ¼ inch slices. Arrange bananas on 4 dessert plates in sunburst pattern. Brush or drizzle with 2 teaspoons lemon juice. Mound raspberries in center of bananas, dividing evenly.

2. Mix ¼ cup reserved syrup and remaining 1 teaspoon lemon juice. Spoon over raspberries, evenly. Refrigerate covered. Sprinkle with almonds at serving time and garnish with mint leaves.

Pineapple-Cheese Salad

YIELDS: 4 servings

An attractive salad served in scooped out pineapple halves.

1 large fresh pineapple	½ cup celery, diced
6 ounces sharp Cheddar cheese	½ medium green pepper, diced
¾ cup mayonnaise (not salad dressing)	8 ounces Swiss cheese, shredded, or cut into bite size pieces
2 tablespoons milk	¾ cup croutons
½ teaspoon salt	

1. With sharp knife, slice pineapple into 4 wedges from bottom through crown, leaving on leafy crown for decoration. Cut off hard core from each wedge; then with paring knife, loosen fruit by cutting close to rind leaving ½ inch thick shell; cover with plastic wrap and refrigerate shells. Cut fruit in bite size pieces.

2. Shred ⅓ cup (2-ounces) Cheddar cheese for garnish; set aside. Cut remaining cheese into bite size pieces or shred.

3. In medium bowl with fork, blend mayonnaise, milk, and salt. Stir in celery, green pepper, pineapple, croutons, and the Cheddar and Swiss pieces. Mound mixture in the chilled pineapple shells. Sprinkle Cheddar cheese on top.

May be prepared early in the day.

Layered Fruit Salad

Impress your guests!

In a trifle dish, make layers of five fruits in a variety of colors. Some suggestions are peaches, blueberries, kiwi, strawberries, oranges, and cherries. Spread a layer of Lemonade Fruit Dressing or Luscious Fruit Dip over the top layer of fruit. This makes a lovely presentation at a brunch buffet.

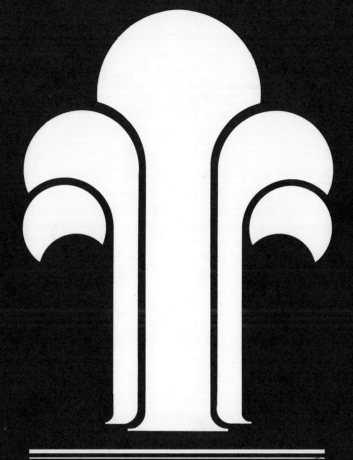

SOUPS AND SANDWICHES

SOUPS AND SANDWICHES

Avgolemono Soup
(Egg Lemon Soup)

YIELDS: 6-8 servings

Serve with salad and bread for a nice meal.

3½ **pound chicken**	¾ **cup rice or very thin**
2 **carrots, sliced**	**noodles (Fethe)**
1 **stalk celery, sliced**	4 **eggs, room temperature**
1 **medium onion, chopped**	**dash of water**
1¼ **teaspoons salt**	**juice of 1 large lemon**
1/16 **teaspoon pepper**	**(4 tablespoons)**
water to cover	1 **cup chicken pieces**
	(optional)

1. Place chicken, carrots, celery, onion, salt, and pepper in a large pot. Cover chicken with water. Bring to a boil. Cover and simmer for 1½ hours. Remove chicken. Skin, debone, and cut into small chunks. Strain the broth. Add more salt and pepper, if necessary. Remove fat.

2. Combine broth and rice. Boil, then reduce heat. Cover and simmer until rice is tender, about 30 minutes. Remove pan from heat. Add chicken pieces.

3. In bowl, beat eggs until fluffy and pale yellow, adding water. Beat in lemon juice. Slowly pour 2 cups of hot broth into egg mixture, beating so eggs do not curdle. Pour mixture into remaining broth and stir over low heat for one minute. Remove from heat. Stir occasionally until ready to serve.

Note: May substitute 8 cups chicken broth, 1¼ teaspoons salt, and 1/16 teaspoon pepper in place of first seven ingredients.

Caldo
(Spanish Soup)

YIELDS: 12 servings

A unique chicken soup.

2½	quarts water	4	garlic cloves, minced
1	3-pound chicken	1	tablespoon oregano
1	tablespoon chicken bouillon granules	¼	teaspoon cloves
2	teaspoons salt	2	cups carrots, sliced
2	teaspoons cumin	1	green pepper, diced
½	teaspoon basil	2	cups zucchini, sliced
1	teaspoon pepper	1	medium onion, sliced
3	bay leaves	1	(14-ounce) can garbanzo beans

1. Bring water to a boil. Add chicken, stock base, salt, cumin, pepper, bay leaves, and basil.

2. Mix garlic, oregano, and cloves to a paste. Add to soup mixture.

3. Simmer chicken 45 minutes to an hour until cooked. Remove chicken to cool.

4. Add carrots, pepper, zucchini, onions, and beans to the soup mixture and bring to a boil. Simmer 15 minutes.

5. Skin and debone chicken, slice, and add to soup.

Chicken and Ham Burgoo

YIELDS: 18-20 servings

Serve with a salad and cornbread for a complete meal.

1	(3-pound) roasting chicken	1	package frozen corn
4	ham hocks or ham, diced	2	cups cabbage, shredded
3	teaspoons salt	2	cups celery, thinly sliced
½	teaspoon chili powder	2	cups tomatoes, diced
2	cups potatoes, diced	2	tablespoons Worcestershire sauce
2	cups carrots, diced	1	cup green pepper, diced
2	large onions, diced	2	tablespoons parsley
1	package frozen green beans	1	teaspoon basil
1	package frozen peas	½	teaspoon pepper
1	package frozen okra	¼	cup margarine

1. Put chicken and ham hocks in large soup kettle. Add enough water to cover chicken and ham hocks. Cook over medium heat until done. Cool.

2. Let broth from ham and chicken cool, then remove fat. Measure broth and return 12 cups to the kettle. Skin and debone chicken. Dice chicken and ham. Add other ingredients. Bring to a boil, then simmer for 2 hours or until thick.

May be prepared ahead.

Chili-5 Ways

YIELDS: 16 servings

Serve it up your way or all 5 ways!

2½ pounds ground beef
1 pound ground lean pork
5 large onions, chopped
3 large green peppers, chopped
2 garlic cloves, crushed
2 (32-ounce) cans whole, peeled tomatoes, undrained
2 cups tomato juice
1 (16-ounce) can kidney beans
⅓ cup chili powder
2 teaspoons cumin
1 teaspoon monosodium glutamate

1 tablespoon oregano
2 bay leaves
1 tablespoon sugar
1 tablespoon sweet paprika
2 tablespoons salt
1½ teaspoons pepper
16 ounces spaghetti, cooked and drained
1 (16-ounce) can kidney beans, warmed
1 large onion, finely chopped
2 cups Cheddar cheese, grated
oyster crackers

1. Cook ground meat, onion, garlic, and green pepper until meat loses its color and onion is transparent.

2. Add tomatoes, tomato juice, and beans. Add all seasonings. Simmer, covered, for 1 hour. Skim. Remove bay leaves. For best flavor, refrigerate overnight before reheating.

3. To construct the plate of 5-way, layer spaghetti on a plate (a small oval plate is traditional), top it with chili, then with a sparse layer of kidney beans, and then chopped onions. Sprinkle on the cheese while the chili is still hot and serve immediately, with oyster crackers on the side. You may, if desired, omit either the beans or onions, or both, for 3-way or 4-way chili.

Italian Sausage Zucchini Soup

YIELDS: 6 servings

Serve with Parmesan cheese and garlic bread.

1	pound Italian sausage, mild or hot	1	teaspoon salt
2	cups celery, sliced in ½ inch pieces	1	teaspoon Italian dressing
2	pounds zucchini, sliced in ½ inch pieces	1	teaspoon oregano
1	cup onion, chopped	1	teaspoon sugar
2	(28-ounce) cans tomatoes, undrained, fresh may be used	½	teaspoon basil
		¼	teaspoon garlic powder
		2	green peppers, cut into ½ inch pieces

1. Brown sausage in large Dutch oven; drain off fat. Add celery and cook for 10 minutes.

2. Add remaining ingredients, except green pepper. Simmer, covered, for 20 minutes.

3. Add green pepper and cook, covered, for an additional 10 minutes.

May be made ahead and frozen.

Italian Wedding Soup

YIELDS: 6-8 servings

A traditional Italian delight!

MEATBALLS

¾ pound ground beef, pork, and veal mixture
1 egg, beaten
¼ cup dry bread crumbs
2 tablespoons Parmesan cheese, grated
1 tablespoon parsley flakes

¼ teaspoon garlic salt
¼ teaspoon ground black pepper
1 teaspoon oregano, crumbled
1 tablespoon vegetable oil

1. Combine all ingredients, except oil; mix well. Form mixture into 50 small meatballs. Brown meatballs in hot oil; drain; set aside.

SOUP

3 (13¾-ounce) cans chicken broth
1 cup water
½ cup carrots, thinly sliced
½ cup celery, thinly sliced
½ cup green onions, thinly sliced

½ teaspoon sweet basil, crumbled
½ cup broken spaghetti, uncooked
½ pound escarole, chopped and cooked

1. Combine first 6 ingredients in large saucepan. Bring to boil. Reduce heat, cover, and simmer until vegetables are almost tender. Add spaghetti, escarole, and meatballs; simmer 10 minutes longer.

Pozole
(Pork and Hominy Soup)

YIELDS: 6-8 servings

This is a Mexican soup. Serve with big squares of hot cornbread, three-bean salad, and beer!

1	pound fresh pork ribs	2	medium onions, chopped
1½	quarts water	4	teaspoons salt
1	(1-pound) can whole tomatoes or 1 pound fresh	¼	teaspoon hot pepper seasoning
2	(1-pound) cans hominy, drained		

1. Put pork, water, tomatoes, hominy, onions, and salt into large kettle. Simmer 2-3 hours.

2. Remove meat from soup; cool broth and meat. Remove meat from bones and cut into small chunks.

3. Skim fat off soup. Just before serving, add meat to soup and heat. Season to taste.

Serve with an assortment of condiments, to be added to individual servings, such as: shredded lettuce, chopped green onions, hot chiles, cubes of cream cheese, Monterey Jack cheese, Cheddar cheese, or chopped avocados.

Helpful Hints: A lettuce leaf dropped in a pot of soup absorbs grease from the top of the soup. Remove lettuce as soon as it has absorbed grease.

Savory Winter Vegetable Soup

YIELDS: 6 servings

Tastes even better if prepared ahead 3-4 days.

8 tablespoons butter, divided	½ teaspoon basil
2 cups onion, chopped	½ teaspoon white pepper
6 tablespoons flour	1 cup celery, diced
6 cups rich chicken broth (College Inn, canned)	3-4 carrots, julienned
2 cups potatoes, diced	2 large leeks, julienned
1 bay leaf	6 large mushrooms, sliced
1½ teaspoons salt	½ to ¾ cup whipping cream

1. Saute onion in 4 tablespoons butter until soft but not brown. Add flour and stir over moderate heat for about 2 minutes. Gradually add chicken broth, whisking until smooth.

2. Add potatoes and seasonings; simmer, uncovered, until potatoes are almost tender.

3. Saute strips of carrots, mushrooms, and leeks in 4 tablespoons of butter until just softened, but not brown.

4. When potatoes in the soup are just barely cooked, add the chopped celery, which should remain crisp. Add the whipping cream, stir until smooth. Taste for seasonings, adding salt and pepper, if needed. Serve very hot, garnished with strips of leeks, carrots, and mushrooms.

Variation: Add 2 cups cooked, cubed chicken.

Tortilla Soup

YIELDS: 4-6 servings

Hot and spicy!

2 tablespoons oil	2 tablespoons chili powder
1 onion, chopped	2 teaspoons cumin
2 cloves garlic, chopped	1 tablespoon oregano
1 jalapeno pepper, chopped	salt and pepper to taste
2 cups peeled tomatoes, chopped	1 package flour tortillas
4 cups chicken broth	Mozzarella cheese, grated

1. Saute onion, garlic, and jalapeno pepper in oil. Add tomatoes, chicken broth, chili powder, cumin, oregano, salt, and pepper. Bring to a boil. Simmer 3-5 minutes.

2. Cut flour tortilla into strips. Deep fry.

3. To serve, place large amount of tortilla chips in bowl. Cover with soup. Sprinkle with Mozzarella cheese. If necessary, place in oven or microwave to melt cheese.

Doritos or Tostitos may be used instead of flour tortillas. May be made ahead and frozen 2-3 months.

Artichoke Soup

YIELDS: 8 servings

Elegant and simple!

½	cup butter	8	cups chicken broth
2	bunches green onions, chopped		dash of cayenne pepper
			salt
2	stalks celery, chopped	1	tablespoon Worcestershire
3	cloves garlic, minced		sauce
2	(14-ounce) cans artichoke hearts, cut into quarters	¼	teaspoon thyme
		⅓	cup sherry
3	tablespoons flour	2	cups half and half

1. Melt butter. Saute onions, celery, and garlic. Add artichoke hearts and mix gently.

2. Sprinkle with flour and add broth. Add Worcestershire sauce and thyme; simmer, covered, for 1 hour.

3. Add sherry and simmer for 10 minutes. Add half and half and simmer an additional 10 minutes. Do not allow soup to boil.

Company Crab Chowder

YIELDS: 4 servings

A seashore request that will come your way again and again.

1	(10-ounce) package frozen cauliflower	1	cup light cream
2	cups milk	3	tablespoons flour
2	tablespoons green onion, sliced	1	(7 ½-ounce) can crabmeat, drained, cartilage removed, and cut up
2	tablespoons pimento, diced	1	(3-ounce) package cream cheese, cubed
½	teaspoon salt		

1. In a 3 quart saucepan, cook cauliflower according to package directions. Do not drain. Cut up large pieces of cauliflower. Add milk, onion, pimento, and salt, and heat until just boiling.

2. Combine light cream and flour. Add to milk mixture and cook, stirring constantly, until bubbly and thick.

3. Add crabmeat and cubed cream cheese and heat until cheese melts and soup is hot. Season to taste with salt and pepper.

Creamy Cheese Soup

YIELDS: 6 servings

This creamy soup is a dreamy addition to an elegant meal.

2 cups water	1 (8-ounce) package
1 cup carrots, shredded,	cream cheese, cubed
about 3 medium carrots	2 cups milk
1 medium onion, chopped	2 tablespoons margarine
½ cup celery, chopped	2 tablespoons flour
1 teaspoon salt	parsley flakes
several dashes bottled	Parmesan cheese
hot pepper sauce	

1. In a 3 quart saucepan, combine water, carrots, onion, celery, salt, and hot pepper sauce. Bring to a boil. Reduce heat and cook, covered, for 15 minutes or until vegetables are tender. Add cream cheese and stir until melted. Add milk.

2. In small saucepan, melt margarine and blend in flour. Add to soup mixture. Cook, stirring until mixture thickens and bubbles. Garnish each serving with parsley flakes and lots of grated Parmesan cheese.

Fresh Tomato Soup

YIELDS: 4 servings

Although frozen tomatoes may be used, what a wonderful use for those fresh garden beauties.

2 cups fresh tomatoes,	2 tablespoons butter
canned or frozen may be	salt and pepper to taste
used	1 tablespoon dill weed or
¼ teaspoon baking soda	1 tablespoon basil
2 cups half and half	(optional)
2 cups milk	

1. Peel and quarter tomatoes. In a 2 quart saucepan, bring tomatoes to a boil; cook until soft.

2. Add baking soda. (Milk will curdle without baking soda.) Add half and half, milk, butter, salt, pepper, and seasonings. Heat until hot but not boiling.

Carrot Soup

YIELDS: 6 servings

2 tablespoons butter	2 teaspoons tomato paste
¾ cup onions, finely chopped	3 tablespoons rice, uncooked
3 cups carrots, finely diced	salt and white pepper, to taste
1 quart chicken stock or canned chicken broth	½ cup cream or evaporated milk

1. In a medium saucepan, melt butter. Stir in onions and cook, stirring occasionally, until they are soft but not browned. Add carrots, chicken stock, tomato paste, and rice, and simmer, uncovered, for 30 minutes.

2. Puree in a food processor in small batches and return soup to a clean saucepan. Season with salt and white pepper and stir in cream. Heat but do not boil.

3. Ladle into soup bowls. Garnish with a pat of butter and carrot curls or parsley sprigs.

Seafarer's Delight

YIELDS: 6 servings

1 pound fresh scallops	1 teaspoon salt
1 large onion	dash pepper
2 tablespoons butter	½ cup dry white wine
¼ cup flour	½ cup Swiss cheese, shredded
3½ cups milk	1 tablespoon parsley
1 (4-ounce) can mushrooms, sliced	

1. Halve large scallops. Set aside.

2. Cut onion into thin wedges and cook in butter over low heat until tender but not brown. Stir in flour. Add milk and stir. Cook over medium heat until bubbly.

3. Add mushrooms, scallops, salt, and pepper. Cover and simmer for 5 minutes. Stir in wine and heat. Garnish each bowl with cheese and parsley.

Hearty Potato Soup

YIELDS: 4-6 servings

A thick soup accented with bacon and a touch of curry. May be served as a main dish.

4	slices bacon	½	cup water
2	medium onions, sliced	1	teaspoon salt
2½	cups potatoes, diced	¼	teaspoon curry powder
1	(10¾-ounce) can chicken broth	1	(12-ounce) can evaporated milk

1. Fry bacon until crisp in Dutch oven. Remove bacon and reserve 2 tablespoons bacon grease in pan.

2. Cook onion in bacon grease until tender. Add potatoes, chicken broth, water, salt, and curry powder. Cover and bring to a boil. Simmer for 10 minutes or until potatoes are tender.

3. Mash potatoes slightly with a fork or potato masher. Stir in evaporated milk. Crumble bacon and add to soup. Do not boil after adding evaporated milk.

This is a very thick soup. If thinner soup is preferred, add more broth. This soup will keep well in refrigerator for several days.

The Inn's Creamed Onion Soup

YIELDS: 6-8 servings

Easy!

4	tablespoons butter	16	ounces chicken broth
3	medium onions, chopped	16	ounces milk
½	cup flour		croutons
1	teaspoon salt	½	cup Parmesan cheese

1. Melt butter in double boiler. Add onions. Simmer until onions are cooked but not browned.

2. Add flour, salt, and chicken broth. Gradually add milk. Do not boil. Top with croutons and Parmesan cheese. Put under broiler or in oven to melt cheese.

Chilled Cantelope Soup

YIELDS: 10 servings

Serve this soup in cantalope shells with a short straw and garnish with a sprig of mint.

5 **large cantelopes, halved**	1½ **cups orange juice**
½ **cup dry sherry**	**mint leaves**
(optional)	
¾ **cup sugar**	

1. Scoop pulp from cantelope leaving shells ½ inch thick. If shell does not sit level, cut a thin slice from the bottom of each shell, being careful not to cut through the shell. With a sharp knife, notch or scallop top edges of cantalope.

2. Combine cantalope pulp and next 3 ingredients in a blender and puree until smooth. Chill thoroughly.

Soup may be made 1 day ahead.

Rosy Strawberry Soup

YIELDS: 6 servings

A pretty cold soup.

2 **pints fresh strawberries,**	1 **cup red wine**
hulled and halved	½ **cup sugar**
1 **tablespoon cornstarch**	1 **cup sour cream**
1 **cup orange juice**	**mint leaves**

1. Place half of the strawberries in food processor or blender and spin. Add remaining berries and puree.

2. Blend cornstarch with ¼ cup of orange juice in a 2 quart saucepan; add remaining orange juice, red wine, sugar, and pureed strawberries. Heat just to boiling over medium heat, stirring frequently.

3. Remove from heat. Stir in sour cream with whisk. Cover and refrigerate until cold. Garnish with mint leaves.

Big Sandwich Loaf

YIELDS: 6-8 servings

Perfect for break time on poker night.

1	8 inch round bread loaf	4	slices Swiss cheese
2	teaspoons prepared horseradish	2	tablespoons mayonnaise
½	pound roast beef, thinly sliced	6	slices bacon, cooked
		1	tomato, thinly sliced
2	tablespoons prepared mustard	4	slices American cheese
		1	medium onion, sliced
½	pound baked ham, thinly sliced	¼	cup butter
		1	tablespoon sesame seeds
			onion salt to taste

1. Slice bread into five equal layers.

2. Spread first slice with horseradish and top with roast beef. Layer with second piece of bread.

3. On second slice of bread, spread mustard and top with ham and Swiss cheese. Layer with third piece of bread.

4. Spread on third layer, the mayonnaise and top with bacon and tomatoes. Layer with fourth piece of bread.

5. Place American cheese and onion on the fourth layer of bread. Top with remaining piece of bread.

6. Combine the remaining ingredients in small bowl and spread over top and sides of sandwich.

7. Place loaf on baking sheet. Bake, uncovered, in a preheated 400 degree oven for 15-20 minutes. Slice.

Make ahead one day. Freezes up to two weeks. Slicing is easier with an electric knife.

D.P.'s Tailgate Sandwiches

YIELDS: 16 sandwiches

A must for fall football parties. Men love these!

½ cup butter, softened	16 small buns
3 tablespoons hot mustard	1 pound shaved ham
1½ tablespoons poppy seeds	¾ pound Swiss cheese,
1 teaspoon Worcestershire	thinly sliced
sauce	
1 medium onion, finely	
chopped	

1. Mix together butter, mustard, poppy seeds, Worcestershire sauce, and onion.

2. Spread the buns with butter mixture. Place ham and cheese on buns. Wrap individually with aluminum foil. Heat in a preheated 400 degree oven for 10 minutes.

May be frozen before heating.

Grilled German Bratwurst

YIELDS: 4 sandwiches

Bratwurst "boats"—perfect for half time.

4 bratwurst	½ teaspoon onion salt
cooking oil	4 frankfurter buns
1½ cups onions, chopped	½ cup sharp Cheddar cheese,
1 (12-ounce) can beer	grated
2 tablespoons butter	4 slices bacon, fried
	and crumbled

1. Brown bratwurst over medium heat in a little oil. Add onions and beer. Simmer, uncovered, for 20-30 minutes.

2. Stir together butter and onion salt. Spread on buns.

3. Make a lengthwise cut in each bratwurst to within ½ inch from end. Place brats on buns. Spoon on drained onions and sprinkle with cheese.

4. Place in foil "boat". Broil 4 inches from heat for 2 minutes. Top with crumbled bacon. Serve with German potato salad.

Easy.

Party Beef Pitas

YIELDS: 12 sandwiches

A terrific make-ahead to free the hostess at party time.

1 pound ground beef	1 teaspoon oregano, crushed
1 cup onion, sliced	¼ teaspoon rosemary,
½ cup green pepper,	crushed
cut in strips	1 bay leaf
1 clove garlic, minced	2 cups Swiss cheese,
8 ounces fresh mushrooms,	shredded
sliced	½ cup Parmesan cheese,
¼ cup catsup	grated
1 tablespoon parsley	6 small Pita bread rounds,
1 tablespoon Dijon style	halved
mustard	alfalfa sprouts (optional)
1 tablespoon steak sauce	tomato slices (optional)
¼ teaspoon salt	
¼ teaspoon pepper	

1. Cook beef, onion, green pepper, and garlic until meat is just brown. Drain fat. Stir in mushrooms, catsup, parsley, mustard, steak sauce, salt, pepper, and herbs. Cook and stir for about 5 minutes. Remove bay leaf and stir in cheeses. Remove from heat.

2. Line Pita halves with vegetables and fill with ⅓ cup meat.

May be prepared 1 day ahead.

Quesadillas

YIELDS: 8 sandwiches

These resemble grilled cheese sandwiches and make a sensational light lunch.

16 slices bacon, fried and crumbled
8 ounces sharp Cheddar cheese, shredded
½ bunch green onions, chopped (tops included)

8 large flour tortillas
1 (8-ounce) carton sour cream

1. Drain grease from skillet after frying bacon. Divide cheese, green onions, and bacon among the 8 tortillas, putting cheese on one half of tortilla topped by onion and bacon.

2. Fold tortilla over and fry in skillet until tortilla begins to brown. Turn and fry other side (like a grilled cheese sandwich). These may be kept in a warm oven until all are finished.

SALSA
2 fresh tomatoes, chopped
2 tablespoons green onion, chopped

½ small can green chilies, chopped

1. Combine all above ingredients.

GUACAMOLE
2 ripe avocados

4 teaspoons lemon juice

1. Mash ripe avocados with fork; mix in lemon juice.

2. Pass around salsa, guacamole, and sour cream to put on top of warm tortillas.

Mediterranean Chicken Pitas

YIELDS: 8 sandwiches

A luncheon idea—just add fresh fruit.

4	Pita bread rounds, halved	6	ounces chicken breast, cooked, chopped into bite size pieces
1	(3-ounce) package cream cheese, softened	4	ounces alfalfa sprouts
1	tablespoon mayonnaise or salad dressing	3	tablespoons cucumber, chopped (optional)
2	cups lettuce, torn	3	tablespoons creamy Italian dressing
1	medium tomato, diced		

1. Combine cream cheese and mayonnaise and spread inside Pita pockets.

2. Combine all other ingredients in bowl and toss well. Spoon salad mixture into pocket breads and serve immediately.

Easy.

Sensational Shrimp Sandwiches

YIELDS: 6 servings

A nutritional seafood pleasure.

1	loaf French or Italian bread	½	cup alfalfa sprouts
	butter	⅓	cup ripe olives, sliced
	mayonnaise	1	small avocado, peeled and sliced
	lettuce leaves	1½	cups shrimp, cooked and peeled
2	tomatoes, sliced		
½	cup mushrooms, sliced		

1. Split bread lengthwise. Spread butter, then mayonnaise on top half.

2. Layer lettuce, tomatoes, mushrooms, sprouts, olives, avocado, and shrimp on bottom half. Add top half.

3. Serve with mayonnaise or Thousand Island dressing to be spread on as desired.

Easy.

Stroganoff Steak Sandwiches

YIELDS: 6 sandwiches

Buy an eight-pack. Use one—drink one while preparing—and serve the other six with these hearty sandwiches!

⅔	cup beer		dash salt
⅓	cup salad oil	4	cups onions, sliced
1	teaspoon salt	12	slices French bread,
¼	teaspoon garlic powder		toasted
¼	teaspoon pepper	1	cup sour cream, warmed
1	(2-pound) flank steak	1	teaspoon prepared
2	tablespoons butter		horseradish
½	teaspoon paprika		paprika

1. Combine beer, oil, salt, garlic powder, and pepper. Place flank steak in mixture, cover, and marinate overnight in refrigerator. Drain.

2. Broil steak 3 inches from heat for 5-7 minutes on each side for medium rare.

3. While doing step 2, melt butter and blend in paprika and dash of salt. Add sliced onions, cooking until tender (not brown).

4. To serve, slice meat on the diagonal across grain. For each serving, arrange meat slices over two slices toasted French bread. Top with cooked onions. Mix together warm sour cream with horseradish. Spoon mixture onto sandwiches and sprinkle with paprika.

Must begin preparing 1 day ahead.

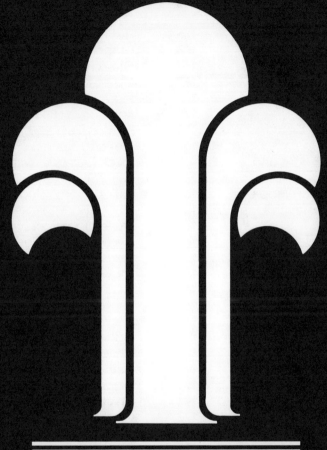

MAIN DISHES

MAIN DISHES

MAIN DISHES

Grasping for Grapes

Wines for this book have been selected along the classic guidelines of matching food and wine. These wine suggestions, however, are merely a guide and not intended to be the last word in grasping for grapes. A perfect match is often accomplished only by much trial and error. The search for a food and wine union should never be boring as there are thousands of vineyards, hundreds of grape varieties, and always a new vintage to tantalize the palate.

To match a food and wine, keep in mind these simple guidelines. For lighter food, choose lighter wine and vice versa. That does not always mean white wine with white food. Adventure is always fun.

An uncomplicated dish should be joined with an uncomplicated wine. A rich, full-flavored recipe needs to be accompanied by wine with some complex characteristics.

The social event being celebrated is vital to consider when deciding to opt for quality or quantity. A reasonable amount of wine per person for the main course of a meal is approximately 8 to 10 ounces. Most formal events call for less wine than a neighborhood picnic. Leftover wine will keep up to one week if refrigerated.

Finally, be proud of the wine you have chosen to serve. Present the meal and the wine, and enjoy the fruits of your labor.

Karen W. Davis

 MAIN DISHES

Bacon and Tomato Pie

YIELDS: 6 servings

1½ cups soft bread crumbs
1 medium onion, sliced thin
¼ pound Cheddar cheese, grated
3 fresh tomatoes, peeled and sliced

½ teaspoon salt
⅛ teaspoon pepper
2 eggs, slightly beaten
4 strips bacon, halved

1. Butter 9 inch pie plate. Cover bottom with one cup bread crumbs. Make layers of onions, cheese, and tomatoes in that order.

2. Beat eggs with salt and pepper and pour over top. Sprinkle with remaining bread crumbs. Arrange bacon in spoke-like fashion over top. Bake in a preheated 350 degree oven for 30 minutes or until bacon is crisp.

Wine Suggestion: Serve champagne before the brunch, then a rich coffee.

Blueberry Topping

YIELDS: 1⅓ cups

An excellent spread for toast, English muffins, or pancakes.

2 cups fresh or frozen unsweetened blueberries
¼ cup frozen apple juice concentrate

1½ tablespoons cornstarch
½ teaspoon vanilla extract or lemon juice

1. Place blueberries and apple juice in blender; add cornstarch and blend until smooth. Transfer to saucepan and heat mixture over medium heat, stirring frequently, until thickened. Stir in vanilla or lemon juice.

MAIN DISHES 🌷

Company Souffle

YIELDS: 6 servings

An elegant morning greeting for your out of town guests.

6 bacon slices, cooked and crumbled	1 tablespoon parsley, chopped
1 tablespoon reserved bacon grease	½ teaspoon salt
⅓ cup onion, chopped	1 cup (4-ounces) Cheddar cheese, shredded
8 eggs, beaten slightly	1 cup (4-ounces) Swiss cheese, shredded
1 cup milk	1 tablespoon flour
1 (2-ounce) jar pimentos, chopped	

1. Saute onion in reserved bacon grease until tender.

2. Combine onion, bacon, eggs, milk, pimentos, parsley, and salt. Toss Cheddar cheese and Swiss cheese in flour; add to egg mixture. Pour into 1½ quart souffle dish. Bake in a preheated 350 degree oven for 40 minutes.

Wine Suggestion: For a change of pace try a Beaujolais or serve wine only before the meal.

Honey Orange French Toast

YIELDS: 4-6 servings

Good recipe for the cook! Everyone can eat at the same time. Nice for larger crowds if doubled or tripled.

¼ cup butter	½ cup orange juice
2 tablespoons honey	⅛ teaspoon salt
1 teaspoon cinnamon	1 loaf French bread, uncut
3 eggs	

1. Melt butter and honey in a 9 x 13 inch casserole. Sprinkle with cinnamon. Set aside.

2. In medium size mixing bowl, beat together eggs, orange juice, and salt. Cut French bread into 1 inch slices. Soak bread in egg mixture and place on top of honey mixture (6-8 slices fit a 9 x 13 inch casserole). Bake in a preheated 400 degree oven for 20 minutes. Serve with warm honey or syrup.

Crab Quiche

YIELDS: 6-8 servings

A touch of seashore tastiness.

½ cup mayonnaise (not salad dressing)	4 ounces Monterey Jack cheese, grated
2 tablespoons flour	4 ounces Swiss cheese, grated
2 eggs, beaten	1 (3-ounce) package cream cheese, softened
½ cup half and half	½ cup green onions, chopped
1 (6-ounce) package frozen crabmeat, thawed, and drained or substitute 7 pieces bacon, fried crisp and crumbled	1 pie shell, unbaked

1. Combine mayonnaise, flour, and eggs. Add half and half. Stir in crab or bacon and the cheeses. Add green onions and stir well. Pour into unbaked pie shell.

2. Bake in a preheated 350 degree oven for 40 to 45 minutes, or until golden brown and puffed up.

Wine Suggestion: French Sancerre or Spanish Extra Dry Champagne.

Day After Easter Casserole

YIELDS: 6-8 servings

Relax in the morning with your overnight guests as you prepare this a day ahead.

3 cups cooked ham, diced	2 teaspoons Worcestershire sauce
6 hard boiled eggs, sliced	6 drops Tabasco sauce
1 (6-ounce) can mushroom crowns, drained	¾ cup dry medium bread crumbs
2 cups dried bread cubes	2 tablespoons butter, melted
1 can cream of celery or cream of mushroom soup	Parmesan cheese, grated
½ cup milk	parsley for garnish
2 cups sharp Cheddar cheese, grated	

1. In a two quart oblong casserole dish, alternate layers of ham, eggs, mushrooms, and dried bread cubes.

2. In a saucepan, combine soup and milk, stirring well. Stir in cheese, Worcestershire sauce, and Tabasco sauce. Heat until cheese is melted and pour over ham.

3. Toss crumbs in melted butter and sprinkle over top of casserole. Sprinkle with Parmesan cheese. Bake, uncovered, in a preheated 375 degree oven for 25 minutes. Garnish with additional egg slices and parsley.

Easy and may be prepared 1 day ahead.

Wine Suggestion: Ham is nice with Rose D'Anjou.

Dutch Babies

YIELDS: 6-8 servings

Oven pancakes, no matter what size, are often called "Dutch Babies". The batter is full of eggs and puffs up dramatically in the oven. You'll want to have everyone seated before you bring it to the table for a spectacular presentation!

BATTER

⅓ cup butter	1 teaspoon sugar
4 eggs, slightly beaten	⅛ teaspoon nutmeg
1 cup milk	2 tablespoons powdered
1 cup flour	sugar

1. Melt butter in the pan you will use to bake the pancakes. A 3 inch deep quiche dish or 2 glass pie pans work best.

2. Mix remaining batter ingredients, except powdered sugar, in blender. Pour this into pan and bake in a preheated 425 degree oven for 20 minutes until puffy and brown. It will rise about 4-5 inches along the edges and form a well in the center.

3. Sprinkle with powdered sugar during last few minutes of baking.

TOPPING

2 cups sliced fruit (strawberries, bananas, peaches, blueberries, etc.)	½ cup brown sugar, packed
	4 ounces sour cream

1. Spoon fruit or combination of fruits into center of pancakes, sprinkle with brown sugar, and top with dollops of sour cream. Cut in wedges. Serve immediately.

Variation: Fill with hot glazed apples or use canned cherry or apple pie filling warmed. You may serve pancake without fruit and pass favorite syrup.

Eggs Cancun

YIELDS: 6 servings

A reminder of a sunny Mexican island. Accent with bright napkins and a pinata centerpiece.

1	(8-ounce) package tortilla chips	1	teaspoon oregano
1	pound sausage, mild	1	teaspoon salt
2	cups onion, chopped	⅛	teaspoon cayenne pepper
½	pound mushrooms, sliced	2	cups Monterey Jack cheese, shredded
3⅓	cups tomato puree	6	eggs
½	cup water		

1. Cover bottom of 12 x 7½ x 2 inch baking dish with half of tortilla chips.

2. Brown crumbled sausage in skillet. Add onion; cook until tender. Add mushrooms; cook until tender. Stir in puree, water, oregano, salt, and cayenne pepper; blend well. Simmer, uncovered, 15 minutes, stirring occasionally.

3. Spoon half of tomato mixture over chips. Top with one cup of cheese. Add remaining chips and tomato mixture.

4. Make 6 depressions for eggs in casserole. Break an egg into each spot. Cover with foil. Bake in a preheated 375 degree oven for 25 minutes or until eggs are almost done. Remove foil. Top with remaining cheese. Bake, uncovered, 5 minutes longer or until cheese bubbles.

Wine Suggestion: Fruit punch or for wine drinkers a California Chablis.

Eggs Fiesta

YIELDS: 6 servings

Fantastic egg dish enhanced by two cheeses and Picante sauce.

1 pound bulk sausage, crumbled	½ teaspoon salt
1½ pounds fresh mushrooms, chopped	½ teaspoon pepper
	6 tablespoons Old El Paso mild Picante sauce
½ medium onion, diced	10 ounces Cheddar cheese, grated
6 eggs	
3 tablespoons sour cream	10 ounces Mozzarella cheese, grated

1. Saute sausage, mushrooms, and onion. Drain and set aside.

2. Combine eggs, sour cream, salt, and pepper in a blender. Whip for one minute. Pour egg mixture into a greased 9 x 13 inch baking pan. Bake in a preheated 400 degree oven until soft set, usually about 5-8 minutes.

3. Spoon Picante sauce over eggs. Then spoon on sausage mixture. Top with cheeses.

4. To serve immediately broil until cheeses are melted, about 10 minutes. To serve next day, bake in a preheated 325 degree oven for 30 minutes or until cheeses are melted.

Wine Suggestion: Mexican beer for dinner, pleasant Rose for brunch.

Eggs with Asparagus and Chicken

YIELDS: 4 servings

Best served with warm croissants and fresh fruit.

- 2 tablespoons butter or margarine
- 2 tablespoons flour
- ¼ teaspoon salt
- ⅛ teaspoon white pepper
- ⅛ teaspoon nutmeg
- 1 teaspoon dry mustard
- 2 cups milk
- 1¼ cups Cheddar cheese, shredded
- 1 (8-ounce) package frozen asparagus spears, cooked and drained

- 2 cups chicken, cooked and diced
- 4 eggs
- 4 teaspoons butter or margarine, melted and cooled
- 1 (8-ounce) package frozen asparagus spears, cooked and drained (optional)

1. In a pan over medium heat, melt the 2 tablespoons butter. Stir in flour, salt, pepper, nutmeg, and mustard; cook until bubbly. Gradually stir in milk and cook, stirring constantly, until thick and smooth. Stir in cheese until it is melted and the sauce is smooth. Stir in asparagus pieces and chicken; remove from heat.

2. Pour equal amounts of mixture into 4 buttered 1½ to 2 cup ramekins. Make a hollow in center of each and carefully break an egg into each hollow. Pour 1 teaspoon melted butter over each egg.

3. Bake, uncovered, in a preheated 375 degree oven for 15-20 minutes or until eggs are set to your liking. Garnish each ramekin with warm asparagus spears, if desired.

Wine Suggestion: Perrier would be best but don't hesitate to serve a dry white wine.

Ham and Spinach Wrap-Ups

YIELDS: 18 servings

A great brunch recipe to celebrate happy memories.

1 can cream of celery soup	1 cup small curd cottage cheese
1 cup sour cream	2 eggs
2 tablespoons Dijon mustard	½ cup onion, chopped
1 cup Minute Rice, uncooked	¼ cup flour
1 (10-ounce) package frozen spinach, chopped, thawed, and drained	18 slices boiled ham
	¾ cup Pepperidge Farm stuffing
	¼ cup butter, melted

1. Mix soup, sour cream, and Dijon mustard; reserve half of this mixture for later. Add rice, spinach, cottage cheese, eggs, onion, and flour to half of the soup mixture.

2. Place about 2 tablespoons of mixture on a slice of boiled ham. Roll into log shape and place in baking dish with seam side down. Repeat until all 18 slices of ham are used.

3. Pour remaining half of soup mixture over ham rolls. Combine Pepperidge Farm stuffing and melted butter and sprinkle over top.

4. Bake in a preheated 350 degree oven for 45 minutes, covered. Remove lid last 5 to 10 minutes to toast bread crumbs. Let stand 10 to 15 minutes before serving.

May be prepared ahead and freezes well.

Wine Suggestion: Good quality Rose of semi-dry persuasion.

Italian Frittata

Good use of zucchini and tomatoes in summer. A frittata is an open face omelet.

1½ cups onion, chopped
2-3 tablespoons butter or
   best quality olive oil
½ pound zucchini, peeled
   and shredded
12 eggs, beaten
2 tablespoons fresh basil
   or 2 teaspoons dried
2 teaspoons salt
   cracked pepper to taste

3 tablespoons dry bread
   crumbs
2 cloves garlic, minced
   (optional)
2 tomatoes, peeled and
   sliced
1 cup Cheddar cheese, grated
½ cup Parmesan cheese,
   grated

1. Saute onion in butter or oil until soft, add zucchini and cook about 2 minutes.

2. To beaten eggs, add basil, salt, and pepper. Fold in onion-zucchini mixture, bread crumbs, and garlic, if desired. Pour into 10 inch buttered quiche dish.

3. Arrange tomatoes on top and sprinkle with Cheddar and Parmesan cheese. Bake in a preheated 350 degree oven for 30-35 minutes or until set.

Wine Suggestion: The best recommendation is for a nice Kir Champagne and Cassis before brunch.

Helpful Hints: Use eggs at room temperature to keep egg whites from becoming tough when frying or poaching.

Mexican Cheese Souffle

YIELDS: 8 servings

A festive Mexican brunch dish.

5 (4-ounce) cans whole green chiles	4 eggs, separated
1 pound sharp Cheddar cheese, sliced	3 tablespoons flour
1 pound Monterey Jack cheese, sliced	1 (12-ounce) can evaporated milk
	dash of salt and pepper

1. Wash, flatten, and remove seeds from chilies. Place half the chilies in the bottom of a 9 x 13 inch casserole. Cover chilies with Cheddar cheese slices. Add remaining half of chilies and cover with Monterey Jack slices.

2. Beat egg yolks, flour, and milk. Add salt and pepper. Beat egg whites until stiff and fold into egg yolk mixture. Pour over chilies and cheese layers.

3. Bake in a preheated 325 degree oven for 45 minutes to 1 hour or until top is brown. Allow to set 15-20 minutes before serving.

Serve with Spanish hot sausages (chorizos), fresh fruit with lime, hot Tortilla Crisps, and assorted Mexican breads. Tempting also as a side dish with steak.

Wine Suggestion: Bloody Marys, plain or altered.

Puffy Apple Pancake

YIELDS: 6 servings

Great to serve on Sunday morning. It will always impress your brunch guests. For company, prepare two!

6	eggs	¼	teaspoon cinnamon
1½	cups milk	½	cup butter or margarine
1	cup flour	2	apples, pared and thinly
3	tablespoons sugar		sliced
1	teaspoon vanilla	3	tablespoons brown sugar
½	teaspoon salt		

1. In blender mix eggs, milk, flour, sugar, vanilla, salt, and cinnamon until blended.

2. Melt butter in 12 inch fluted porcelain quiche dish or 9 x 13 inch baking dish in a preheated 425 degree oven. Add apple slices to melted butter in pan and return to oven until the butter sizzles. Do not brown butter.

3. Remove dish from oven and immediately pour batter over apples. Sprinkle with brown sugar. Bake in middle of preheated 425 degree oven for 20 minutes or until puffed and brown. Serve immediately. It will collapse soon after removal from oven.

Reuben Brunch Casserole

YIELDS: 10 servings

10	slices rye bread, cut in ¾ inch cubes	6	eggs, lightly beaten
1½	pounds corned beef, cooked	3	cups milk
2½	cups (10-ounces) Swiss cheese, shredded	¼	teaspoon pepper

1. Cut rye bread and place in a greased 9 x 13 x 2 inch baking dish. Coarsely shred corned beef with knife. Layer meat over bread. Sprinkle with cheese.

2. Beat eggs, milk, and pepper in bowl until well blended. Pour over corned beef mixture. Cover with foil and refrigerate overnight. Bake, covered, in a preheated 350 degree oven for 45 minutes. Bake, uncovered, 10 minutes longer or until bubbly. Serve immediately.

Must be prepared 1 day in advance.

Wine Suggestion: Flavored Perrier or a fruit punch would be a pleasant accompaniment.

Sauces for Pancakes

Versatile—a great addition to bread pudding, ice cream, or apple pie—serve warm or cold!

MAPLE BUTTER   **YIELDS: 2 cups**
1½ cups powdered sugar,   ½   cup maple syrup
     sifted   1   egg, separated
½   cup butter or margarine

1. Cream sugar and butter. Beat in syrup and egg yolk.

2. Beat egg white stiff and fold into mixture. Chill. If it separates when cool, just beat.

ORANGE SYRUP   **YIELDS: 1½ cups**
½   cup butter   ½   cup frozen orange juice
1   cup sugar   concentrate, undiluted

1. Combine all ingredients in a saucepan. Bring to a boil, stirring occasionally. Cook until slightly thickened. Serve warm. Store in refrigerator, but heat before serving.

CREAMY CINNAMON SYRUP   **YIELDS: 2 cups**
1   cup sugar   ¼   cup water
¾   teaspoon cinnamon   ½   cup evaporated milk
½   cup light Karo syrup

1. In small saucepan, combine sugar, cinnamon, corn syrup, and water. Bring to a boil over medium heat, stirring constantly. Cook and stir 2 minutes more.

2. Remove from heat and cool 5 minutes. Stir in evaporated milk. Store in refrigerator.

May be made ahead 1 week. Do not freeze.

Sausage Apple Pie

YIELDS: 6 servings

¾ pound Keilbasa sausage link	¼ teaspoon salt
⅔ cup sugar	4-5 medium baking apples, pared and sliced
1 teaspoon cinnamon	pastry for 9 inch double
⅛ teaspoon nutmeg	crust pie, unbaked
3 tablespoons flour	

1. Slice the sausage link into thin rounds like pepperoni slices. Fry slices in skillet until lightly browned. Drain on paper towels.

2. Combine sugar, cinnamon, nutmeg, flour, and salt. Add apples and sausage to the mixture.

3. Put filling into unbaked pie crust. Put on top crust. Seal edges and crimp. Cut several slits in top of crust to prevent excessive browning.

4. Bake in a preheated 375 degree oven for 50 minutes, or until crust is golden brown and apples are tender.

May be prepared 1 day ahead. Freeze unbaked. Bake frozen by increasing baking time by 30 minutes.

Wine Suggestion: Alastian Gewurztraimer will be spicy enough for the sausage.

MAIN DISHES ❡

Sensational Mandarin Ham Roll-Ups

YIELDS: 4 servings

A garnish of orange slices makes this a pretty springtime dish.

1 (11-ounce) can mandarin oranges, drained	1 tablespoon green onions, sliced
1½ cups cooked white rice	8 large thin slices boiled ham
⅓ cup mayonnaise	½ cup orange marmalade
2 tablespoons pecans, chopped	1 tablespoon lemon juice
2 tablespoons fresh parsley, snipped	¼ teaspoon ground ginger

1. Reserve 8 orange sections. Chop remainder and combine with the cooked rice, mayonnaise, pecans, parsley, and onion.

2. Divide mixture among ham slices. Roll ham around filling and place seam side down in 10 x 6 x 2 inch baking dish.

3. Combine marmalade, lemon juice, and ginger. Brush on top of rolls. Bake in a preheated 350 degree oven for 25-30 minutes, brushing occasionally with remaining sauce, and garnish with remaining oranges.

Freezes well and may be prepared ahead.

Wine Suggestion: A beautiful Rose D'Anjou will be a credit to this meal.

Sicilian Quache

YIELDS: 6 servings

A recipe that tastes as good as it looks.

1	loaf frozen bread dough, thawed	¼	cup fresh parsley, chopped
1	pound Italian sausage, browned and drained	1-2	cloves garlic, minced
1	cup Mozzarella cheese, diced	½	cup walnuts, chopped

1. Roll or stretch dough out to form a large rectangle.

2. Press sausage lightly and evenly into dough. Sprinkle other ingredients over dough. Roll up jelly roll fashion and pinch to seal.

3. Slice about 1 inch thick and place slices flat on a cookie sheet. Bake in a preheated 300 degree oven for 45 minutes.

Wine Suggestion: If using this recipe as a snack, a friendly jug of wine of Italian heritage will do nicely.

Spinach-Sausage Quiche

YIELDS: 6 servings

Men like this quiche too!

1   9 inch frozen deep
    dish pastry shell
6   ounces bulk pork sausage
¼   cup green onion, chopped
1   clove garlic, minced
½   cup frozen chopped
    spinach, cooked and
    well drained
½   cup herb seasoned
    stuffing mix

1   cup Monterey Jack cheese,
    shredded
3   eggs, slightly beaten
1¼ cups half and half
2   tablespoons Parmesan
    cheese, grated
    paprika

1. Place a cookie sheet in oven to be preheated.

2. In a medium skillet, cook sausage, green onion, and garlic over medium-high heat until sausage is done, stirring occasionally. Drain sausage mixture. Stir in spinach and stuffing mix.

3. Sprinkle Monterey Jack cheese and then sausage mixture in the pastry shell.

4. In a medium bowl, combine eggs and half and half with a fork or whisk until mixed well but not frothy. Pour egg mixture over sausage mixture in the pastry shell.

5. Place on the cookie sheet and bake in a preheated 375 degree oven for 30 minutes. Sprinkle with Parmesan cheese and paprika. Bake an additional 15 minutes or until knife inserted off-center comes out clean. Let stand 10 minutes before serving.

Wine Suggestion: California Gamay Beaujolais.

 MAIN DISHES

Spring Sandwich Puff

YIELDS: 6 servings

6	slices American cheese	¼	cup mayonnaise
6	slices bread, toasted on one side under broiler	¼	teaspoon salt
			dash pepper
24	cooked asparagus spears	3	egg whites, stiffly beaten
3	egg yolks, beaten		

1. Place slice of cheese on toasted side of bread; broil to partially melt cheese. Remove from heat, and place 3-4 spears of cooked asparagus on top of each cheese slice.

2. Beat 3 yolks until thickened and lemon colored; stir in mayonnaise, salt, and pepper; fold in beaten egg whites. Mound mixture atop asparagus.

3. Bake in a preheated 350 degree oven for about 12 minutes, or until egg mixture is set.

Wine Suggestion: Try a German Mosel.

Sunday Morning Sausage Ring

YIELDS: 8 servings

2	pounds bulk pork sausage	1½	cups bread crumbs
2	eggs, beaten	¼	cup parsley, chopped
2	tablespoons onion, grated		

1. Lightly grease a 9 inch ring mold. Mix ingredients well with hands and pack lightly into mold.

2. Bake in a preheated 350 degree oven for 20 minutes and remove from oven, pour off excess fat, and return to oven and bake an additional 20 minutes. Turn onto platter. Fill center with scrambled eggs or fresh cherry tomatoes.

Variation: To make sausage ring for supper, fill instead with scalloped potatoes or Cinnamon Skillet Apples.

Wine Suggestion: Recommend champagne before brunch, then coffee.

Wine and Cheese Souffle

An elegant souffle that's worth the extra effort.

1	large loaf day old French or Italian bread, broken in small pieces
6	tablespoons butter, melted
¾	pound Swiss cheese, shredded
½	pound Monterey Jack cheese, shredded
12	slices hard salami, cut in small pieces
16	eggs

3¼	cups milk
½	cup dry white wine (dry vermouth)
4	large whole green onions, minced
1	tablespoon Dijon mustard
¼	teaspoon black pepper
⅛	teaspoon cayenne pepper
1½	cups sour cream
1	cup Parmesan cheese, freshly grated

1. Butter two 9 x 13 inch baking dishes. Spread bread over bottom and drizzle butter over. Spread Swiss and Monterey Jack cheeses and salami over bread.

2. Beat together next 7 ingredients until foamy. Pour over bread mixture and cover tightly with foil. Refrigerate overnight or up to 24 hours. Remove from refrigerator 30 minutes before baking.

3. Bake, covered, in a preheated 350 degree oven for one hour. Uncover, spread sour cream on top, and sprinkle Parmesan cheese over all. Bake until crusty and lightly browned or put under broiler a few minutes.

Must be made 1 day ahead.

Wine Suggestion: A simple white table wine or a Rose of Cabernet.

Williamsburg Shrimp Casserole

YIELDS: 4 servings

A delicious seafood strata.

5 slices bread, buttered and cut in 1 inch cubes	2 eggs, beaten
10 ounces fresh shrimp, cooked and cut in bite size pieces	1½ cups milk
	½ teaspoon salt
	1 teaspoon dry mustard
8 ounces sharp Cheddar cheese, grated	pepper to taste
	paprika to taste

1. In buttered 2 quart casserole dish, layer bread, shrimp, and cheese twice.

2. Combine eggs, milk, and seasonings; pour over layered mixture. Cover and let set in refrigerator at least 4 hours or overnight.

3. Bake, uncovered, in a preheated 325 degree oven for 40 to 50 minutes.

Must be prepared 4 to 24 hours ahead. Tuna or ham may be substituted for the shrimp.

Wine Suggestion: Pouilly Fume or Rose D'Anjou.

Barbecue Beef

YIELDS: 8-10 servings

Serve on warm, crusty buns for a fulfilling sandwich treat.

3 pounds chuck roast	2 tablespoons brown sugar
2 tablespoons Crisco	1 tablespoon prepared mustard
1 large onion, chopped	
2 tablespoons vinegar	2 tablespoons chili powder
2 tablespoons lemon juice	
¾ cup water	1 teaspoon salt
½ cup celery, chopped	¼ teaspoon pepper
2 cups catsup	
3 tablespoons Worcestershire sauce	

1. Trim meat and brown in Crisco. Add the remaining ingredients. Bring to a boil; reduce heat to low. Cover and simmer 2-3 hours, or until meat is tender. Remove meat to platter. Using 2 forks, shred or pull meat apart. Place meat back into sauce and cook until meat is very tender. Cooking time varies from 4-5 hours.

May be prepared ahead and frozen.

Wine Suggestion: A full flavored Red wine. A good inexpensive choice is Romanian Cabernet.

♠ MAIN DISHES

Beef and Zucchini Tortilla Pie

YIELDS: 6-8 servings

A mild tasting touch of old Mexico.

TORTILLA SHELL DOUGH

1	cup flour	2	tablespoons Crisco
½	teaspoon salt	⅓	cup lukewarm water

1. Mix all ingredients to form dough. On lightly floured surface, roll tortilla shell dough to a 12 inch circle. Fit into a 9 inch pie plate. Roll edges to make high rim. Prick bottom and sides with fork. Bake in a preheated 350 degree oven for 20-25 minutes or until edges begin to brown.

BEEF AND ZUCCHINI FILLING

1	pound ground beef	½	cup processed American cheese, shredded
½	cup onion, chopped		
1	clove garlic, minced		
1	teaspoon dried basil	2	tablespoon Parmesan cheese, grated
1	teaspoon dried oregano		
¾	teaspoon salt	2	tablespoons parsley, snipped
⅛	teaspoon pepper		
5	cups zucchini, unpeeled, cut in 1 inch pieces	1	teaspoon Worcestershire sauce
2	eggs, slightly beaten	½	teaspoon dry mustard
1	cup cream style cottage cheese	¼	teaspoon salt

1. In skillet cook meat, onion, and garlic until meat is brown. Drain. Add basil, oregano, ¾ teaspoon salt, and pepper.

2. Cook zucchini in boiling unsalted water for 7 minutes. Drain. Mash, drain thoroughly, pressing out excess water. (Should have 1½ cups mashed drained zucchini.)

continued

Beef and Zucchini Tortilla Pie *continued*

3. In bowl combine eggs, zucchini, cottage cheese, American cheese, Parmesan cheese, parsley, Worcestershire sauce, dry mustard, and the ¼ teaspoon salt.

4. Turn meat mixture into tortilla shell; spoon zucchini mixture over meat. Bake in a preheated 350 degree oven for 35 minutes or until set. Cool 10 minutes before serving.

May be prepared early in the day.

Wine Suggestion: The style of this dish would meld well with a dry Rose.

Baked Steak

YIELDS: 4 servings

The sauce adds a zesty flavor.

1	large flank steak	1	(4-ounce) can whole button mushrooms, drained
2	large tomatoes, quartered	2	tablespoons butter, cut into pieces
1	large green pepper, sliced into thin rings	3	tablespoons chili sauce
1	large Bermuda onion, sliced into thin rings	3	tablespoons catsup
		1	tablespoon Worcestershire sauce

1. Place steak in shallow pan. Cover with tomatoes, green peppers, onions, and mushrooms. Dot with butter.

2. Combine remaining ingredients and pour over top. Bake, uncovered, until tender, about 45 minutes, in a preheated 350 degree oven. Thinly slice across grain to serve.

Wine Suggestion: A zesty Zinfandel!

Beef Brisket in Wine Sauce

YIELDS: 6-8 servings

Great with a green salad, buttered noodles sprinkled with poppy seeds, and hot dinner rolls.

5	pounds beef brisket or rump roast	1	tablespoon paprika
3	strips crisp bacon, crumbled	1	green pepper, sliced thin
1	strip orange peel, finely diced		red wine (Burgundy or Bordeaux) to cover
1	bay leaf		salt and pepper to taste
2	cloves garlic, minced	½	pound (more or less to
3	medium onions, quartered		your liking) mushrooms, sliced

1. In a Dutch oven, brown meat and drain fat.

2. Add bacon, orange peel, bay leaf, garlic, onions, paprika, and green pepper. Cover with wine and bake, covered, in a preheated 300 degree oven for 3 hours. Remove from oven and cool overnight.

3. Skim off fat and reheat slowly. Add salt and pepper to taste.

4. Forty minutes before serving, saute mushrooms in butter and add to brisket.

Must be prepared 1 day in advance.

Wine Suggestion: The wine that goes in the sauce should continue to the table. Use a good quality wine in a very reasonable price range.

Beef Tenderloin Deluxe

YIELDS: 8 servings

1 whole beef tenderloin, approximately 3 pounds	4 tablespoons soy sauce
4 tablespoons butter, softened, divided	2 teaspoons Dijon mustard
½ cup onions, chopped	⅛ teaspoon freshly ground pepper
	1 cup dry sherry

1. Spread tenderloin with 2 tablespoons butter. Put on rack in shallow baking pan. Bake, uncovered, in preheated 400 degree oven for 20 minutes.

2. Meanwhile, in 1 quart saucepan, cook onions in 2 tablespoons butter until tender. Add soy sauce, mustard, and pepper. Stir in sherry. Heat to just boiling and pour over tenderloin.

3. Bake 20-25 minutes more for rare beef. Use meat thermometer. Baste frequently with sauce. (If beef is thicker in middle than ends, slice 3 inches from each end to bake middle faster.) Serve sliced according to personal preference with sauce.

Wine Suggestion: Estate bottled St. Emilion or good Cabernet Sauvignon.

Egg Foo Yung

YIELDS: 2 dozen (3 inch rounds)

5 eggs, well beaten	1 cup canned bean sprouts, well drained
½ cup tiny shrimp, cooked	¼ teaspoon salt
½ cup onion, chopped	½ cup cooking oil
½ cup water chestnuts, sliced	

1. Beat eggs in a large bowl. Add remaining ingredients, except cooking oil, and stir.

2. Heat cooking oil in large skillet.

3. From large measuring spoon, drop dollops of batter into the hot oil and fry so that both sides are golden brown, turning over once.

4. Drain between paper toweling. Serve hot and pass the soy sauce!

Wine Suggestion: Best served with fruit juice. If you want wine, use a very light White wine.

Black Tie Standing Rib Roast

YIELDS: 10 servings

This definitely deserves a candlelight presentation.

2 teaspoons salt	1 (10 pound) standing rib of
1 teaspoon dried thyme,	beef (4 ribs), trimmed,
crumbled	fat scored, chine removed
1 teaspoon freshly	and tied onto roast
ground pepper	

1. Combine salt, thyme and pepper in small bowl and blend well. Rub into roast, covering entire surface.

2. Transfer meat to rack in large roasting pan. Let stand at room temperature 1 hour until ready to use.

SAUCE

⅔ cup water	¼ cup butter
1½ tablespoons butter	½ cup shallots, minced
juice of ½ lemon	1 cup beef stock
¼ teaspoon salt	½ cup Madeira wine
½ pound small white	1 tablespoon tomato paste
mushrooms, trimmed	salt and freshly ground
(sliced or halved)	pepper

1. Combine water, butter, lemon juice, and salt in non-aluminum medium saucepan and bring to boil over medium high heat. Reduce heat to low and stir in mushrooms. Cover and cook gently about 5 minutes. Uncover and set aside. (May be prepared several hours ahead to this point. Let stand at room temperature until ready to use.)

2. Roast meat in a preheated 500 degree oven for 10 minutes. Reduce oven temperature to 350 degrees and continue roasting until meat thermometer inserted in thickest portion of meat (without touching bone) registers 130 degrees (for rare), about 17 minutes per pound. Do not baste. Transfer roast to heated serving platter. Tent with foil and keep warm.

continued

Black Tie Standing Rib Roast *continued*

3. Discard as much fat as possible from roasting pan. Add butter to pan and melt over medium high heat. Stir in shallots and saute until tender. Drain mushroom cooking liquid into measuring cup and add water, if necessary, to equal one cup. Pour into roasting pan with beef stock, Madeira, and tomato paste and blend well. Reduce heat to low and cook, stirring up any browned bits, until liquid is reduced to 2 cups. Stir in mushrooms and cook just until heated through. Season with salt and pepper to taste. Transfer to heated sauce boat. Carve roast at table and serve immediately with sauce.

Wine Suggestion: Consider breaking out a fine Burgundy from the Cote-De-Nuits to accent the meal.

Burgundy Burgers

YIELDS: 4 servings

Burgundy turns a humdrum burger cookout into an elegant patio party.

1 pound ground chuck	1 teaspoon Dijon mustard
⅔ cup dry bread crumbs	1 teaspoon Worcestershire
⅓ cup dry red wine	sauce
(Burgundy suggested)	½ teaspoon salt
3 tablespoons chili sauce	⅛ teaspoon garlic powder
1 tablespoon instant	¼ teaspoon pepper
minced onion	2 English muffins, split,
1 teaspoon horseradish	toasted, and buttered

1. Combine all ingredients except English muffins in a medium size bowl. Shape into four patties.

2. Grill four inches from hot coals for about six minutes on each side for medium doneness. Serve on English muffin half.

Wine Suggestion: Burgundy is best. Get a big bottle and serve the rest with dinner.

Cheese and Pasta in a Pot

YIELDS: 18 servings

Good recipe for large get-togethers.

2 pounds lean ground beef, chuck, or round	1 (3-ounce) can mushrooms, sliced and undrained
2-3 tablespoons vegetable oil	1 (8-ounce) box shell macaroni, pinwheels, rotini, etc.
2 medium onions, chopped	
1 clove garlic, crushed	1½ pints dairy sour cream
1 (14-ounce) jar spaghetti sauce	8 ounces Provolone cheese, sliced
1 (16-ounce) can stewed tomatoes	8 ounces Mozzarella cheese, sliced

1. Cook ground beef in vegetable oil in a large, deep frying pan until brown. Stir often with a fork. Drain off excess fat. Add onion, garlic, spaghetti sauce, stewed tomatoes, and undrained mushrooms. Mix well. Simmer 20 minutes or until onions are soft.

2. Meanwhile, cook macaroni according to package directions. Drain and rinse with cold water.

3. Pour half of the shells into a lightly greased, deep casserole dish. Cover with half of the meat-tomato mixture and half of the sour cream. Top with slices of Provolone cheese. Repeat the layering process of macaroni, meat-tomato mixture, and sour cream, ending with a topping of the Mozzarella cheese.

4. Cover and bake in a preheated 350 degree oven for 35 minutes. Remove cover and continue baking until Mozzarella melts and browns slightly.

May be made in a 5 quart crock pot. Cook on low 5 to 6 hours.

Wine Suggestion: If you are serving a crowd, try "Burgundy wine in a box", or a simple Beaujolais will also be pleasant.

Company at Six Stroganoff

YIELDS: 4 servings

Any time this stroganoff is served you'll be a success.

3 tablespoons flour	½ pound fresh mushrooms, sliced
1 teaspoon salt	½ cup dry sherry
¼ teaspoon pepper	½ cup beef broth
1½ pounds sirloin steak	1 teaspoon chervil
2 tablespoons olive oil	zest of ½ lemon, very finely grated
4 tablespoons butter	½ teaspoon paprika
½ cup onion, finely chopped	1 cup sour cream
1 clove garlic, finely minced	2 teaspoons fresh parsley, chopped

1. Mix flour, salt, and pepper. Slice steak into thin strips and dredge lightly with flour.

2. Heat oil and 2 tablespoons butter in skillet until very hot. Add steak and saute until lightly browned. Do not overcook, steak should be rare.

3. Remove meat from pan and reduce heat. Add remaining butter to skillet. Then add onion, garlic, and mushrooms. Cook, stirring constantly, until onion and mushrooms are tender, but not brown.

4. Return steak to skillet along with sherry, beef broth, chervil, zest of lemon, and paprika. Mix well. Season to taste with salt and pepper. Simmer for five minutes or until most of the liquid has evaporated. Stir in sour cream and heat through, taking extreme care not to boil sauce.

5. Serve over freshly steamed rice or wide egg noodles. Garnish with parsley.

Wine Suggestion: French Cotes-Du-Rhone or Italian Valpolicella.

Classic Beef Wellington

YIELDS: 10-12 servings

Treasure this two day preparation time and serve a truly elegant entree.

4-5 **pounds beef tenderloin**
1½ **cups dry red wine**
1 **tablespoon Worcestershire sauce**

juice of 1 lemon
pepper

TWO DAYS BEFORE

1. Place tenderloin in shallow dish. Mix red wine, Worcestershire, lemon juice, and pepper. Pour over tenderloin, cover, and refrigerate for 24 hours. Turn occasionally.

ONE DAY BEFORE

2 **bacon strips**
½ **cup beef consomme**
salt and pepper to taste

½ **cup Madeira wine**
2 **teaspoons cornstarch**

1. Drain marinade from meat and reserve. Dry meat. Rub with oil or melted butter. Place bacon strip in bottom of shallow pan. Place beef on bacon and put another piece of bacon on top. Bake in a preheated 425 degree oven for 30 minutes to sear. Cool meat and refrigerate until next day.

MADEIRA SAUCE

1. Put juices from meat in saucepan. Add beef consomme, Madeira wine, salt, and pepper. Add 3 tablespoons of reserved marinade, allow to cook down 5 minutes. Dissolve 2 teaspoons of cornstarch in 3 tablespoons cold water and add to sauce. Stir over low heat until slightly thickened. Refrigerate until time to reheat. (May use any recipe for a Brown Sauce or Bordelaise instead of Madeira Sauce.)

continued

184

Classic Beef Wellington *continued*

PATE

2	tablespoons butter
4	chicken livers
½	pound mushrooms, chopped
¼	pound cooked ham, finely ground

⅓	cup sherry
1	egg yolk, beaten
1	tablespoon catsup

1. Saute chicken livers in butter until brown, then chop fine. Return to skillet and add mushrooms, ground ham, catsup, and sherry. Cook, stirring occasionally, 10 minutes. Cool, stir in beaten egg yolk. Remove to bowl. Cover and refrigerate.

PASTRY

3	cups flour
2	teaspoons salt
1¾	sticks butter, chilled

4	tablespoons Crisco shortening
¾	cup ice water

1. Mix flour and salt in bowl. Cut in chilled butter and Crisco. Sprinkle in ice water, a little at a time, tossing all the while, until dough holds together. Wrap in wax paper and refrigerate.

3-4 HOURS PRIOR TO SERVING

1 egg, lightly beaten with
1 teaspoon water

1. Remove meat and pate from refrigerator and allow to reach room temperature. (Time beef to be ready no more than 30 minutes before serving.) Stir pate to soften, may need to be drained.

2. Roll out pastry in rectangle, 9 x 14 inches, and ¼ inch thick. (Large enough to envelope meat.)

continued

Classic Beef Wellington *continued*

3. Place meat in center of pastry and spread pate over the top. Fold pastry over meat and seal seams and ends with water. Place seam side down on buttered cookie sheet and brush top and sides with egg mixture. Make hatch marks over top of pastry with a knife. (May decorate with pieces of pastry.) Prick sides with a fork.

4. Bake in a preheated 425 degree oven for 15 minutes, then reduce temperature to 375 degrees and bake 20 to 30 more minutes until golden brown. Using 2 spatulas, lift to serving platter, let set 20 minutes before carving into 1½ inch slices. Serve with reheated Madeira sauce.

Must start preparing 2 days ahead.

Wine Suggestion: Check your cellar for a fine, aged Medoc or older California Cabernet Sauvignon. Spare no expense on wine for this meal.

Bearnaise Sauce

YIELDS: 1½ - 2 cups

Excellent on broiled beef, fish, or eggs.

½	cup white wine	2	egg yolks
1	tablespoon shallots or scallions, finely chopped	1	tablespoon whipping cream
		⅜	teaspoon salt
1½	teaspoons tarragon	½	cup unsalted butter

1. Combine wine, shallots, and tarragon in a small saucepan and cook until wine is reduced to a glaze. Combine glaze with egg yolks, whipping cream, and salt in blender. Turn blender on and off to blend ingredients.

2. Melt butter until bubbling hot. Turn on blender and allow to run while gradually pouring melted butter in a steady stream until sauce thickens. Keep warm by placing over a pan of warm water.

Individual Beef Wellington

YIELDS: 6-8 servings

An elegant touch.

8 **(5 to 6-ounce) filets**	4 **ounces pate de foie gras**
2 **tablespoons oil**	1 **egg white, room**
1 **teaspoon salt**	**temperature**
½ **teaspoon pepper**	1 **teaspoon water**
3 **tablespoons flour**	
2 **(10-ounce) packages of**	
6 puff patty shells,	
thoroughly defrosted	

1. Place filets in freezer 20 minutes. Remove and brush with oil. In a skillet, sear filets 3 minutes on each side. Remove, sprinkle with salt and pepper, and refrigerate 20 minutes.

2. Lightly flour each patty shell and your rolling pin. On wax paper, roll out to ⅛ inch thickness. Shape pate into small, flat circles and place in center of dough. Place filets on top of pate and fold dough around meat. Pinch to seal. Place in shallow roasting pan, sealed side down. Make hole in center of crust. Cut designs from remaining dough, moisten, and decorate top of crusts. At this point, you may cover Wellingtons with foil and refrigerate overnight.

3. Place Wellingtons 1 inch apart on baking sheet (do not use non-stick sheets). Beat egg white with water and just before cooking, brush crusts.

4. In the upper third of a preheated 450 degree oven, bake 10 minutes for rare, 12 minutes for medium rare, or 15 minutes for medium. If crusts are not brown, place on a low rack under broiler 2 or 3 minutes until golden. Transfer to a heated platter and serve with Bearnaise sauce.

Wine Suggestion: A fine estate bottled Bordeaux or your oldest and best California Cabernet from Napa Valley.

Delicious Flank Steak

YIELDS: 6 servings

Although this can be done under a broiler, it's a specialty done on a grill…a favorite of most men.

1½	pounds flank steak	⅓	cup brown sugar, packed
⅓	cup oil	2	cloves garlic,
⅓	cup soy sauce		minced, or use garlic
1	teaspoon ground		salt
	ginger	¼	cup onions, chopped

1. Score flank steak and place in large dish.

2. Combine remaining ingredients for marinade. Pour marinade over steak and let set for several hours or overnight.

3. Grill steak approximately 5 minutes on each side, depending on doneness. May also be prepared under broiler. Slice meat in thin, cross-grain manner. Warm marinade and serve with steak.

Must be prepared 4 to 24 hours ahead. Easy.

Wine Suggestion: A fruity red young Zinfandel.

Helpful Hints: When frying, broiling or grilling meat turn only once to retain maximum juices.

Dijon Mustard Steak

YIELDS: 4 servings

A pleasant addition to your grill out choices.

1 **flank steak (1½ - 2 pounds)**	2 **tablespoons Worcestershire sauce**
1 **to 1½ tablespoons olive oil**	**freshly ground pepper**
1 **tablespoon Dijon mustard**	**juice of ½ lemon**
1 **teaspoon garlic salt**	

1. Rub olive oil on both sides of flank steak. Spread each side with mustard, sprinkle with garlic salt, Worcestershire sauce, and pepper. Place in a shallow dish and top with lemon juice. Cover and refrigerate overnight turning once.

2. Grill steak over glowing coals for 5-7 minutes per side or until desired doneness is reached. Do not overcook. Slice steak diagonally across the grain into very thin slices.

3. Steak may be grilled in oven. Place in broiler pan and broil 4-6 inches from broiler. Broil 5-7 minutes on each side or until done to taste. Do not overcook.

Must be made ahead 1 day.

Wine Suggestion: An affordable French Burgundy or a nice California Pinot Noir.

Ginger Beef

YIELDS: 2-3 servings

Prepare your ingredients ahead of time or include your company in the fun of Wok cooking.

8	large dried Chinese mushrooms*	1	tablespoon cornstarch
⅔	pound flank steak	1	inch piece ginger root, diced
1	clove garlic, finely minced	½	pound Chinese pea pods
1	tablespoon soy sauce	1	small bunch green onions
6	drops sesame oil		

1. Soak mushrooms in warm water for ½ hour. While they are soaking, slice steak thinly, across grain.

2. Mix steak with the next 4 ingredients and marinate at room temperature for ½ hour. While steak marinates, dice ginger root; wash and string pea pods; and slice onion into ½ inch pieces, on the diagonal.

SAUCE

½	cup dry sherry	2	tablespoons soy sauce
2	tablespoons Hoisin sauce*	4	tablespoons water mixed with 2 tablespoons cornstarch
6	drops sesame oil		
½	teaspoon sugar		
2	tablespoons water left over from soaking mushrooms		peanut oil

1. Combine ingredients for sauce.

2. When mushrooms are soft, squeeze out all of the water, cut off the stems, and slice into strips.

continued

Ginger Beef *continued*

3. Heat 2 tablespoons peanut oil in Wok until very hot. Add steak and stir fry until meat loses its pink color. Remove meat and juices from Wok.

4. Add 2 more tablespoons peanut oil to Wok and heat. Add ginger and stir fry 1 minute. Add vegetables and stir fry 2 additional minutes.

5. Return meat and juices to Wok along with the sauce. Stir fry just until meat is heated and sauce thickens. Serve at once with steamed rice.

Available in gourmet section of supermarket.

Wine Suggestion: Break the Red wine habit and serve a German Rhine or Alsatian Gewurztraimer

5 Hour Beef Stew

YIELDS: 6-8 servings

It's the V-8 juice that gives this recipe its tasty and unusual flavor.

3	pounds beef stew meat	4	tablespoons tapioca
6	large carrots	2	teaspoons salt
6	large potatoes	1	teaspoon pepper
1	cup celery, sliced	1	tablespoon sugar
1	small green pepper, diced	4	cups V-8 juice
1½	large onions, chopped	½	cup water

1. Add ingredients in order given in roaster pan or any large, deep baking dish (a Dutch oven works well).

2. Bake in a preheated 300 degree oven for 5 hours, uncovered, stirring occasionally.

Easy and tasty.

Wine Suggestion: An interesting selection for this dish would include a Red wine from the Rioja Region of Spain or a peppery Cabernet from Sonoma, California.

191

Greek Fetaburgers

YIELDS: 6 burgers

A unique pocket sandwich.

6	small Pita breads
1	pound lean ground beef or ground lamb
6	tablespoons creamy cucumber salad dressing

	pinch of dried marjoram or dried oregano
3	ounces part skim Feta cheese, crumbled sliced onions and tomatoes for garnish

1. Carefully slit the Pita pockets around the perimeter and open each into 2 rounds. Use half a pocket for each burger or use hamburger buns.

2. Mix ground meat with salad dressing and marjoram. Shape into 6 flat patties and broil. May pan fry in a nonstick skillet with no fat added.

3. After flipping burgers, place Feta cheese on top so it will melt.

4. Arrange each patty on top of a Pita bread round. Add onions and tomatoes, if desired.

May prepare ahead up to point of cooking.

Wine Suggestion: Jug Red for the adults and Classic Coke for the kids.

Grilled Korean Beef Ribs

YIELDS: 6 servings

Marinate these ribs for 24 hours to bring out their best flavor.

⅓ **cup sesame seeds**	1 **tablespoon sugar**
¼ **cup salad oil**	2 **cloves garlic, minced**
½ **cup soy sauce**	1 **medium onion, thinly**
⅓ **cup lemon juice**	**sliced**
2 **tablespoons white**	4-5 **racks of meaty beef**
wine vinegar	**ribs (12-15 ribs or about**
	7 to 8 pounds)

1. Toast seeds in salad oil. Combine the remaining ingredients, excluding the beef, in a glass bowl.

2. Pour marinade mixture over meat in the largest size heavy plastic cooking bag. Marinate in refrigerator for 24 hours, turning 2 or 3 times.

3. Trim fat off back of ribs, if necessary. Do not cut the slabs of ribs apart until after grilling for easier turning and juicer meat. Grill on solid bed of coals for 25-30 minutes. Turn every 5 minutes while cooking.

4. Skim oil off remaining marinade and heat to boiling. Serve as a sauce.

Wine Suggestion: A California Burgundy or Zinfandel.

Italian Roast Beef

YIELDS: 8-10 servings

Save the leftovers. This unique way of serving a roast can be enjoyed in sandwiches too.

4	pounds rump roast	2	teaspoons salt
⅛	teaspoon onion salt	⅛	teaspoon garlic
½	teaspoon dried parsley		powder
	flakes	2	tablespoons Worcestershire
½	teaspoon basil		sauce
½	teaspoon black pepper	2	beef bouillon cubes
½	teaspoon Italian	1	cup water
	seasoning		Italian bread, sliced

1. Place meat, fat side up, in ungreased baking pan on rack. Bake in a preheated 325 degree oven for 1 hour.

2. Mix herbs, spices, and salt together and crush to pulverize. Sprinkle on top of meat with Worcestershire sauce, rubbing in with hand. Continue roasting until done to desired degree (usually 25 minutes per pound for medium rare). Remove roast from oven.

3. Dissolve bouillon cubes in water and add to meat drippings to make au jus gravy. Slice meat thinly and add to au jus. Serve over Italian bread with juices.

Easy. May be prepared ahead and freezes well.

Wine Suggestion: Italian Barbera or a Chateauneuk Du Pape.

London Broil

YIELDS: 4-6 servings

An appealing summer grill-out rated excellent in flavor.

1   (2-3 pound) sirloin
     steak, cut 2½
     inches thick

MARINADE

⅔ cup beer
⅓ cup oil
1   teaspoon salt

¼   teaspoon garlic
    powder
¼   teaspoon pepper

1. Combine marinade ingredients. Pour over meat. Marinate overnight. Cook meat on grill until desired doneness. Slice thin. Serve with the following toppings.

TOPPING 1

2   tablespoons butter
½   teaspoon paprika

4   cups onions, sliced

1. Combine all ingredients in saucepan. Cook until onions are tender. Place over sliced steak.

TOPPING 2

¾ cup sour cream

½   teaspoon horseradish sauce

1. Combine ingredients and pour over Topping 1 when ready to serve.

Must be prepared 1 day ahead.

Wine Suggestion: An easy wine. California Pinot Noir or Gamay.

Mexican Pizza

YIELDS: 8 servings

An unusual Mexican flair to serve to your pizza lovers.

1½ cups Bisquick
½ cup yellow cornmeal
½ cup cold water
1 pound ground beef
1 (4-ounce) can green
   chilies, drained,
   seeded, chopped
1 package taco
   seasoning mix

¾ cup water
1 can refried beans
1½ cups Cheddar cheese,
   shredded
1 cup lettuce, shredded
2 medium tomatoes, chopped
½ cup onion, chopped

1. Mix Bisquick, cornmeal, and ½ cup water until soft dough forms. Roll or pat dough into 12 inch circle on ungreased pizza pan or cookie sheet forming ½ inch rim. Bake in a preheated 425 degree oven for 10 minutes.

2. Cook and stir ground beef until brown. Drain. Stir in chilies, seasoning mix, and ¾ cup water. Heat to boiling. Simmer uncovered 5-10 minutes.

3. Spread beans over baked crust, top with beef mixture, and sprinkle with cheese. Bake 10 minutes longer. Top with lettuce, tomatoes, and onion. Serve with taco sauce on top, if desired.

Wine Suggestion: Lots of your favorite California Generic Red table wine.

Mock Tournedos with Bearnaise

YIELDS: 4 servings

A unique recipe for the ever popular flank steak.

1½ **pounds flank steak, pound to ⅛ inch thick**	½ **teaspoon garlic powder**
1 **teaspoon salt**	¼ **teaspoon pepper**
1 **tablespoon fresh tarragon or 1½ teaspoons dried**	2 **tablespoons fresh parsley, chopped**
	12 **slices bacon**

1. Pound steak into a rectangle. Sprinkle with spices.

2. Saute bacon until half done. Drain. Place bacon lengthwise on the steak. Roll up jelly roll style starting at the narrower end of the meat. Secure the roll with toothpicks down the edge at 1 inch intervals. Cut the roll into 1 inch slices.

3. Broil tournedos for 6-7 minutes on each side for medium rare or grill over medium coals. Serve with Bearnaise Sauce.

Wine Suggestion: A moderately priced California Cabernet will make a nice accompaniment to this dish.

Helpful Hints: To correct lumpy gravy, blend a little salt into flour or cornstarch before adding water to the thickening.

 MAIN DISHES

Pete's Sirloin Tip Roast

YIELDS: 10-12 servings

This roast makes quite a bit of luscious brown sauce. Serve with mashed potatoes or spoon over sliced beef.

5-6 **pound sirloin tip roast**	¼ **cup soy sauce**
½ **cup Wesson oil**	½ **cup Worcestershire sauce**
3 **cans cream of mushroom soup**	⅛ **teaspoon salt**
2 **medium onions, diced**	⅛ **teaspoon pepper**
1 **package Lipton's onion soup**	½ **teaspoon garlic powder**

1. Roll roast in flour, pressing flour into roast with your fingers. Braise roast in Dutch oven in oil.

2. In large mixing bowl, combine rest of the ingredients and pour over meat. Be sure meat is three-fourths covered with sauce. Turn once while cooking. Bake in a preheated 350 degree oven for 1½ hours.

Easy. Leftovers freeze well.

Wine Suggestion: For a new taste sensation use an Australian Shiraz.

Helpful Hints: When cooking meat, never prick it, this allows juices to escape. Use tongs to turn meat.

Quick Cheese Steaks

YIELDS: 4-6 servings

2	tablespoons onion, grated	1	teaspoon sugar
1	tablespoon shortening	¼	teaspoon basil
4-6	cubed steaks	1	teaspoon salt
1	can tomato soup	¼	cup Parmesan cheese

1. Cook onion in melted shortening. Add steaks and fry until brown. Add other ingredients, except cheese. Put into a 2 quart casserole and cover tightly. (May freeze at this point. Cool first, then seal, and freeze.)

2. Bake in a preheated 350 degree oven for 55 minutes or until steaks are tender. Sprinkle with Parmesan cheese and bake 5 more minutes. (Thaw frozen steaks before baking.)

Wine Suggestion: Open an unpretentious Red table wine and enjoy.

Ray's Barbecue Sauce

This sauce is great for chicken, ribs, kabobs, or anything on the grill and keeps 2-3 months refrigerated.

1	cup catsup	2	teaspoons chili powder
¼	cup vinegar	¼	teaspoon cayenne pepper
¼	cup Worcestershire sauce	1	medium onion, chopped fine
¼	cup brown sugar, packed	2	dashes Tabasco sauce
1	teaspoon salt	1½	cups water
1	teaspoon black pepper	1	lemon, cut in quarters

1. Mix all of the above ingredients together in a heavy saucepan. Simmer for 20 minutes, stirring occasionally. Remove the lemon pieces before refrigerating.

Stuffed Flank Steak

YIELDS: 4-6 servings

An interesting way to see flank steak.

1¼ **pounds flank steak**	1 **clove garlic, minced**
½ **cup soy sauce**	1 **cup water**
¼ **cup cooking oil**	½ **cup long grain rice**
2 **tablespoons molasses**	½ **cup carrots, shredded**
2 **teaspoons dry mustard**	½ **cup water chestnuts,**
1 **teaspoon ginger**	**sliced**
root, grated	¼ **cup green onions, sliced**

1. Have butcher cut a pocket lengthwise in flank steak, open at both ends.

2. Combine soy sauce, oil, molasses, mustard, ginger, and garlic. Pour in pocket and over meat, and let stand at room temperature for 30 minutes.

3. In a saucepan, combine water, rice, carrots, water chestnuts, and onion. Bring to boil, cover, reduce heat, and simmer 8 minutes. Remove from heat and set aside.

4. Drain meat, reserving marinade. Add ¼ cup marinade to rice mixture. Mix well and stuff into pocket of steak. Close ends of pockets and secure with skewers or toothpicks. Place in shallow baking pan, cover with foil, and bake in a preheated 350 degree oven for 1 hour. Brush occasionally with marinade.

May be prepared early in the day and refrigerated.

Wine Suggestion: Use a sturdy but mellow Red Zinfandel Merlot from California.

Stuffed Tomatoes

YIELDS: 4-6 servings

May be made one day ahead. Bake halfway and finish baking on serving day.

7 medium to large tomatoes	1 teaspoon salt
1 pound ground beef	1/16 teaspoon pepper
1 medium onion, chopped	1 (6-ounce) can tomato paste
½ cup green pepper, chopped	½ cup long grain rice

1. Cut tops off tomatoes and carefully clean them out. Set aside. Save tomato tops.

2. Brown meat with onion, green pepper, salt, and pepper. Drain off excess fat. Add ½ can tomato paste. Blend and cook 1 minute. Add rice and cook for 5 minutes, stirring frequently.

3. Lightly salt inside of tomatoes. Stuff tomatoes with meat mixture. Cover with tomato top. Place tomatoes close together in roasting pan. Combine remaining tomato paste with enough water to pour in pan, about ¼ inch high. Cover. Bake in a preheated 350 degree oven for 45 minutes or until rice is tender.

Wine Suggestion: California Charbono or Petit Sirah.

Helpful Hints: When saving oil that has been used for deep frying, line a funnel with a paper coffee filter to clarify the oil as it is poured into the storage jar.

Sweet and Sour Beef Stew

YIELDS: 4-5 servings

A welcomed dinner for a nippy winter day.

1½ pounds beef chuck or round steak, cut in cubes	¼ cup brown sugar, packed
	¼ cup vinegar
2 tablepoons cooking oil	1 tablespoon Worcestershire sauce
1 cup carrots, chopped	½ cup water
1 cup onions, sliced	1 teaspoon salt
1 (8-ounce) can tomato sauce	4 teaspoons cornstarch
	¼ cup cold water

1. Brown meat in oil.

2. Add carrots, onions, tomato sauce, brown sugar, vinegar, Worcestershire sauce, ½ cup water, and salt. Cover and cook over low heat until meat is tender, approximately 1½ - 2 hours.

3. Combine cornstarch and ¼ cup water and add to beef mixture; cook and stir until thickened. Serve over buttered noodles or rice.

May be prepared ahead and reheated.

Wine Suggestion: A very young Beaujolais, Cotes-Du-Rhone, or Pinot Noir.

Texas Grill

This unique grill out calls for bandana print napkins and a red checkered tablecloth!

5-7	pound sirloin tip roast or brisket	1	teaspoon paprika
½	teaspoon garlic powder	1	cup tomato sauce
½	cup salad oil	1	cup chili sauce
1	teaspoon cayenne (red) pepper	1	teaspoon oregano
		1	tablespoon ground black pepper

1. Mix all ingredients for basting sauce.

2. Place meat on grill, away from coals. Roast 3½ - 4 hours, basting generously every 30 minutes. Turn meat after each basting. Cook with lid closed. If meat thermometer used, cook until 160 degrees. Outside of meat will be crusty.

Start to prepare early in the day.

Wine Suggestion: Spanish Sangre De Toro. (The blood of the bull and plenty of it!)

Helpful Hints: Allow 1 pound of ice per guest.

Top Blade Steak with Creamy Dill Sauce

YIELDS: 4 servings

This recipe leaves plenty of sauce to serve as a side dish with noodles.

1	tablespoon salad oil	⅛	teaspoon pepper
4	beef chuck top blade boneless steaks, cut 1 inch thick (1½ pounds)	1	(8-ounce) package medium egg noodles
⅓	cup water	8	ounces sour cream
1	beef bouillon cube	½	teaspoon dill weed
½	teaspoon salt	½	teaspoon parsley, snipped
		¼	teaspoon Worcestershire sauce

1. In large skillet over medium high heat, cook steaks in hot oil until well browned on both sides. Stir in water, bouillon, salt, and pepper; heat to boiling. Reduce heat to low, cover, and simmer steaks 1¼ hours or until tender, turning steaks once during cooking.

2. Prepare noodles as directed on package.

3. When steaks are done, remove to platter. Drain noodles, place on same platter, and keep warm.

4. Stir sour cream, dill weed, parsley, and Worcestershire sauce into hot liquid in skillet. Cook, stirring until slightly thickened (do not boil). Spoon sauce over steaks. Pass remaining sauce.

Wine Suggestion: A Red wine from the Graves area of France or try a Cabernet from Livermore Valley, California.

Youvarlakia
(Greek Meatballs in Sauce)

YIELDS: 4 servings

MEATBALLS

1	pound very lean ground beef	dash	pepper
¼	cup rice	1	teaspoon cumin
½	cup onion, chopped	1	teaspoon parsley
½	teaspoon salt	1	egg

1. Combine all ingredients. Shape into 2 inch balls. Set aside.

SAUCE

1½	tablespoons butter	2	cups water
½	teaspoon salt	2	eggs, room temperature
6	ounces tomato sauce		juice of ½ large fresh lemon

1. In large saucepan, melt butter until bubbly. Add salt and tomato sauce. Stir to blend.

2. Add water and bring to a boil. Add meatballs carefully. Sauce should cover meatballs. Add more water if necessary. Bring to a boil. Cover and lower heat. Simmer for 30 minutes or until rice is tender. (At this point, meatballs can be refrigerated for next day's use. When ready to serve, bring meatballs to a boil and continue with recipe.)

3. Beat eggs until frothy. Add lemon juice.

4. Using low speed of mixer, slowly add hot liquid from pan to eggs. Pour this back into pan over meatballs.

5. Serve immediately, spooning sauce over meatballs. Dip French or Italian bread in sauce, if desired.

Wine Suggestion: Greek food—serves Greek Domestic Red.

Cheese Chache Chicken

YIELDS: 4 servings

Rated high in the ease of preparation.

2	whole chicken breasts, skinned, boned, and halved	½	cup flour
		2	eggs
4	pieces Monterey Jack cheese, ¼ inch thick by 3 inches long	1	teaspoon Parmesan cheese, grated
	sage	¼	teaspoon salt
1	tablespoon parsley, minced	¼	teaspoon pepper
		¼	cup oil

1. Pound chicken breasts to flatten. Place 1 piece of cheese and pinch of sage on each breast. Fold chicken around cheese.

2. Combine parsley and flour.

3. Beat eggs with Parmesan cheese, salt, and pepper.

4. Dip folded chicken breast into flour, then into egg mixture. Saute in oil until golden and crisp. Transfer to baking dish and bake in a preheated 375 degree oven for 20 minutes.

May be prepared ahead to baking point.

Wine Suggestion: Try a very light red wine or Chenin Blanc, semi-dry.

Chicken and Artichokes

YIELDS: 6-8 servings

A pleasant luncheon entree.

2	(14-ounce) cans artichoke hearts	6	chicken breasts, halved and boned
½	pound fresh mushrooms or 1 (4-ounce) can mushrooms	¾	can water chestnuts, sliced
2	cans cream of chicken soup	1	cup Pepperidge Farm herb seasoned stuffing
½	cup white wine	¼	cup butter or margarine
⅛	teaspoon salt		
⅛	teaspoon pepper		

1. Rinse and drain artichoke hearts. Slice mushrooms.

2. Mix soup, wine, salt, and pepper. Pour ⅓ of the mixture into a buttered 9 x 13 inch baking dish.

3. Add chicken, cover with mushrooms, water chestnuts, and artichoke hearts. Pour remaining soup and wine mixture over top. Cover with stuffing and dot with butter.

4. Cover with foil and bake in a preheated 350 degree oven for 45 minutes. Remove foil and bake for an additional 30 minutes.

Easy. May use 1 can of artichoke hearts.

Wine Suggestion: Artichokes sometimes fight the flavors of wine, but wine drinkers serve alot of bread so that the flavors meld better. Try a Beaujolais with this dish.

 MAIN DISHES

Chicken and Peppers Piccata

YIELDS: 4 servings

2-3 tablespoons vegetable oil
2 large red peppers, seeded and cut into squares
2 large sweet onions, peeled and cut into wedges
6-8 mushrooms, quartered
1½ pounds boneless chicken thighs, cut in 1 inch cubes

2 large cloves garlic, minced
1 dried hot red pepper, crumbled, or ¼ teaspoon Tabasco sauce
rind and juice of 1 lemon
2 tablespoons butter
2 tablespoons parsley, finely chopped
salt and pepper to taste

1. In large skillet, heat 2 tablespoons of oil. Saute red pepper squares, onion wedges, and mushrooms until vegetables begin to soften slightly. Remove vegetables from oil with slotted spoon and set aside.

2. In oil in pan, brown chicken cubes, adding additional oil if necessary. When chicken is lightly browned, add garlic and hot pepper. Reduce heat slightly, and cook, covered, for 1-2 minutes.

3. Stir in lemon rind and juice. Stir well to dissolve browned particles in bottom of pan. Add butter, blending well into sauce. Return cooked vegetables to chicken mixture with chopped parsley. Season to taste with salt and pepper. Heat well. Serve over hot rice.

Wine Suggestion: A favorite with this dish is Malon-Lugny.

Chicken Bundles

YIELDS: 4 servings

A flavorful asparagus and ham wrap-up.

1	cup water	¼	cup butter or margarine
18	fresh, trimmed asparagus spears or 9-ounce package frozen asparagus spears, thawed and drained	½	teaspoon salt
		3	whole chicken breasts, skinned, boned, halved
		6	slices cooked ham

1. In 10 inch skillet bring water to boil, add fresh asparagus, cover and cook until asparagus is partially cooked. Drain and set aside. (No need to precook frozen asparagus.)

2. In 13 x 9 inch baking dish, melt butter in preheated oven. Add salt, stir to blend. Dip both sides of chicken breasts in seasoned butter. Place 1 ham slice and 3 cooked asparagus spears on top of each chicken breast. Wrap each breast around ham and asparagus and secure with toothpicks.

3. Place chicken in same baking dish and cover with foil. Bake near center of a preheated 350 degree oven for 35-45 minutes or until chicken is fork tender.

SAUCE

¼	cup butter or margarine	¾	teaspoon salt
⅓	cup flour	¾	teaspoon tarragon
1½	cups half and half	1	tablespoon lemon juice
½	cup water	⅛	teaspoon hot pepper sauce
2	tablespoons parsley		

1. In heavy 2 quart saucepan, melt butter over medium heat. Add flour, stirring to blend; add remaining ingredients.

2. Cook over medium heat, stirring occasionally until mixture comes to a full boil. Boil one minute. Spoon ⅓ cup sauce over each chicken breast and serve.

May be assembled ahead.

Wine Suggestion: A nice quality Red Burgundy would be a different approach. Alternative could be Chardonnay.

Chicken Lasagna

YIELDS: 8-10 servings

3 tablespoons butter	8 ounces lasagna noodles, cooked and drained
¼ pound fresh mushrooms, sliced	1 (16-ounce) carton small curd cottage cheese
½ cup onion, finely chopped	4 cups chicken, cooked and cubed
1 can cream of chicken soup	2 cups sharp Cheddar cheese, shredded
⅓ cup milk	½ cup Parmesan cheese

1. Melt butter in saucepan, over medium heat, about 2 minutes. Add mushrooms and onion. Saute 5 minutes or until tender. Remove from heat. Stir in chicken soup and milk.

2. Arrange 4 lasagna noodles, overlapped, in a greased 9 x 13 x 2 inch glass baking dish. Top with layers of sauce, ½ of cottage cheese, ½ of chicken, ½ of Cheddar cheese, and ½ of Parmesan cheese. Add remaining noodles and repeat layers.

3. Bake in a preheated 350 degree oven for 45 minutes or until hot and bubbly. Let stand 10 minutes before serving.

Wine Suggestion: A party needs a jug of premium White wine.

Chicken Marengo

Flamed in Cognac, caressed in vermouth, and served with the elegance of white wine.

1	large chicken, cut into 8 pieces	6	large tomatoes, peeled, seeded, and coarsely chopped
	salt and freshly ground pepper	¼	cup dry white wine (vermouth)
4	tablespoons olive oil	¼	cup pitted black olives
¼	cup Cognac	6	large cooked shrimp, shells left intact
4	medium white onions, cut into eighths		salt and pepper to taste
2	cloves garlic, minced		chopped parsley
1	teaspoon sugar		

1. Sprinkle chicken with salt and pepper and brown evenly in olive oil.

2. Heat Cognac over high heat. Pour over chicken and ignite, shaking pan until flame subsides. Remove chicken and set aside.

3. Saute onions and garlic in drippings remaining in skillet until golden. Add tomatoes, sugar, salt, and pepper. Saute a few minutes and then turn up heat to remove any juices from tomatoes.

4. Add vermouth and return chicken to skillet. Spoon sauce over chicken. Simmer, covered, for 30 minutes. Add olives and cook additional 10 minutes or until chicken is tender.

5. Place chicken on platter, cover with sauce, and garnish with cooked shrimp. Sprinkle with parsley.

May be prepared ahead and reheated.

Wine Suggestion: Try a Chianti Classico with this dish.

Chicken Parmigiana

YIELDS: 12 servings

SAUCE

3   medium onions, chopped
3   cloves garlic, crushed
1   (28-ounce) can whole tomatoes

⅓   cup red wine
1   bay leaf, crushed
½   teaspoon oregano

1. Lightly brown onions and garlic in small amount of oil.

2. Add whole can of slightly mashed tomatoes, wine, bay leaf, and oregano. Salt to taste. Bring to a boil, stirring; then simmer 20 minutes.

CHICKEN

6   chicken breasts, split, skinned, and boned
    salt and pepper
    flour
3   eggs, beaten
2¾ cups Ritz crackers, crushed

    oil
1   pound Mozzarella cheese, sliced
½   cup Parmesan cheese, grated

1. Flatten chicken between wax paper.

2. Sprinkle with salt and pepper. Dip in flour, then egg. Coat with cracker crumbs and brown slowly in hot oil.

3. Pour half the sauce in a 9 x 13 inch baking dish. Lay chicken on top. Cover with Mozzarella cheese. Add remainder of sauce. Top with grated Parmesan cheese.

4. Bake in a preheated 350 degree oven for 20 minutes, covered, and an additional 20 minutes, uncovered.

Early day preparation. Must refrigerate. Freezes well.

Wine Suggestion: A Red wine from the Piedmont region of Italy will enhance the rich flavors of this dish.

Chicken Teriyaki

YIELDS: 4 servings

Add this specialty to your summer picnic basket.

3	pounds frying chicken, cut up, or chicken breasts	4	tablespoons brown sugar
1	cup soy sauce	⅛	teaspoon pepper
½	cup oil	1	clove garlic, finely minced
		1	large onion, finely minced

1. Combine soy sauce, oil, brown sugar, pepper, garlic, and onion. Place chicken in marinade. Marinate for at least 8 hours. Preferably overnight.

2. Grill over medium coals until tender. Turn frequently to prevent burning.

Easy. May be prepared ahead.

Wine Suggestion: Use a well-chilled Gamay Rose.

Chicken Veronique

YIELDS: 4 servings

Lightly tossed in a simmering white wine sauce.

2	large whole chicken breasts	½	cup light white wine or white grape juice
¼	cup vegetable oil	¾	cup green grapes, sliced
¼	cup onions, chopped		brown rice
½	cup mushrooms, sliced		

1. Skin and cut breasts into small bite size pieces.

2. Place oil in skillet and add chicken pieces. Brown chicken. Add onions, mushrooms, and wine.

3. Cover and simmer gently 30 to 40 minutes. Add grapes the last 3 to 5 minutes.

Easy. Brown rice is a good accompaniment.

Wine Suggestion: A classy California Sauvignon Blanc that is on the drier side, or a good quality Chardonnay.

Chicken with Leeks and Dried Tomatoes

YIELDS: 4 servings

2	whole chicken breasts, skinned, boned, and halved
3	tablespoons unsalted butter
½	teaspoon salt
¼	teaspoon freshly ground black pepper
1	large leek, minced
⅔	cup whipping cream
½	cup dry white wine
⅛	teaspoon oregano (optional)
¼	cup Genovesi dried tomatoes, coarsely chopped

1. Slice breast halves crosswise on the diagonal into 6 equal pieces. Season the chicken with salt and pepper. Cook the pieces in a large skillet in the butter over moderate heat until the chicken is just cooked through, about 4 or 5 minutes.

2. Remove chicken with slotted spoon. Add leek to skillet and saute, stirring until softened, about 1 minute. Stir in cream, wine, oregano, and dried tomatoes and bring to a boil over moderate heat.

3. Reduce heat slightly and simmer, uncovered, stirring occasionally until sauce thickens slightly, about 5 minutes. Return chicken to the skillet and simmer gently, spooning with sauce, until heated through, 2-3 minutes.

Wine Suggestion: Sauvignon Blanc or Chardonnay.

Chicken Yucatan

The slow cooking is the essence of this recipe.

4	large chicken breasts, halved	2	large tomatoes, chopped
	salt and pepper	3	large stalks celery, chopped
	chili powder	1	large green pepper, chopped
	curry powder	1	quart orange juice
1	large onion, finely chopped		

1. Place chicken in an 11 x 13 inch glass baking dish. Season with salt and pepper. Sprinkle curry and chili powders thickly over breasts. Distribute remaining vegetables evenly over chicken. Pour in orange juice and marinate 4-6 hours or overnight. Cover with foil and bake in a preheated 300 degree oven for 4 hours. Serve over saffron rice.

Wine Suggestion: Interesting flavors call for a Spanish Chardonnay.

Brazil Nut Dressing

Complimented nicely by a cranberry salad.

8	cups soft bread cubes or according to size of turkey (8 cups for 13 pound turkey)	½	teaspoon powdered sage
		2	cups Brazil nuts, chopped
		½	can cream of chicken soup
			salt to taste
2	onions, chopped		pepper to taste
½	cup butter, melted		giblet broth

1. Let bread cubes set out overnight to dry.

2. Combine all ingredients and moisten with giblet broth. Stuff a 13 pound turkey. The remaining one-half can of cream of chicken soup may be used to baste the turkey.

Chinese Chicken and Cashews

YIELDS: 4-6 servings

This serves well over a bed of fluffy white rice.

3	whole chicken breasts	¾	cup regular roasted cashews (not dry roasted)
5	tablespoons soy sauce		
1	tablespoon dry white wine or sherry	3	green peppers, cut bite size
1½	tablespoons cornstarch		
¾	tablespoon sugar	1	medium onion, cut bite size
⅛	teaspoon monosodium glutamate	6	tablespoons safflower oil
1	clove garlic, crushed		

1. Skin, bone, and cut chicken into ¾ inch cubes.

2. Mix together soy sauce, wine, cornstarch, sugar, monosodium glutamate, and garlic. Add chicken cubes and marinate in refrigerator for 1 to 2 hours.

3. Heat 2 tablespoons oil in Wok or frying pan. Cook cashews in oil 1 to 2 minutes or until golden brown. Remove from pan.

4. Wipe pan and heat 3 tablespoons oil; add chicken and marinade. Stir fry over high heat until no longer pink, about 5 minutes. Remove from pan.

5. Wipe pan and heat 1 tablespoon oil. Cook green peppers and onions, about 3 minutes. Add chicken and cashews and stir quickly until heated. Arrange on platter and serve immediately.

Variation: Add ¾ pound snowpeas instead of green peppers.

Wine Suggestion: A spicy Gewurztraimer or California Green Hungarian.

Crab Stuffed Chicken Breast

YIELDS: 6-8 servings

A surf 'n turf combo highlighted by the gentle flavoring of white wine.

½ cup green onions, thinly sliced	½ cup milk
¼ pound mushrooms, thinly sliced	½ cup dry white wine
	salt and pepper to taste
3 tablespoons butter	½ pound fresh crabmeat, chopped
3 tablespoons flour	¼ to ⅓ cup parsley
¼ teaspoon thyme	⅓ cup bread crumbs
½ cup regular strength chicken broth	1 cup (4-ounces) Swiss cheese, shredded
	4 whole chicken breasts, boned, skinned (8 pieces)

1. Saute mushrooms and onions in butter until juice evaporates. Stir in flour and thyme. Blend in broth, milk, and wine. Cook until thickened. Add salt and pepper to taste.

2. Take ¼ cup of the sauce and mix it together with the crab, parsley, and bread crumbs.

3. Pound chicken flat. Spoon crab mixture on chicken and roll. Place seam side down. Pour remaining sauce over top. Sprinkle with Swiss cheese.

4. Cover and bake in a preheated 400 degree oven for 40 minutes.

May be assembled in the afternoon. Easy.

Wine Suggestion: Delicate flavors, delicate wine—French Muscadet or Rose of Cabernet.

 MAIN DISHES

Crusty Mustard Chicken

YIELDS: 4 servings

Good hot or cold for a picnic.

1	large frying chicken, cut into pieces	2	teaspoons dry rosemary
3	tablespoons Dijon mustard	⅛	teaspoon pepper
3	cloves garlic, finely minced	½	cup Parmesan cheese, freshly grated

1. Place chicken, skin side up, in a 9 x 13 inch baking dish or pan.

2. Mix together mustard and garlic and spread over each piece of chicken. Sprinkle on rosemary and pepper. Dust with Parmesan cheese. Bake, uncovered, in a preheated 350 degree oven for 45 minutes.

Wine Suggestion: California Chardonnay goes well with this meal.

Oriental Turkey

YIELDS: 6-8 servings

3	cups turkey, cooked and diced	1	(3-ounce) can Chinese noodles
2	cans cream of chicken soup	1	cup celery, chopped
1	(16-ounce) can chop suey vegetables, drained	½	cup Miracle Whip
1	(8-ounce) can water chestnuts, sliced and drained	1	teaspoon lemon juice
		2	tablespoons green onions, diced
		½	to ¾ cup cashews

1. Combine all ingredients together except cashews. Mix well. Place in greased 2 quart shallow casserole dish. Sprinkle with cashews. Bake in a preheated 350 degree oven for 30 minutes.

Wine Suggestion: California Chenin Blanc, German Rhine.

Gourmet Chicken Casserole

YIELDS: 6-8 servings

4	half chicken breasts	½	cup mayonnaise
1	(6-ounce) box Uncle Ben's wild rice mix (original recipe), cooked	2	tablespoons pimento, chopped
		2	tablespoons onion, chopped
1	can cream of celery soup	1	teaspoon salt
1	(8-ounce) can water chestnuts, sliced	¼	teaspoon pepper
		½	cup Chablis white wine
			paprika

1. Cook chicken; cut into pieces.

2. Combine cooked rice, soup, mayonnaise, water chestnuts, pimento, onion, salt, pepper, and wine. Add chicken pieces and mix well. Pour into casserole dish and sprinkle with paprika. Bake, uncovered, in a preheated 350 degree oven for 25 minutes.

May prepare ahead 2 days. Freezes well.

Wine Suggestion: Buy enough California Chablis for the sauce and the cook.

Oyster Dressing

YIELDS: 10-12 servings

A true reminder of your favorite colonial inn.

1½	cups onions, chopped	¾	teaspoon thyme
1½	cups celery, chopped	¾	teaspoon sage
6	tablespoons margarine	¾	teaspoon marjoram
6	tablespoons oil	¾	teaspoon oregano
6-8	slices bread, broken into small pieces		salt and pepper to taste
		2	eggs
3	tablespoons parsley, minced	1½	cups oysters, chopped

1. Slowly cook onions and celery in the margarine and oil until soft and yellow. Add bread and the remaining ingredients, adding the oysters last. Stuff into turkey or put into buttered casserole dish and bake in a preheated 350 degree oven for 1 hour.

Greek Chicken and Rice

YIELDS: 6 servings

CHICKEN

1	2½ to 3½ pound chicken, whole or cut up	¼	cup onion, chopped
1	cup water	⅛	cup green pepper, chopped
	salt and pepper	8	ounces tomato sauce

1. Rinse chicken and place in roaster with a tight-fitting lid. Pour water in pan. Sprinkle chicken with salt and pepper. Add onion and green pepper. Cover and bake in a preheated 350 degree oven for 35 minutes.

2. Pour ½ of the tomato sauce on chicken and the remainder in the juices. Cover. Bake 35-45 minutes longer or until chicken is tender. Remove chicken from pan and place on platter. Cover with foil to keep warm.

RICE

	juices from cooked chicken	½	teaspoon salt
2	cups water	1½	cups rice

1. Turn oven up to 450 degrees. Heat juices in roaster on stove on high heat. Add salt and water. Heat until boiling. Add rice and stir, continuing to boil for 3 minutes. Cover and place in oven. Reduce oven to 400 degrees. Bake for about 20 minutes or until rice is tender. Stir occasionally. Serve with chicken.

Wine Suggestion: A lighter style California Pinot Noir or French Cotes-Du-Rhone.

Herbed Chicken

The zip of Swiss cheese adds a delightful touch.

8	to 10 chicken breast halves, boned and skinned	2	cups Swiss cheese, grated
1	(4-ounce) can mushroom pieces, drained (or fresh mushrooms in amount desired)	1	can cream of mushroom soup
		1	can cream of chicken soup Pepperidge Farm herb seasoned stuffing

1. Place chicken breasts in shallow baking dish. Sprinkle mushrooms on top of chicken. Add Swiss cheese. Pour combined soups over all.

2. Bake in a preheated 350 degree oven for approximately 1 hour. Remove from oven and add finely crumbled stuffing over top. Bake 10 minutes longer. May be held in warm oven for ½ hour or until ready to serve.

May be made ahead 1 day.

Wine Suggestion: A German Rhine or California Chenin Blanc.

MAIN DISHES

Honey Glazed Herb Chicken

These herbs add flavor without salt.

1 cup honey	½ teaspoon thyme
1 cup bread crumbs, fresh	½ teaspoon pepper
¼ cup wheat germ	3 whole chicken breasts, halved
1 teaspoon basil	
¼ teaspoon rosemary	½ cup oil

1. Pour honey into shallow baking dish.

2. In separate shallow dish blend crumbs, wheat germ, and seasonings.

3. Dip chicken into honey, coat well, and cover each piece of breast in crumb mixture.

4. Pour oil ⅛ inch deep into large baking dish. Add chicken. Bake in a preheated 350 degree oven for one hour.

May prepare early in the day.

Wine Suggestion: Use a sweet style Rose or California Rhine to stand up to the honey.

Keeng Wha Chicken

YIELDS: 2 servings

An oriental delight worth the preparation time.

1 whole chicken breast, split, skinned, boned, and diced	¼ teaspoon ginger
	⅛ teaspoon pepper
	¼ cup celery, diced
1 egg white, beaten until foamy	¼ cup green pepper, diced
	¼ cup onion, diced
1 teaspoon cornstarch	10 straw mushrooms (optional)
¼ cup oil	8 water chestnuts, sliced
½ teaspoon cooking wine	2 teaspoons chicken stock
2 tablespoons soy sauce	2 cloves garlic, minced
½ teaspoon sugar	1 teaspoon cornstarch
½ teaspoon garlic powder	1 tablespoon cold water

1. Combine chicken and egg white in a bowl. Add 1 teaspoon cornstarch and thoroughly coat chicken.

2. Heat oil in large frying pan or Wok. Add wine, soy sauce, sugar, garlic powder, ginger, and pepper to oil. Stir fry chicken in oil and spices until meat turns from pink to white. Remove chicken from pan leaving the spices and liquid.

3. Place celery, green pepper, onion, water chestnuts, and mushrooms in pan and stir fry vegetables 3 to 5 minutes (crisp cooked).

4. Return chicken to pan, mixing with vegetables. Add chicken stock, minced garlic, 1 teaspoon cornstarch, and cold water. Toss mixture until liquid is thickened. Add additional soy sauce to taste at this time. Serve over rice.

RICE

1¼ cups rice   2½ cups water

1. Place rice and water in covered pan. Heat on high until boiling. Turn heat to simmer and continue cooking in covered pan until water is absorbed.

Wine Suggestion: Fu Gai wine made in New Zealand especially for Chinese food or California wines with Chinese names.

 # MAIN DISHES

Lemon Chicken

YIELDS: 4 servings

Use a pound of fresh shrimp in place of chicken for a delightful change.

1 pound boneless chicken breasts, cut into 1½ inch pieces	½ pound snow peas, strings removed
2½ tablespoons peanut oil, divided	¼ cup fresh mushrooms, sliced
1 teaspoon cornstarch	4 teaspoons fresh lemon juice
1 teaspoon salt	½ tablespoon cornstarch, mixed with ½ tablespoon water
2 teaspoons lemon peel, finely grated	pinch of white pepper
⅓ cup chicken stock	salt

1. In a small bowl, combine chicken, 1 tablespoon of oil, and the cornstarch; blend well.

2. Heat remaining oil with salt in Wok until very hot. Add chicken and saute until meat is white. (Recipe may be prepared ahead to this point.) Sprinkle with lemon peel. Add stock, snow peas, and mushrooms; cook an additional minute.

3. Combine remaining ingredients and pour over chicken. Continue cooking, stirring constantly until sauce thickens. Adjust seasoning with salt and white pepper. Serve immediately over rice.

Wine Suggestion: White Graves or crisp Sauvignon Blanc from California.

Mexican Chicken Kiev

YIELDS: 4-6 servings

8	chicken breast halves, skinned and boned	¼	cup Parmesan cheese, grated
1	(7-ounce) can green chilies, diced	1	tablespoon chili powder
4	ounces Monterey Jack cheese, cut in 8 strips	½	teaspoon salt
		¼	teaspoon cumin
½	cup fine dry bread crumbs	¼	teaspoon black pepper
		6	tablespoons butter, melted
			tomato sauce (optional)

1. Pound chicken pieces to about ¼ inch thickness.

2. Put about 2 tablespoons chilies and 1 strip cheese in center of each chicken piece. Roll up and tuck ends under.

3. Combine bread crumbs, Parmesan cheese, chili powder, salt, cumin, and pepper. Dip each stuffed chicken piece in a shallow bowl containing the melted butter. Roll in crumb mixture.

4. Place chicken rolls, seam side down, in an oblong baking dish and drizzle with a little melted butter.

5. Cover and chill 4 hours or overnight.

6. Bake, uncovered, in a preheated 400 degree oven for 20 minutes or until done. Serve with a side dish of warmed tomato sauce, if desired.

Must start preparation early in the day.

Wine Suggestion: Mexican beer served in wine glasses will dazzle your guests.

Mozzarella Chicken

YIELDS: 4-6 servings

3 whole chicken breasts, boned, and skinned
2 eggs
1½ cups Pepperidge Farm herb bread stuffing, finely crumbled
6 tablespoons butter

1 chicken bouillon cube
1 cup water
2 small jars button mushrooms
1 (8-ounce) package sliced Mozzarella cheese

1. Beat eggs. Marinate chicken in this for one hour in refrigerator.

2. After one hour, roll chicken in bread crumbs to coat completely. Fry chicken in butter.

3. Place fried chicken in a 9 x 13 inch baking dish. Place at least 3 mushrooms on each breast.

4. Dissolve chicken bouillon cube in 1 cup hot water. Pour this over chicken. Bake, covered, in a preheated 300 degree oven for 45 minutes. Uncover and place slices of Mozzarella cheese on top. Bake for 15 minutes or until cheese is melted and slightly brown.

Easy. May be prepared 1 day ahead.

Wine Suggestion: For an elegant presentation use a French Pouilly-Fuisse; or select a simple California French Colombard.

Pesto Chicken Linguine

YIELDS: 4 servings

A dish with Italian P-zzazz!

1½ cups torn fresh spinach
½ cup fresh parsley, chopped
¼ cup chicken broth (may use bouillon)
1 egg yolk
2 tablespoons Parmesan cheese, grated
1 teaspoon dried basil, crushed

4 cloves garlic
¼ cup olive oil
8 ounces linguine
2 whole chicken breasts boned, skinned, and cut into thin strips
2 medium tomatoes

1. For pesto sauce combine spinach, parsley, chicken broth, egg yolk, Parmesan cheese, basil, garlic, and olive oil in blender or food processor. Cover and blend until mixture is pureed.

2. Cook pasta according to package directions. Drain. Keep hot.

3. In a large skillet, heat cooking oil; stir-fry chicken strips 3 to 4 minutes or until done.

4. Reduce heat, remove chicken, and keep hot. Add pesto sauce to skillet. Cover and cook 1 to 2 minutes. Add tomatoes and cook until heated through. Toss the pesto sauce with the linguine. Place chicken on top.

Wine Suggestion: Italian dry white such as Verdicchio or Frascati.

Rolled Chicken Breasts

YIELDS: 6 servings

Serve for dinner or slice thin as a tasty appetizer.

6	half chicken breasts, boned and skinned	½	cup water
6	slices boiled ham	1	chicken bouillon cube
6	ounces Swiss cheese, cut into strips	½	cup Sauterne
¼	cup Dijon mustard (optional)	½	cup mushrooms, sliced, slightly sauteed
¼	cup flour	1	tablespoon margarine, melted
2	tablespoons margarine, melted		

1. Pound chicken breasts to ¼ inch thick. If using Dijon mustard, spread each cutlet with 2 teaspoons. Cover with ham slice and strip of cheese. Roll up and secure with a toothpick.

2. Coat chicken rolls in flour and brown in margarine in skillet. Remove chicken to baking dish.

3. Combine water, bouillon, and wine in same skillet. Heat thoroughly until cube is dissolved, mixing with chicken drippings. Pour over chicken rolls.

4. Saute mushrooms in 1 tablespoon margarine. Add to top of chicken rolls. Bake in a preheated 350 degree oven for 1-1¼ hours.

SAUCE

2	tablespoons flour	½	cup water

1. Remove chicken from baking pan. Blend 2 tablespoons flour and ½ cup water together. Add slowly to baking dish to make sauce. Stir until thickened.

Serve as gravy over chicken rolls. May be made ahead a few hours.

Wine Suggestion: A fresh Beaujolais or a French Vouray.

Szechuan Chicken

An easy Wok treat!

3	whole chicken breasts, skinned and boned
¾	cup soy sauce, divided
3	tablespoons cornstarch
1½	teaspoons sugar
3	cloves garlic, minced
4	tablespoons cornstarch
¾	teaspoon crushed red pepper
3	cups water

⅓	cup vegetable oil, divided
6	carrots, cut diagonally into ⅛ inch slices
3	medium onions, chunked and separated
6	very small zucchini, cut in half lengthwise, then diagonally
1½	cups cashews (optional)

1. Cut chicken into thin, narrow strips. In medium bowl, combine ¼ cup soy sauce and next 3 ingredients. Stir in chicken and set aside.

2. Blend remaining soy sauce, 4 tablespoons cornstarch, red pepper, and 3 cups water. Set aside.

3. Heat half of the vegetable oil in Wok or large skillet over high heat. Add chicken, stir fry 2 minutes or until chicken is tender, remove.

4. Heat remaining oil in same Wok or skillet. Add vegetables and stir fry for 2 minutes. Stir in chicken and soy sauce mixture; cook and stir until sauce boils and thickens. Just before serving, stir in nuts. Serve over hot cooked rice.

Wine Suggestion: Chinese style California wines. Beer or California Gewurztraimer.

Turkey in Phyllo

YIELDS: 6-8 servings

A delicious way to use leftover Thanksgiving turkey.

8 ounces frozen phyllo (10-12 sheets)	2 tablespoons parsley, chopped
1 cup celery, chopped	½ teaspoon salt
¾ cup onion, chopped	½ teaspoon nutmeg, grated
½ cup butter	⅛ teaspoon pepper
2 cups cooked turkey, chopped	1 egg, beaten
2 tablespoons turkey or chicken broth	

1. Thaw phyllo in package.

2. Saute celery and onion in 1 tablespoon butter in a covered skillet until just tender. Add turkey and broth. Cook and stir, uncovered, until broth is absorbed. Stir in parsley, salt, nutmeg, and pepper. Remove from heat. Blend in egg. Set aside.

3. Melt remaining butter.

4. Make 3 stacks of phyllo, using 3-4 sheets for each; butter each sheet generously. Spread ⅓ of mixture over each stack, to within 1 inch of edges. Roll jelly roll fashion, starting with shorter side. Place seam side down on a lightly buttered baking pan. Brush each roll with melted butter. Score each roll 3-4 times.

5. Bake in a preheated 350 degree oven for 40 minutes or until browned and crisp. Cut where scored.

Wine Suggestion: A dry Sauvignon Blanc or Pouilly Fume from the Loire Valley.

Vegetable-Cracked Wheat Stuffing

YIELDS: 11 cups

For the whole-wheat eater in your family.

1 (1-pound) loaf cracked wheat or whole wheat bread, cubed	2 cups onion, chopped
	2 cups celery with leaves, chopped
2 teaspoons leaf sage	2 cups carrots, chopped
1 teaspoon marjoram	½ pound fresh mushrooms, chopped
1 teaspoon thyme	
1 teaspoon salt	¼ cup vegetable water or turkey broth
½ teaspoon pepper	
¾ cup butter or margarine	

1. To get a head start on stuffing, prepare bread and vegetables the day before. In large bowl combine bread cubes, sage, marjoram, thyme, salt, and pepper. Cover and set aside. Chop vegetables and refrigerate in plastic bag until the next day.

2. Melt butter in a large skillet; add onion, celery, carrots, and mushrooms. Saute until soft, about 10 minutes. Add to bread mixture and mix well. Stir in water. Spoon into a 12 cup baking dish. Cover with foil. Bake in a preheated 325 degree oven for 1 hour.

Helpful Hints: Never salt turkey. This draws out the juices.

Walnut Chicken

YIELDS: 4 servings

Crunchy, nutty, tasty, and easy!

1 pound whole chicken breasts, boned and skinned	6 cups peanut oil (may strain and reuse)
¼ pound walnuts, coarsely chopped	

1. Slice chicken in 1½ x 2 x ¼ inch pieces and place in glass bowl.

MARINADE

1 egg white, slightly beaten	1 teaspoon salt
½ tablespoon white wine	2 tablespoons cornstarch

1. Combine marinade ingredients and pour over chicken. Let set for 15 minutes.

2. Dredge chicken pieces in walnuts.

3. Heat oil. It is ready for frying when chicken sizzles. Deep fry chicken for 1½ minutes or until golden brown. (Fry half of chicken at a time.) Drain on paper towel. Serve with pepper-salt.

PEPPER-SALT

1 teaspoon pepper	4 teaspoons salt

Wine Suggestion: A Brut sparkling wine could add to the celebration if used as an appetizer. For entree, a sturdy Chardonnay.

Walnut Stuffed Chicken Breasts

YIELDS: 4 servings

Perfect for an autumn dinner when accompanied by a fresh green vegetable.

2 cups fresh bread crumbs, toasted	½ cup walnuts, chopped
4 tablespoons butter, melted, divided	⅛ teaspoon salt
	⅛ teaspoon pepper
¼ cup onion, chopped	4 chicken breasts, boned
¼ cup celery, chopped	juice of ½ lemon
2 teaspoons parsley flakes	

1. Combine bread crumbs, 2 tablespoons butter, onion, celery, parsley, walnuts, salt and pepper, and enough water to moisten. Make 4 mounds of stuffing, each on a square of foil. Arrange on a cookie sheet.

2. Brush both sides of chicken breasts with lemon juice, then spoon remaining butter over. Season with salt and pepper. Place an open chicken breast over each mound. Shape around stuffing, tucking sides under. Bake in a preheated 350 degree oven for 45 to 50 minutes.

Wine Suggestion: A White wine from the Macon area of France will agree with the unique flavors. A light Beaujolais.

Calzone
(Italian Easter Bread)

YIELDS: 6-8 servings

This may be served warm or cold with meals, as a snack, or appetizer. Also good with your favorite spaghetti sauce.

1	pound prepared white yeast bread dough (any recipe or frozen dough)	8	slices Genoa salami
3	tablespoons butter, softened	½	pound Ricotta cheese sesame seeds green pepper (optional) onion (optional) jalapeno pepper, sliced (optional)
¼	teaspoon garlic powder		
2	scallions, sliced very thin		
4-5	thin slices very lean boiled ham	6-8	ripe olives, sliced (optional)
8	slices Provolone cheese	2	ounces mushrooms, sliced (optional)
6	slices mortadella (or ⅕ pound thinly sliced prosciutto)	1	tablespoon Parmesan cheese (optional)

1. Have dough properly risen and prepared for baking. Roll dough to 12 x 18 inch rectangle. Cream butter and garlic powder and spread about 2 tablespoons on dough. Sprinkle scallions over dough. Arrange slices of meats and cheeses over dough and spread with Ricotta cheese. There should be an even distribution when dough is folded and later sliced.

2. Fold top ⅓ of dough over middle and bottom ⅓ over the top, like a letter. Transfer roll to a greased baking sheet. Pinch seal all edges firmly. Spread top with remaining garlic butter and sprinkle with sesame seeds.

3. Bake in a preheated 350 degree oven for 30 minutes. Cool at least 10 minutes. Cut slices across the roll.

Variation: Include one or more of the optional ingredients for different tastes.

Wine Suggestion: A light, stylish, fragrant Red wine such as a young Chianti.

Clam Linguine

A good alternative is to substitute shrimp for clams.

1 (16-ounce) package linguine	½ teaspoon oregano
½ cup butter	1 teaspoon parsley or to taste
1 clove garlic	¾ to 1 cup Romano cheese, grated
4 (6½-ounce) cans clams, minced, undrained	

1. Melt butter in pan. Saute garlic. Add clams and liquid, parsley, and oregano. Simmer for 10 minutes.

2. Cook linguine until al dente. Drain. Put in large bowl. Pour clam sauce over and sprinkle Romano cheese on top. Mix.

Wine Suggestion: Italian Frascati or French Saint Veran.

Skillet Tomato Chicken

½ cup butter	2 tablespoons flour
6 whole chicken breasts, skinned, boned, and halved	1 teaspoon salt
1 large onion, sliced	1 (28-ounce) can plum tomatoes, drained
2 cloves garlic, minced	1 cup sour cream
	½ cup Parmesan cheese, grated

1. Melt butter in large skillet. Saute chicken until tender. Remove chicken, set aside, and keep warm. In same skillet, cook onion and garlic until transparent.

2. Blend in flour and salt. Add tomatoes and chicken. Cover and cook 35 minutes on low heat.

3. Add sour cream and Parmesan cheese. Heat gently, but do not boil. Serve over hot noodles, if desired.

Wine Suggestion: California Chenin Blanc or French Vouray.

Fettuccini Carbonara

YIELDS: 6 servings

A nice accompaniment to a salad luncheon or dinner. Easy to prepare.

¼ cup butter	1 cup Parmesan cheese, freshly grated
4 eggs	dash of pepper
¼ cup whipping cream	¼ cup fresh parsley, chopped
½ pound bacon, cooked and crumbled	salt to taste
1 pound fettuccini (or linguine)	

1. Let butter, eggs, and cream stand at room temperature for 2-3 hours.

2. Cook fettuccini according to package directions until al dente. Drain, but do not rinse.

3. Beat eggs and cream together.

4. Heat oven-proof serving dish in 250 degree oven. Turn pasta into dish. Toss pasta with butter. Pour egg mixture over pasta and toss until well coated. Add bacon, cheese, pepper, and parsley. Toss to mix and serve.

Wine Suggestion: Italian Valpolicella at cool room temperature.

Italian Sausage and Pasta

YIELDS: 4-6 servings

A nice light supper to serve with your favorite wine.

1	pound bulk Italian sausage	2	eggs
1	(4-ounce) can mushrooms, drained	¼	cup half and half
2	teaspoons basil, dried or 2 tablespoons fresh basil	½	cup Parmesan or Monterey Jack cheese, freshly grated
½	teaspoon salt	8	ounces spaghetti
1	clove garlic, crushed	4	tablespoons butter
		8	to 10 cherry tomatoes (optional)

1. In 10 inch skillet, brown sausage and drain. Add mushrooms, basil, salt, and garlic. Keep warm.

2. In mixing bowl, beat eggs slightly, stir in half and half and cheese. Set aside.

3. In large saucepan, cook spaghetti according to directions and drain. Add butter and stir until melted. Add meat and egg mixture to spaghetti. Blend well. Serve immediately. Can also toss 8 or 10 cherry tomatoes with mixture.

Wine Suggestion: California Merlot will stand up to the sausage and be pleasant with the cream.

Mushroom-Cheese Lasagna Rolls

YIELDS: 6-8 servings

An interesting, meatless version of lasagna.

12 lasagna noodles	¼ cup butter or margarine
1 (15-ounce) carton Ricotta cheese	¾ pound fresh mushrooms, quartered
8 ounces Mozzarella cheese, shredded, divided	1 (21-ounce) jar Italian cooking sauce
2 eggs	1 teaspoon Italian seasoning
¼ cup parsley, chopped	1 teaspoon sugar
½ teaspoon salt	
½ teaspoon nutmeg	

1. Cook noodles until firm. Drain and return to pot covering with cold water.

2. In a bowl, combine Ricotta, half of Mozzarella, eggs, parsley, salt, and nutmeg. Set aside.

3. Melt butter in a saucepan, add quartered mushrooms and saute until wilted. Remove and cool.

4. In another bowl, combine Italian sauce, seasoning mix, and sugar. Spoon half of sauce into a 13 x 9 inch baking dish.

5. Lift noodles, one at a time, from water. Drain and spread with ¼ cup of cheese mixture. Place 3 or 4 mushrooms along narrow end of noodle and roll up jelly-roll fashion. Spoon sauce over rolls.

6. Cover dish with foil and bake in a preheated 375 degree oven for 25 minutes. Remove foil, sprinkle with remaining cheese, and top with any leftover mushrooms. Bake 5 minutes longer.

May prepare ahead. Freezes well.

Wine Suggestion: A young fruity Chianti.

Pasta with Dried Tomatoes

YIELDS: 4 servings

Similar to a carbonara. Use as a light supper with salad.

2	**eggs**
½	**cup dried tomatoes, reserve oil, cut into strips**
¼	**cup olive oil from the tomatoes**
½	**cup Parmesan cheese, freshly grated**

½	**cup parsley, minced**
2	**cloves garlic, crushed**
1	**tablespoon lemon juice**
¾	**pound linguine**
	salt and pepper

1. In large serving bowl whisk eggs, tomatoes, oil, cheese, parsley, garlic, and lemon juice. Set aside.

2. In a large pot, cook linguine in boiling, salted water until just tender. Drain and add to egg mixture. Toss the mixture with two forks, sprinkle with salt and freshly ground pepper.

Note: If less garlic flavor is desired, crush cloves lightly and remove from egg mixture before tossing with pasta.

Wine Suggestion: Italian crisp Soave or Frascati.

Pesto Sauce for Pasta

YIELDS: 4-6 servings

Choose your pasta and enjoy this delightful blend of Italian seasonings.

2	cloves garlic	2	cups fresh basil leaves, roughly chopped
½	teaspoon coarse sea salt	⅓	cup Parmesan cheese, grated
4	whole black peppercorns or dash of pepper	⅓	cup virgin olive oil
¼	cup pine nuts, lightly toasted		

1. In food processor, process garlic. Add other ingredients in order of use. (Add oil a little at a time through feed tube with processor running.) May be refrigerated at this time.

1	pound linguini, spaghetti, fettuccini, or any pasta	¼	cup melted butter

1. Before serving time, cook pasta and drain. Add melted butter and mix well.

2. Add enough pesto sauce to coat pasta. (The amount is according to taste.) Mix well and serve immediately.

Sausage Stuffed Shells

YIELDS: 6-8 servings

1	pound Jimmy Dean bulk pork sausage
½	cup onion, finely chopped
1	teaspoon salt
4	slices fresh white bread, made into crumbs
1	egg, beaten
¼	cup fresh parsley, chopped, or 1½ teaspoon dried flakes
20	jumbo pasta shells, parboiled and drained
2	(19½-ounce) cans Schiavone's spaghetti sauce
8	ounces Mozzarella cheese, grated

1. Fry sausage and onion until brown and crumbly. Drain well. Add salt, bread crumbs, egg, and parsley. Mix thoroughly. Using a teaspoon, fill parboiled pasta shells with sausage mixture.

2. Pour half a can of spaghetti sauce into a 9 x 13 inch baking dish. Arrange shells in dish. Pour remaining sauce over shells. Sprinkle with cheese. Cover with foil. Bake in a preheated 350 degree oven for 30 minutes or until hot and bubbly. Remove foil and bake, uncovered, for 10 minutes longer.

Wine Suggestion: Alascian Riesling or Italian Red table wine.

Sicilian Spaghetti

YIELDS: 4 servings

The olive oil and bacon make this a flavorful pasta dish.

4 tablespoons olive oil	1 (6-ounce) can tomato paste
1 medium onion, finely chopped	a few dried hot peppers, to taste
1 clove garlic, finely chopped	12 ounces spaghetti
½ pound bacon, cut in small pieces	¼ cup Romano cheese, grated
1 (28-ounce) can whole tomatoes, drained and chopped	¼ cup Parmesan cheese, grated

1. Heat olive oil in skillet. Briefly saute onion and garlic until just soft. Add bacon and cook until crisp. Pour off excess oil and bacon grease, leaving about 1-2 tablespoons in the onion-bacon mixture. Add chopped tomatoes, tomato paste, and peppers to taste.

2. Cook spaghetti. Drain well. Toss spaghetti with cheeses until well coated. Pour tomato mixture over spaghetti and mix well. Serve immediately.

Wine Suggestion: Good quality Cotes-Du-Rhone is an excellent match.

Vermicelli with Shrimp Sauce

YIELDS: 4 servings

A wonderful creamy pasta dish.

- 3½ tablespoons butter, divided
- 1 teaspoon garlic, minced
- 6 ounces (1 cup) shrimp, peeled and deveined
- 2 tablespoons parsley, chopped
- 2 tablespoons dry vermouth or white wine

- ¼ cup Parmesan cheese
- ½ cup whipping cream
- pinch red pepper flakes
- 4 ounces vermicelli, cooked according to package
- ½ ripe avocado, peeled, pitted, and diced (optional)

1. In a large skillet, heat 1 tablespoon of butter over medium heat. When melted, add garlic and cook 1 minute. Add shrimp, parsley, and vermouth and cook 2 minutes longer, stirring constantly, until shrimp turn pink and are just tender. Transfer to a small bowl.

2. Add remaining butter to pan and melt. Reduce heat to low; add cheese, cream, and red pepper flakes and cook 3 minutes, stirring constantly, until cheese melts and sauce is smooth. Remove from heat.

3. Add hot vermicelli, avocado, and shrimp mixture; toss gently to coat. Serve immediately on heated plates.

Wine Suggestion: Try a California Sauvignon Blanc from Livermore Valley.

White Lasagna

YIELDS: 6-8 servings

A tasty variation of a family favorite.

8 ounces lasagna noodles	1 (3-ounce) package cream cheese, cubed
1 pound ground beef	½ cup dry white wine
1 cup celery, finely chopped	2 cups Cheddar cheese, shredded
¾ cup onion, chopped	1½ cups Gouda cheese, shredded
1 clove garlic, minced	12 ounces cottage cheese
2 teaspoons basil	1 egg, beaten
1 teaspoon oregano	12 ounces Mozzarella cheese, sliced
¾ teaspoon salt	
½ teaspoon pepper	
½ teaspoon Italian seasoning	
1 cup light cream	

1. Cook noodles to al dente.

2. Brown meat and drain grease. Add celery, onions, and garlic. Cook until done. Add herbs, cream, and cream cheese. Cook over low heat to melt cream cheese. Add wine and gradually add Cheddar and Gouda cheeses, stirring until nearly melted. Remove from heat.

3. Stir egg and cottage cheese together.

4. In greased 9 x 13 inch pan, layer one-half of each: noodles, meat, cottage cheese, and Mozzarella. Repeat layers. Bake, uncovered, in a preheated 375 degree oven for 30 to 35 minutes. Let stand 10 minutes before cutting.

May be prepared ahead. Freezes well.

Wine Suggestion: Italian crisp Soave or Frascati.

Lamb Roast

YIELDS: 8 servings

Consider this recipe for that special Easter dinner.

¾ cup butter, softened	1 teaspoon rosemary
1 tablespoon parsley	1 teaspoon thyme
6 fresh mint leaves, chopped or 1½ teaspoons dried mint, crushed	1 clove garlic, minced
	3-5 pound Leg of Lamb preferably rolled by butcher

1. Preheat oven to 450 degrees. Combine butter, crushed dried spices, and garlic. Set aside.

2. Remove fell or outer covering from lamb. On fat side, prick lamb in several places with a fork. Spread half of butter mixture on fat side of lamb. Place lamb on rack in shallow baking dish. Insert meat thermometer. Place in oven and lower temperature to 350 degrees. Halfway through roasting, spread remaining mixture on lamb. For medium-rare lamb, cook to 160-165 degrees. Slice and serve immediately.

Wine Suggestion: Mature St. Julien from Bordeaux or Chateauneuf-Du-Pape.

Minted Lamb Ragout

YIELDS: 8 servings

A great way to celebrate spring!

1	pound lamb stew meat
¼	cup flour
½	teaspoon salt
¼	teaspoon paprika
1	tablespoon cooking oil
1	medium onion, chopped
½	teaspoon chervil
¾	teaspoon dried mint
1½	cups water
1	(.19-ounce) packet chicken broth powder
2	large carrots

1. Combine flour, salt, and paprika. Dredge stew meat in mixture.

2. Heat oil and brown meat. Add onions when meat is almost browned. Add chervil, mint, water, and chicken broth powder. Simmer, covered, for 1½ hours. Add carrots, peeled and sliced diagonally. Cook ½ hour longer. Serve with rice.

May be prepared ahead 1 day. Also freezes and reheats well.

Wine Suggestion: A spicy California or an Alastian Gewurztraimer.

Lebanese Lamb Kabobs and Tabouli in Pita Bread

YIELDS: 6 servings

A completely refreshing summer meal that can be made ahead.

LAMB

1 cup bulgur wheat, divided	1-2 cloves garlic, minced
2 cups boiling water	1 teaspoon salt
1 pound lean ground lamb	⅛ teaspoon pepper
1 small onion, chopped	1 teaspoon cinnamon
½ cup fresh parsley, minced	1 egg, beaten
1 tablespoon lemon juice	¼ cup slivered almonds

1. Prepare bulgur wheat by adding the boiling water to the dry wheat in a heat-proof bowl. Allow to stand at least one hour. (The longer it stands, the more liquid is absorbed.) Drain excess water. Set aside.

2. Combine ground lamb, onion, parsley, garlic, salt, pepper, cinnamon, and lemon juice. Add ½ cup of prepared bulgur wheat and beaten egg; mix well. Thoroughly mix in almonds. Shape into 3 inch oblong kabobs. Grill over hot charcoals about 15 minutes, turning frequently.

TABOULI

1 large tomato, cut into small chunks	3 tablespoons lemon juice
4 green onions, finely chopped	¾ cup salad oil salt and pepper to taste
½ cup fresh parsley, minced	6 Pita breads

1. Combine all ingredients and remaining prepared bulgur wheat. Chill until ready to use. To assemble, cut warmed Pita bread in half. Open and add lamb kabob and tabouli.

May be prepared 1 day ahead. Lamb kabobs may be frozen 2 weeks to 1 month.

Wine Suggestion: A well chilled Rose D'Anjou.

Cherry-Almond Glazed Pork

YIELDS: 8 servings

The glaze keeps this pork roast moist and tasty.

1 (3-pound) boneless pork loin roast	¼ teaspoon salt
salt	¼ teaspoon ground cinnamon
pepper	¼ teaspoon ground nutmeg
1 (12-ounce) jar cherry preserves	¼ teaspoon ground cloves
¼ cup red wine vinegar	¼ teaspoon slivered almonds, toasted
2 tablespoons light corn syrup	

1. Rub roast with a little salt and pepper. Place the meat fat side up on a rack in a shallow roasting pan. Insert meat thermometer. Roast, uncovered, in a preheated 325 degree oven for 2 - 2½ hours.

2. About 45 minutes before roast is done, combine in saucepan cherry preserves, red wine vinegar, corn syrup, salt, cinnamon, nutmeg, and cloves. Cook and stir mixture until it boils; reduce heat and simmer 2 minutes more. Add the almonds. Keep the sauce warm so it will not harden.

3. About ½ hour before the roast is done, spoon some of the sauce over the roast to glaze. Continue cooking the roast until meat thermometer registers 170 degrees. Baste roast with sauce several times. Pass remaining sauce with roast. Double sauce recipe if you want to pass.

Wine Suggestion: A rich sweeter style Rose or fruity German Rhine.

Country Fried Pork Chops

YIELDS: 4 servings

4	pork chops, fat and bones removed, cut in bite size pieces	¼	teaspoon thyme, crushed
1	can mushrooms, drained	6	whole small white onions or ½ cup chopped
1	can cream of celery soup	1	cup carrots, sliced rice or noodles
½	cup water		

1. In skillet, brown chops and mushrooms. Pour off fat.

2. Stir in soup, water, and thyme. Add onions and carrots. Cover and cook over low heat 45 minutes, stirring occasionally. Serve over rice or noodles.

Easy and may be prepared ahead.

Wine Suggestion: A pleasant California White Zinfandel is useful here.

Pork Adobo

YIELDS: 4-6 servings

The sauce served with this pork appeals to all ages.

2	pounds fresh pork, cut into bite size pieces	¼	cup vinegar
1	clove garlic, pounded	1	cup beer
1	teaspoon black peppercorns	2	tablespoons soy sauce salt to taste

1. Place pork in saucepan. Add garlic, peppercorns, vinegar, beer, soy sauce, and salt. Cover and cook slowly until meat is tender, about 1 hour. Serve over rice.

Easy.

Wine Suggestion: California Chardonnay or Zinfandel.

Hungarian Pork with Sauerkraut

YIELDS: 6 servings

If you like serving a pork dish on New Year's day, this is a good choice.

2 pounds boneless pork, cut into 1 inch cubes	2 teaspoons paprika
2 tablespoons cooking oil	2 teaspoons chicken bouillon granules
2 (16-ounce) cans sauerkraut, drained and rinsed	½ teaspoon dried dill weed
	1 cup water
½ cup onion, chopped	½ cup sour cream
1 garlic clove, minced	

1. Trim excess fat from pork. Heat cooking oil in a Dutch oven and brown meat on all sides over medium high heat. Stir in remaining ingredients except sour cream. Reduce heat. Simmer, covered, until pork is tender, about 1 hour and 15 minutes. Remove from heat. Stir in sour cream. Serve with mashed potatoes.

Wine Suggestion: Alastian Whites or German Riesling.

Mustard Sauce

Fantastic with ham or on sandwiches. May be prepared ahead 2-3 days.

1 cup sugar	1 egg
1 tablespoon flour	1 cup evaporated milk
2 tablespoons dry mustard	½ cup vinegar

1. Mix dry ingredients. Add egg and evaporated milk. Cook over medium heat until boils. Add vinegar and boil again. Serve warm.

Italian Sausage and Peppers

YIELDS: 8 servings

Serve with hard crusty rolls and a crispy salad.

3 pounds Italian link sausage (Bob Evans)	2 cans all purpose Italian sauce (19 ½-ounce Schiavone's)—if less sauce desired, use 1 can
3-5 tablespoons olive oil	
2 medium onions, chopped	
4 cloves garlic, diced	
9 peppers, green and red (if available)	

1. Slice Italian sausage in 1 inch chunks. Place in large skillet with 1 inch of water. Bring to a boil, then reduce to simmer. Cook, covered, until water evaporates and sausage browns. Remove sausage and drain grease if any remains.

2. In same skillet, add 3-5 tablespoons of olive oil to cover bottom. Saute onions, garlic, and chopped peppers until browned.

3. Return sausage to skillet. Pour sauce over top and simmer 30-45 minutes. Peppers will be tender-crisp.

Wine Suggestion: An uncomplicated sturdy Italian wine is a source of pleasure with sausage.

North Carolina Barbecue Sauce

This is not a thick style sauce. Best used with leftover pork, shredded and simmered in sauce for 30 minutes or more.

1 pint apple cider vinegar	1 tablespoon prepared mustard
1 tablespoon salt	2 tablespoons ketchup
1 teaspoon black pepper	1 teaspoon paprika
1 teaspoon cayenne pepper	1 tablespoon fresh lemon juice

1. Mix all ingredients and bring to a boil over low heat, stirring constantly.

Pork Chops Florentine

YIELDS: 6 servings

Make this dish early in the day for that special dinner in the evening.

6-10 pork chops
    (½ inch thick) use
    boneless chops or
    pork tenderloin cut
    into chops
    salt
    pepper
    flour
    oil
3 (10-ounce) packages
    frozen chopped spinach
1 (10½-ounce) can
    chicken broth

1 onion, sliced
1 carrot, sliced
½ bay leaf
6 tablespoons butter
6 tablespoons flour
1¾ cups milk
2 egg yolks, lightly
    beaten
1 cup Swiss cheese,
    grated

1. Dredge chops with salt, pepper, and flour. Brown chops in oil in skillet. Lower heat, cover pan; cook slowly 30 minutes or until tender.

2. Cook spinach. Drain well.

3. Simmer chicken broth with onion, carrot, and bay leaf for 10 minutes. Strain. Melt butter, add flour; when bubbly, add strained broth and milk, stirring constantly. Cook until thickened. Blend egg yolks into hot sauce.

4. Grease 9 x 13 inch baking dish. Spread spinach on bottom, lay chops on top. Pour sauce over chops, sprinkle with cheese. Bake in a preheated 375 degree oven about 15 minutes to melt and brown cheese.

Wine Suggestion: The pork flavors will be enhanced with a simple California Beaujolais or a Pouilly-Fume from the Loire Valley.

Pork Chops in Orange Wine Sauce

YIELDS: 4-6 servings

8	pork chops	1½	cups orange juice
4	tablespoons vegetable oil	½	cup white wine
2	tablespoons butter	¼	cup brown sugar, packed
2	tablespoons flour	2	teaspoons salt

1. Brown pork chops in oil. Drain.

2. In saucepan, melt butter. Add flour and stir until thick. Slowly stir in orange juice and wine. Cook and stir until thick; add brown sugar and salt.

3. Place chops in shallow casserole and pour sauce over them. Cover and bake in a preheated 350 degree oven for 45 minutes.

May be prepared ahead to the point of baking.

Wine Suggestion: California Chenin Blanc or White Zinfandel are suited to these flavors.

Raisin Sauce for Ham

YIELDS: 2 cups

A recipe handed down for several generations—it's the finishing touch to a warmly baked ham.

¾	cup seedless raisins	1	tablespoon cornstarch
1	cup beer	1	tablespoon red wine vinegar
4	whole cloves	1	tablespoon lemon juice
1	tablespoon butter	¼	teaspoon Worcestershire sauce
¾	cup brown sugar, packed	2	teaspoons horseradish

1. In a saucepan, add raisins with beer and cloves. Simmer very slowly for 10 minutes. Add remaining ingredients and blend thoroughly. Simmer 5 minutes longer. May be served at this point or refrigerated and reheated when desired.

May be prepared ahead 2 to 3 days.

Pork Chops in Dill Gravy

YIELDS: 6 servings

½ cup green onions, thinly sliced	½ cup Chablis or other dry white wine
½ cup fresh mushrooms, sliced	1 teaspoon Worcestershire sauce
3 tablespoons butter or margarine	1 teaspoon dried dill weed
6 (¾ inch thick) pork chops	⅓ cup water
1 teaspoon salt	2 tablespoons flour
¼ teaspoon pepper	1 (8-ounce) carton sour cream
	hot cooked rice

1. In a large skillet, saute onions and mushrooms in butter until tender. Remove from skillet; set aside.

2. Sprinkle pork chops with salt and pepper; place in skillet and brown on both sides.

3. Combine sauteed vegetables, wine, Worcestershire sauce, and dill weed; pour over chops. Cover, reduce heat, and simmer 40 minutes or until pork chops are tender. Remove chops from skillet; set aside.

4. Combine water and flour, stirring until smooth; add to pan drippings in skillet. Cook over low heat, stirring constantly, until thickened and bubbly. Stir in sour cream. Cook until thoroughly heated.

5. Serve chops over hot, cooked rice; spoon gravy over chops, as desired.

Wine Suggestion: The dill flavor will shine with a nice Chablis.

Pork Tenderloin

YIELDS: 6 servings

An appealing blend of seasonings make this a nice dish for company.

1 pound pork tenderloin, sliced, 5 slices to an inch

1 can Italian seasoned bread crumbs

3 tablespoons Parmesan cheese

2 eggs, slightly beaten with 2 tablespoons water

½ pound bacon

2 cups onions, thinly sliced

1 (4-ounce) jar mushrooms, sliced and drained

½ cup chicken or vegetable stock (or Spice Island chicken seasoned stock base

¾ teaspoon to ½ cup water)

1. Call your butcher in advance and have him slice the meat for you. To do it yourself, slightly freeze so it will be firm and easy to slice thin.

2. Add cheese to bread crumbs and dredge meat in crumbs, egg mixture, and again in the crumbs. Let stand on wax paper for 20 minutes turning twice to let the breading dry.

3. Fry bacon until crisp, break into small pieces, and set aside. Save bacon grease. Add onions to bacon grease and saute 7-8 minutes, until lightly golden and soft. Drain and set aside. Brown meat slices in bacon grease until lightly browned.

4. Place meat in a 10 x 6 inch baking dish, overlapping slightly. Spread onions on top. Top with mushroom slices. Sprinkle bacon on top. Pour stock over all and cover. Bake in a preheated 325 - 350 degree oven for about 40 minutes.

5. Casserole may be prepared, refrigerated, and baked later in the day or the following day. If cold, bake a bit longer. Freezes beautifully, but should be baked at least 30 minutes before freezing. If frozen, bake almost an hour in a preheated 325 degree oven, until hot and bubbly. Recipe doubles and triples well.

May be prepared 1 day ahead. Freezes up to 6 weeks.

Wine Suggestion: A full-flavored Chardonnay or Sauvignon Blanc.

⚜ MAIN DISHES

Sweet and Sour Pork and Potato Casserole

A great all-in-one casserole.

4 loin pork chops, cut 1 inch thick (boneless)	1 tablespoon Worcestershire sauce
1 teaspoon cooking oil	1¼ teaspoons salt
2 large onions, peeled and sliced ¼ inch thick	¼ teaspoon pepper
⅓ cup cider vinegar	1 tablespoon cornstarch mixed with 1 tablespoon cold water
⅓ cup light brown sugar, packed	4 large potatoes, peeled and quartered lengthwise
¾ cup fruit juice (orange, pineapple, apple, or combination)	

1. Brown chops 8-10 minutes on each side over moderately high heat in a skillet brushed with oil, then transfer to an ungreased 2½ quart casserole.

2. Saute onions in drippings 8-10 minutes until golden and spread over chops.

3. Add remaining ingredients, except potatoes, to skillet and heat, stirring until slightly thickened. Pour sauce over chops, tucking potatotes in here and there. Cover and bake in a preheated 375 degree oven for ¾ to 1 hour, until chops and potatoes are tender.

May be assembled and baked a day ahead, then reheated.

Wine Suggestion: Serve an Alastian Pinot Gris and enjoy a superb meal.

Zucchini Sausage Imperial

YIELDS: 4-6 servings

A colorful way to use summer zucchini.

1	pound bulk sausage
1	medium onion, chopped
¼	cup green pepper, chopped
4	cups zucchini, sliced
2	cups water
2	eggs
¼	to ½ cup Hellmann's mayonnaise

1	cup (or more) Cheddar cheese, shredded
	salt and pepper to taste
1	tomato, peeled and sliced
	Parmesan cheese, grated

1. Brown sausage with onion and green pepper. Drain and set aside. Cook zucchini in water until just tender. Drain.

2. Mix eggs, mayonnaise, and Cheddar cheese. Add salt and pepper to taste. Add zucchini, sausage, onion, and green pepper. Turn into greased baking dish.

3. Arrange sliced tomato on top of casserole and sprinkle with Parmesan cheese. Bake in a preheated 350 degree oven for 30 minutes.

Easy and may be assembled ahead.

Wine Suggestion: Use an Italian Orvieto or French Beaujolais.

Athenian Shrimp

A wonderful appetizer or a lighthearted main course.

2	pounds raw shrimp in shells
3-4	medium garlic cloves, minced
1	cup fresh parsley, minced
	juice of 3 lemons

2	tablespoons dried oregano
	salt and pepper to taste
1	tablespoon dried basil
½	cup olive oil
½	cup salad oil
1	cup dry sherry or dry vermouth

1. Wash shrimp thoroughly but do not remove shells. Place in a roasting pan large enough so that shrimp do not overlap significantly.

2. Combine remaining ingredients and pour over shrimp. Mix well so that all shrimp are thoroughly coated.

3. Bake in a preheated 450 degree oven for 10-15 minutes or until shrimp turn pink.

4. Serve on a large platter with all pan juices poured over the shrimp. Garnish the edge of the platter with lemon wedges. Serve with plenty of crusty bread to absorb the juices.

Marinade may be prepared ahead 2 days.

Wine Suggestion: This is a fun meal for adults! Have lots of full-bodied premium white table wine.

Caribbean Shrimp Casserole

YIELDS: 6-8 servings

Serve with hot buttered rolls and a spinach salad.

2 cups raw rice, cooked	6 teaspoons onion, grated
2 pounds shrimp, boiled	4 teaspoons lemon juice
2 cans cream of mushroom soup	1 small green pepper, diced
1 pound Velveeta cheese, cubed	⅛ teaspoon garlic salt
4 tablespoons butter	1 teaspoon pepper

1. Mix all ingredients together. Bake in a preheated 350 degree oven for 30 to 40 minutes.

Wine Suggestion: Serve a pleasant, rich California Riesling or White Zinfandel.

Colossal Crab Casserole

YIELDS: 8 servings

2 cups (12-ounces) fresh, cooked crab, cut in small cubes	1 cup celery, chopped
2 cups half and half	1 tablespoon parsley, chopped
1 cup mayonnaise	1 tablespoon onion, chopped
5 slices white bread, cut up slightly	2 teaspoons salt
7 hard boiled eggs, coarsely chopped	⅛ teaspoon pepper
	1 cup corn flakes, crushed

1. Combine all ingredients, except corn flakes. Mix well and put in a 3 quart buttered casserole. Top with corn flakes. Bake in a preheated 350 degree oven for approximately 1 hour.

Wine Suggestion: Vouray or California Chenin Blanc.

MAIN DISHES

Crab-Broccoli Casserole

YIELDS: 4 servings

1 bunch fresh or (10-ounce) package frozen broccoli	2 tablespoons flour
2 tablespoons butter	1 cup milk
2 tablespoons onion, chopped	1 cup Cheddar cheese, shredded
½ teaspoon salt	1 tablespoon lemon juice
	½ pound crab, cooked

1. Cook broccoli until crisp tender. Place in 8 x 11 inch baking dish.

2. Melt butter in pan. Saute onion in butter. Stir in salt and flour. Gradually add milk, stirring constantly. Add cheese and cook over low heat until thickened. Stir in lemon juice. Add crab and pour over broccoli.

3. Bake in a preheated 350 degree oven for 30 minutes.

Wine Suggestion: Vouray or Rose of Provence well chilled will let the crab shine.

Herbed Haddock

YIELDS: 4 servings

Other filets can be used in this recipe, but haddock is the recommended selection.

½ cup butter	½ teaspoon oregano
⅔ cup saltine crackers, crushed	½ teaspoon salt
¼ cup Parmesan cheese	¼ teaspoon garlic powder
½ teaspoon basil	1 pound haddock filets, thawed and drained

1. Melt butter in 9 x 9 inch baking dish.

2. On a separate plate, combine cracker crumbs, cheese, and spices. Dip fish in butter and then the cracker mixture.

3. Drain remaining butter from dish and place breaded filets in dish. Bake in a preheated 350 degree oven for 25 to 30 minutes.

Wine Suggestion: A dry crisp Chablis will go well with the haddock.

East Indian Shrimp Curry

YIELDS: 4 servings

Don't let the number of ingredients scare you - this is a marvelous blending of many flavors. Spicy good!

2 pounds shrimp, freshly boiled	1 tablespoon parsley, chopped
½ cup butter	2 cloves
1 clove garlic, finely chopped	¼ teaspoon basil
3 stalks celery, chopped	2 tablespoons flour
1 large onion, chopped	2 tablespoons curry powder
1 green pepper, seeded and chopped	½ teaspoon salt
1 apple, peeled, cored, and chopped	½ teaspoon pepper
1 carrot, chopped	¼ teaspoon cayenne pepper
2 tomatoes, chopped	¼ teaspoon nutmeg
1 bay leaf, crumbled	2 cups consomme
pinch each of thyme, marjoram and dried mint	1 cup dry white wine
	boiled rice
	chutney

1. Melt ½ cup butter in saucepan and add garlic, celery, onion, green pepper, apple, carrot, tomatoes, bay leaf, thyme, marjoram, dried mint, parsley, cloves, and basil.

2. When vegetables are soft, sprinkle in flour mixed with curry powder, salt, pepper, cayenne pepper, and nutmeg. Mix well with the contents of the pan and cook for five minutes. Slowly add the consomme. When mixture begins to thicken add wine. Cook over low heat for about ½ hour.

3. Add shrimp to sauce. Heat through and serve with rice and chutney.

Wine Suggestion: The distinct flavor of curry sometimes "fights" with wine. However, good types to try are Gewurztraimers from Germany, California, or France. Beer would be a good choice.

Filet of Sole aux Crevettes

YIELDS: 4 servings

French cooking at its best.

1 **pound sole filets**	1 **teaspoon cornstarch**
1 **tablespoon lemon juice**	1 **cup half and half**
¼ **cup parsley, chopped**	1 **cup shrimp (canned or**
1 **(3-ounce) can**	**frozen), cooked**
whole mushrooms	2-4 **tablespoons fine bread**
1 **tablespoon Dijon**	**crumbs**
mustard	1 **teaspoon butter, melted**

1. Cut fish filets in half lengthwise. Brush filets with lemon juice. Season with salt and pepper. Sprinkle one side of filets with parsley. Roll up each filet loosely and secure with toothpick. Stand on end in 8 inch square or round baking dish. Cover and bake in a preheated 425 degree oven for 10 minutes. Meanwhile, prepare sauce.

2. Blend mustard and cornstarch; stir in half and half. Cook and stir until thickened. Sauce will not be too thick. Add shrimp and set aside.

3. Drain juice from fish and remove toothpicks. Place a mushroom in each roll. Pour sauce over fish. Top with bread crumbs and drizzle with butter. Bake, uncovered, for an additional 10 minutes.

Serve with Uncle Ben's long grain wild rice.

Wine Suggestion: A distinguished Mersault will suit the elegance of this recipe.

Filet of Sole Roulades

YIELDS: 4 servings

Two fresh fish favorites (sole and salmon) are combined for an unusual flair.

4 filets of sole	½ cup milk
salt, to taste	1 cup seedless grapes
garlic salt, to taste	¾ cup mushrooms, sliced
pepper, to taste	(fresh or canned)
paprika, to taste	⅛ pound sharp Cheddar
4 strips salmon, 1½	cheese, grated
inches wide (cut to	pimento strips
width of filet)	
½ cup mushroom soup	

1. Season sole with salt, garlic salt, pepper, and paprika.

2. Place a strip of salmon crosswise on each filet. Roll up and fasten with a toothpick.

3. Mix soup, milk, grapes, mushrooms, and cheese to make a sauce.

4. Place fish in au gratin dish and pour sauce over all. Bake in a preheated 350 degree oven for 40-50 minutes. Baste fish halfway through baking period. Baste again when finished. Place pimento strips over center of each roll.

Wine Suggestion: An extra-dry Spanish Champagne will make this meal a celebration.

Filet of Sole with Mornay Sauce

YIELDS: 6 servings

A tender flaky fish enhanced by a mild cheese sauce.

6	filets of sole	1	cup milk
	salt and pepper,	1	cup whipping cream
	to taste	1	cup Gruyere, Swiss, or
	water or white wine		Cheddar cheese, grated
¼	cup butter		(use only one)
¼	cup flour		Parmesan cheese, grated

1. Sprinkle fish with salt and pepper and simmer in water or white wine that barely covers fish. Cook until fish flakes easily when tested with fork. Remove fish to heat-proof dish and keep warm. Reserve fish broth.

2. In a saucepan melt butter, add the flour, and stir with a wire whisk until blended. In a saucepan, bring milk and cream, with fish broth if desired, to a boil. Add, all at once, to the butter-flour mixture, stirring vigorously with whisk until sauce is smooth but not too thick.

3. Remove sauce from heat and let cool for one minute. Stir in one cup of cheese and salt and pepper. Pour sauce over the fish and sprinkle with Parmesan cheese. Place under broiler to glaze. Serve with toast points if desired.

Wine Suggestion: Serve Entre-Deaux-mers or Emerald Riesling.

Fish Plaki

A complete vegetable and seafood dinner nestled in an inviting wine sauce.

2 pounds fish, steaks or filets	¼ cup fresh parsley, minced
¼ to ½ cup olive oil	1 cup celery, diced
2 bunches green onions, chopped	1 cup carrots, grated
2 medium onions, chopped	¼ cup green pepper, minced
2 cups canned tomatoes	¼ cup white wine
	juice of 1 lemon
	salt and pepper to taste

1. Wash and dry fish well with paper toweling. Cut into steaks or filets, if necessary.

2. In a skillet, heat oil and saute onions until soft and transparent. Add tomatoes and all remaining ingredients. Cook the sauce at a low simmer until vegetables are tender, about 45 minutes.

3. Pour ⅓ of the sauce into a shallow baking dish large enough to hold all the fish and sauce. Nestle fish into the sauce.

4. Pour remaining sauce on top of fish. Bake, uncovered, in a preheated 375 degree oven for 20 to 25 minutes.

Wine Suggestion: Crisp, dry Chablis or Muscadet.

 MAIN DISHES

Grilled Swordfish with Horseradish Sauce   YIELDS: 4 servings

4   small swordfish steaks,
about ¾ inch thick

MARINADE
¾   cup dry white wine
¼   cup fresh lemon juice
salt and pepper
to taste

½   teaspoon dry mustard
1   teaspoon dried dill
2   tablespoons onions,
finely chopped

HORSERADISH SAUCE
¾   cup sour cream
¼   cup mayonnaise
2-3 tablespoons prepared
horseradish

½   teaspoon prepared mustard
1   tablespoon fresh lemon
juice

1. Place fish in shallow dish and cover with marinade and chopped onions. Marinate at room temperature for 1 hour, turning steaks over after 30 minutes.

2. Barbecue over medium coals for about 6-8 minutes per side (depending on the thickness of the fish) or put under broiler of oven. Baste the fish once or twice on each side with some of the marinade. Serve with Horseradish Sauce.

Variation: Use any firm fish such as halibut or sea bass.

Wine Suggestion: Swordfish can accommodate many varieties of wine. Try Cotes-Du-Rhone, Rose of Cabernet, or Soave.

Herb Baked Filets

YIELDS: 4 servings

2 **pounds fish filets**	½ **cup bread crumbs**
salt and pepper to taste	1 **teaspoon fresh tarragon,**
½ **cup olive oil**	**minced**
2 **tablespoons lemon juice**	1 **teaspoon fresh thyme,**
¼ **cup green onions,**	**minced**
chopped	1 **teaspoon fresh rosemary,**
2 **tablespoons fresh**	**minced**
parsley, chopped	**butter**
3-4 **tablespoons Dijon**	½ **cup Gruyere (or Swiss)**
mustard	**cheese, grated**

1. Season fish with salt and pepper. Marinate fish in mixture of olive oil, lemon juice, onions, and parsley for 4 hours.

2. Transfer fish to a baking dish and lightly coat top surface of filets with mustard.

3. Combine bread crumbs and herbs. Spread over fish. Dot with butter and sprinkle with cheese.

4. Bake, uncovered, in a preheated 400 degree oven until fish is done, approximately 15-20 minutes.

Wine Suggestion: California Chardonnay will let herb flavors shine.

Helpful Hints: Always freeze fresh fish in water to retain freshness and to cut down on odor when cooking.

Lemon Roll-Ups

YIELDS: 8 servings

Tender fish filets wrapped around a lemon-y surprise of broccoli and sharp Cheddar.

⅓ cup butter or margarine	1 cup (4-ounces) sharp Cheddar cheese, shredded
⅓ cup lemon juice	
2 teaspoons chicken bouillon or 2 bouillon cubes	8 fish filets (about 2 pounds), fresh or frozen Flounder and Sole work well
1 teaspoon Tabasco sauce	
1 cup cooked rice (not Minute Rice)	paprika
1 (10-ounce) package frozen chopped broccoli, thawed	

1. In small saucepan, melt butter. Add lemon juice, bouillon, and Tabasco. Heat slowly until bouillon dissolves; set aside.

2. Combine rice, broccoli, cheese, and ¼ cup of lemon butter sauce in medium bowl; mix well.

3. Divide broccoli mixture equally between filets. Roll up and place seam side down in shallow baking dish. Pour remaining sauce over roll-ups.

4. Bake in a preheated 375 degree oven for 25 minutes or until fish flakes with fork. Spoon sauce over individual servings; garnish with paprika. Refrigerate leftovers.

May be prepared to baking point several hours ahead and refrigerated.

Wine Suggestion: White wine from Macon or Spanish Chardonnay.

Marinated Flounder

YIELDS: 8 servings

Serve cold. A great luncheon dish.

8 large flounder filets	2 cups prepared Italian or
8 sprigs fresh dill	garlic salad dressing
8 green onions, cut into	1 red onion, cut into rings
16 (3 inch) pieces	lime wedges
1 teaspoon salt	leaf lettuce leaves
1 cup orange juice mixed	Boston lettuce leaves
with juice of one lime	

1. Put the dill and two pieces of onion on each filet. Fold the filet over and put it into a large skillet. Sprinkle with salt and pour on the orange and lime juice mixture. Cover and simmer gently 15 to 20 minutes, until flouder is white and cooked.

2. Remove the fish with a spatula and put it in a shallow dish. Cover with salad dressing and onion rings and chill. When ready to serve, arrange filets on a serving platter with lime wedges and lettuce.

Wine Suggestion: Good quality Brut Champagne will form a pleasing attraction.

New Zealand Orange Roughy

YIELDS: 4 servings

4 tablespoons butter, melted	¼ cup dried bread crumbs
1 pound orange roughy	salt
4 green onions, chopped	paprika

1. Preheat oven to 325 degrees. Melt 2 tablespoons butter in baking dish in oven. Add fish and top with green onions (save a few for the end). Cover and bake for 10-12 minutes.

2. Remove from oven. Brush with remaining melted butter. Top with bread crumbs. Sprinkle lightly with paprika and salt. Broil 3-5 minutes or until crumbs become crisp and fish flakes easily. Top with remaining green onions, if desired.

Wine Suggestion: A first class Sauvignon Blanc.

 MAIN DISHES

Prawns in Parmesan Butter

YIELDS: 3-4 servings

If you're visiting the seashore consider taking this recipe along to utilize the abundance of fresh shrimp while there. It's easy and delicious.

36 large raw shrimp, peeled and deveined	2 cloves garlic, minced
1 cup butter	2 tablespoons lemon juice
3 tablespoons capers, including liquid (optional)	4 ounces Parmesan cheese, grated

1. Butterfly shrimp by cutting each piece lengthwise halfway through and separate the two sides to form a thin, flat piece of shrimp.

2. Place butter in a one quart measure, microwave at high for one minute or until melted. Stir in capers, garlic, and lemon juice.

3. Pour two-thirds of butter in 12 x 8 x 2 inch dish. Arrange shrimp in sauce. Top with cheese, then remaining butter. Cover with wax paper. Microwave at high for 6 to 7 minutes, rotating dish one-half turn after 3 minutes, until shrimp is opaque and firm.

Wine Suggestion: A very dry White wine such as Muscadet French or Brut Champagne.

Scallops Supreme

1	pound fresh, tiny bay scallops	2	tablespoons butter, melted
¼	cup flour	2	tablespoons lemon juice
½	teaspoon salt	1	teaspoon lemon rind
⅛	teaspoon pepper	1	tablespoon parsley, chopped
¼	cup butter, melted		

1. Coat scallops with mixture of flour, salt, and pepper. Saute in ¼ cup butter over low heat until tender and lightly browned on all sides.

2. In a small saucepan, combine 2 tablespoons butter, lemon juice, lemon rind and parsley. Heat just to boiling. Pour over scallops. Serve immediately.

Wine Suggestion: Sweet bay scallops need a mellow White wine, Vouray, or Johannisberg Riesling.

Shrimp in Foil

6	tablespoons butter	½	teaspoon salt
2	tablespoons parsley		dash pepper
	Tabasco sauce to taste, start with ⅛ teaspoon	2	pounds large shrimp, peeled and deveined
1	clove garlic, minced		

1. Melt butter; stir in parsley, Tabasco, garlic, salt, and pepper. Add shrimp and stir to coat.

2. Divide equally among four 12 x 18 inch pieces of heavy duty foil. Seal edges well.

3. Grill over hot coals for 8 minutes, turn and grill for 8 more minutes. Serve over rice, if desired.

Wine Suggestion: For a great picnic with class, use Muscadet or California premium White table wine.

 MAIN DISHES

Seashore Breadcups

YIELDS: 6-8 servings

If you've never made "breadcups", try these for fun and then enhance them with this seashore recipe.

½ cup butter
    garlic salt
½ pound fresh mushrooms,
    sliced
½ cup green onions, chopped
3 rounded tablespoons
    flour
1 can cream of shrimp soup
1 cup half and half
¾ cup white wine

1 pound fresh shrimp, peeled
   and deveined
½ pound crabmeat
1 cup (4-ounces) sharp
   Cheddar cheese, grated
   (reserve some for garnish)
   chopped parsley

1. Melt butter, seasoned with garlic salt, in a skillet. Saute mushrooms and onions until tender. Sprinkle with flour. Add shrimp soup, half and half, and white wine.

2. When mixture thickens slightly, add raw shrimp and crab meat. Stir in grated cheese and salt and pepper to taste.

3. Simmer in covered skillet gently until thickened and shrimp are pink. Transfer shrimp to chafing dish until ready to serve. Serve shrimp over bread cups. Top lightly with grated cheese and chopped parsley.

BREADCUPS
8-12 slices fresh white
   bread

6 tablespoons butter
   garlic salt

1. Trim crust from slices of bread. Press bread in muffin cups. Melt butter with garlic salt. Spread garlic butter over bread. Bake in a preheated 300 degree oven 35 to 40 minutes or until crispy.

May be made 1 day ahead.

Wine Suggestion: A good Chardonnay with substance or an equally elegant California Sauvignon Blanc.

Sherried Fish au Gratin

YIELDS: 6-8 servings

May be made with frozen filets—but fresh is best.

2 **pounds fresh flounder filets**	1 **tablespoon flour**
salt and pepper	1½ **cups whipping cream**
½ **cup chopped parsley**	2-3 **tablespoons sherry**
2 **tablespoons butter**	2 **tablespoons Parmesan cheese, grated**
2 **tablespoons fresh lemon juice**	2-3 **tablespoons bread crumbs**
1 **pound fresh mushrooms, sliced**	**paprika**

1. Sprinkle separated filets with salt and pepper. Arrange in shallow baking dish; sprinkle with parsley.

2. In small skillet melt butter with lemon juice. Add mushrooms and saute over low heat 10-12 minutes, stirring occasionally. Blend in flour. Gradually add cream, simmer until thickened, stirring. Simmer 10 minutes longer, stirring occasionally. Add sherry and a pinch of salt and pepper.

3. Pour sauce over fish and sprinkle with cheese, bread crumbs, and a dusting of paprika. Bake in a preheated 450 degree oven for 20 minutes or until fish is white and flakes easily and top is well browned.

Wine Suggestion: Luscious Washington State Riesling or a full California Sauvignon Blanc.

Sole Divan

YIELDS: 4 servings

A divan that's simply divine!

1 bunch fresh broccoli, steamed or (10-ounce) package frozen broccoli spears
1 pound fresh sole filets
1 tablespoon butter
1 cup (4-ounces) fresh mushrooms, sliced
1 cup milk, divided
1 teaspoon chicken bouillon granules
1 tablespoon cornstarch
4 ounces Cheddar cheese, shredded
½ cup almonds, slivered

1. Cook broccoli according to package directions or until crisp tender. Drain well. Line bottom of 1½ quart baking dish with cooked broccoli. Place sole filets on top of broccoli.

2. In medium skillet melt butter and saute mushrooms. Spoon mushrooms over fish.

3. Add ¾ cup milk and bouillon granules to butter remaining in skillet and stir. Add cornstarch to ¼ cup milk and mix well. Add cornstarch mix to pan and stir until thick. Stir in cheese until melted and pour mixture over fish.

4. Sprinkle almonds on top and bake in a preheated 400 degree oven for 15 minutes or until fish flakes easily.

Frozen filets may be used, thaw first.

Wine Suggestion: Chenin Blanc or German Riesling.

Southview Salmon

An enjoyable way to enhance your summertime zucchini. Save the leftovers—they're worth reheating.

1 **(7¾-ounce) can pink salmon**	3 **cups milk**
3-4 **medium zucchini**	½ **cup Hellmann's mayonnaise**
½ **cup butter, divided**	½ **cup Parmesan cheese, grated**
1½ **teaspoons garlic powder**	**juice of 1 lemon**
4-5 **tablespoons flour**	**paprika**
¾ **cup green onions, sliced (tops included)**	
2 **teaspoons dill weed**	

1. Drain and debone salmon; set aside.

2. Slice each zucchini into 4 lengthwise slices and steam until crisp tender (5-7 minutes, do not overcook). Arrange slices of zucchini in 9 x 13 inch dish. (Use any extra zucchini in another small casserole.)

3. Cut 4 tablespoons of butter into thin slices. Place randomly over zucchini slices. Sprinkle with garlic powder.

4. Melt 4 tablespoons butter in skillet. Stir in flour until well blended. Add green onions and dill weed. Cook for 1 minute, stirring constantly. Gradually add milk and cook until thickened. Remove from heat.

5. Stir in Hellmann's mayonnaise, Parmesan cheese, and lemon juice. Fold in salmon. Spoon sauce mixture over zucchini. Sprinkle with additional Parmesan cheese and paprika.

6. Bake in a preheated 350 degree oven for 15 to 20 minutes or until bubbly. Cool 5 to 10 minutes before serving. Garnish with parsley and lemon slices.

Prepare early in the day.

Wine Suggestion: Gamay Rose or Semillon.

Whitefish in Tomato Sauce

YIELDS: 4 servings

The secret here is to make sure that your fish is broiled thoroughly but not dried out.

1 (16-ounce) can stewed tomatoes	½ cup Parmesan cheese, grated
1 teaspoon oregano	parsley, chopped
½ teaspoon garlic salt	lemon wedges
dash pepper	
2 pounds whitefish or halibut filets	

1. Mash tomatoes in saucepan. Add oregano, garlic salt, and pepper. Simmer 15 minutes.

2. Preheat broiler 10 minutes.

3. Brush filets with vegetable oil and place skin side up on broiler pan. Broil on bottom shelf about 8 minutes, depending on thickness of filet. Do not turn over. Skin may char.

4. Place on platter, fleshy side up, and spoon sauce over. Sprinkle with cheese and parsley. Garnish with lemon.

Wine Suggestion: Tavel Rose or lighter style Italian Red wine will stand up to the tomatoes.

Cordon Bleu

YIELDS: 1 serving

FOR EACH SERVING

1 veal cutlet or	1 thin slice boiled
2 pork tenderloins	ham
	1 thin slice Swiss cheese

COATING

1-2 eggs	2 cups seasoned bread
2-4 tablespoons water	crumbs

1. Pound cutlet or tenderloin to ¼ inch. Cut cutlet in half.

2. Layer as follows: Slice of meat, ½ slice of Swiss cheese, 1 slice of ham folded same size as meat, ½ slice Swiss cheese, and top with slice of meat.

3. Beat eggs and water together. Dip prepared meat into egg mixture, then into bread crumbs. Cover all sides and repeat. Let stand 20 minutes or until ready to cook.

4. Fry in oil at medium heat for 10-15 minutes, until cheese melts and cutlets are golden brown and crispy.

Wine Suggestion: A light dry Merlot.

French Veal Rolls

YIELDS: 6 servings

6	large veal cutlets
½	cup bread crumbs
¼	cup milk
¼	pound pork sausage, cooked
¼	cup onion, chopped
½	clove garlic, minced
2	slices bacon, cooked and diced
1	tablespoon parsley, minced
1	egg yolk
2	tablespoons shortening
2	cups consomme
1	tablespoon flour
	parsley
6	lemon slices

1. Pound veal to ¼ inch thick.

2. Combine bread crumbs with milk; mix with sausage, onion, garlic, bacon, parsley, and egg yolk. Put 2 tablespoons filling across center of each piece of veal. Roll up, securing with wooden pick.

3. Heat shortening in skillet. Saute veal rolls until browned. Add consomme and simmer 45 minutes. Place veal rolls on platter. Thicken cooking liquid with flour. Pour over veal rolls. Garnish with parsley and lemon slices.

May be prepared ahead to cooking point. Pork may be used in place of veal.

Wine Suggestion: A red Graves.

Veal Almondine

Garnish with fresh parsley and lemon slices for a truly elegant presentation.

6 **(4 to 6-ounce) veal cutlets**	⅓ **cup fresh parsley, minced**
salt and pepper to taste	3 **tablespoons lemon rind, grated**
2½ **cups stale bread crumbs**	3 **egg whites**
1½ **cups sliced almonds, toasted lightly**	¾ **cup clarified butter or margarine**
	2 **lemons, sliced**

1. Flatten veal to ¼ inch thick and season with salt and pepper.

2. In a shallow bowl, combine bread crumbs, almonds, parsley, and lemon rind. In another bowl, beat egg whites lightly.

3. Dip cutlets into egg whites and then into crumb mixture, pressing the mixture onto them. Chill cutlets on baking sheet for at least 30 minutes.

4. In a large skillet, saute veal in butter for 1-2 minutes per side until golden. Transfer to platter and garnish with lemon slices.

You may freeze the cutlets after cooking and reheat in a 350 degree oven until warmed, about 20 minutes.

Wine Suggestion: A nice light fruity Mosel.

Veal and Spinach Fettuccini

YIELDS: 6 servings

An adaption of a favorite chicken dish served at the Netherland Plaza in Cincinnati.

SPICED NUTS

1	tablespoon butter	¼	teaspoon cinnamon
½	cup walnuts or pecans, coarsely chopped	⅛	teaspoon allspice
		¼	teaspoon salt
2	teaspoons sugar	¼	teaspoon vanilla

1. In a small nonstick skillet, over medium heat, melt the butter. Add nuts and then all other ingredients.

2. Toss nuts until thoroughly coated. Saute for 3-5 minutes, or until nuts are slightly browned. Stir frequently to prevent burning.

3. Place on paper towel to remove excess butter. Store in an airtight container.

4. May be made up to 3 months in advance and kept frozen.

VEAL

2	tablespoons butter	¼	teaspoon salt
2	tablespoons flour	¼	teaspoon pepper
1	pound veal, thinly sliced and cut into 1 inch strips	¼	cup vermouth

1. In a large nonstick skillet melt the butter and saute the lightly floured veal until tender.

2. Season with salt and pepper. Add the vermouth and cook until most of the liquid is absorbed. Remove to a warm platter.

continued

Veal and Spinach Fettuccini *continued*

SAUCE

8 ounces spinach fettuccini, cooked and drained	½ teaspoon basil
	½ teaspoon salt
	1 ounce Bleu cheese
½ cup butter	¼ cup Romano cheese,
1 cup whipping cream	freshly grated

1. In same pan, melt butter. Add cream and cook until it begins to thicken. Stir frequently. Reduce heat and add basil and salt. Add Bleu cheese and stir until melted and smooth. Add Romano cheese and prepared veal. Add cooked fettuccini and toss until thoroughly coated.

2. Remove to platter and sprinkle with half of nut mixture. Freeze remaining nuts. Serve immediately.

Chicken breast filet may be substituted; do not flour.

Wine Suggestion: A sturdy Cotes-Du-Rhone like Hermitage.

Veal Scaloppine ala Marsala

YIELDS: 4 servings

This is good served with spaghetti or wide buttered-dill noodles.

4	pieces of veal, cut into thin even slices	2	dashes pepper
¼	cup flour	¼	cup butter
⅔	cup Italian bread crumbs	¼	cup Marsala wine
¼	teaspoon garlic salt	½	cup canned beef bouillon (concentrated)
½	teaspoon oregano	2	tablespoons Marsala wine

1. Mix flour, bread crumbs, garlic salt, oregano, and pepper together. Coat veal pieces in mixture.

2. Melt butter in skillet and brown breaded veal on both sides; add ¼ cup Marsala, cook one minute longer, and put on warm platter.

3. Add bouillon and 2 tablespoons Marsala wine slowly to pan drippings, scrape pan particles, and heat. (If more sauce is needed or sauce is too thick, add more bouillon.) Pour over veal and serve.

Wine Suggestion: A Haut-Medoc would make an elegant meal.

ACCOMPANIMENTS

ACCOMPANIMENTS

ACCOMPANIMENTS

ACCOMPANIMENTS ⚜

Asparagus Supreme

Excellent!

4 cups fresh asparagus or 2 (8-ounce) packages frozen asparagus
1 can cream of shrimp soup, undiluted
½ cup sour cream
2 tablespoons carrots, shredded

1 teaspoon onion, grated
⅛ teaspoon pepper
½ cup herb seasoned stuffing mix
1 tablespoon butter, melted

1. Cook fresh asparagus in boiling salted water 3 minutes or cook frozen asparagus according to package directions. Drain.

2. Combine soup, sour cream, carrots, onion, and pepper. Fold in asparagus. Turn mixture into a greased 1 quart baking dish.

3. Combine stuffing mix with butter and sprinkle around the edge of the casserole. Bake in a preheated 350 degree oven for 30 to 40 minutes.

Baked Vidalia Onions

YIELDS: 6 servings

The light, delicate flavor of these onions has made the tiny town of Vidalia, Georgia famous. They are available only in the spring, but worth the wait!

6 cups sliced onion rings, Vidalia or Texas Sweet
4 tablespoons butter
½ cup long grain rice, uncooked

1¾ cups boiling, salted water
¾ cup Swiss cheese, grated
¾ cup half-and-half

1. Saute onions in butter until just softened.

2. Add rice to boiling water and cook for 5 minutes. Drain and mix well, but gently, with onions, cheese, and cream. Spoon mixture into a greased casserole. Bake, uncovered, in a preheated 300 degree oven for 45 minutes.

Au Gratin Vegetables

YIELDS: 4-6 servings

A gratifying blend of four vegetables in a creamy cheese sauce.

1 **pound total-fresh cauliflower, broccoli, and Brussels sprouts**	½ **cup Cheddar cheese, shredded**
½ **cup onion, chopped**	**salt and pepper**
3 **tablespoons butter or margarine**	¼ **cup Parmesan cheese**
2 **tablespoons flour**	**paprika**
	bread crumbs (optional)

1. Cut cauliflower and broccoli into florets; halve Brussels sprouts. Cook in a small amount of water, 5 minutes or until tender crisp. Drain, reserving liquid, add enough water to make 1 cup. Keep vegetables warm.

2. In a small saucepan, cook onion in butter or margarine until tender, but not brown. Stir in flour; add reserved liquid, all at once. Cook and stir until thick and bubbly. Stir in Cheddar cheese; cook 1-2 minutes more or until cheese melts. Season with salt and pepper.

3. Pour vegetables into a greased baking dish. Top with sauce. Sprinkle with Parmesan cheese and paprika. Broil 4 inches from heat until lightly browned. Sprinkle with bread crumbs and serve at once.

Herb Butter

YIELDS: ¾ cup

½ **cup butter or margarine, melted**	2 **tablespoons fresh parsley, finely chopped**
1 **tablespoon chives, snipped**	½ **teaspoon dried tarragon**
2 **tablespoons lemon juice**	

1. In small bowl, combine all of the above and mix until well blended. Pour over cooked fresh green vegetables and serve immediately.

Bari's Carrot Delight

YIELDS: 4 servings

Cook everything in the microwave. Just be sure to stir the sauce frequently.

6-8 large carrots	1½ cups orange juice
½ cup sugar	2 tablespoons lemon juice
2 tablespoons cornstarch	2 tablespoons butter
½ teaspoon salt	

1. Peel and slice at an angle 6-8 large carrots. Cook in salted water until fork tender. (Stove top or microwave.)

2. Mix sugar, cornstarch, and salt in separate pan. Slowly add orange juice and lemon juice and cook until bubbly and thick. Stir in butter and pour over carrots. Serve warm.

May prepare sauce ahead and serve over fresh carrots.

Broccoli and Artichoke Casserole

YIELDS: 8-10 servings

2 (10-ounce) packages frozen broccoli, chopped	1 (8-ounce) package cream cheese, softened
1 can artichoke hearts	1 teaspoon lemon juice
½ cup butter, melted	cracker crumbs

1. Cook broccoli and drain. Drain artichoke hearts.

2. Blend butter, cream cheese, and lemon juice. Add to broccoli.

3. Place artichoke hearts (cut in half) in bottom of greased 3 quart casserole. Add mixture. Top with cracker crumbs; dot with butter. Bake in a preheated 350 degree oven for 25 minutes.

Easy to prepare.

ACCOMPANIMENTS

Broccoli-Onion Deluxe

YIELDS: 8 servings

A favorite vegetable highlighted by an appetizing wine and cheese sauce.

2	(10-ounce) packages frozen cut broccoli	¾	cup milk
2	cups frozen whole small onions	1	(3-ounce) package cream cheese, softened
2	tablespoons butter	⅓	cup dry white wine
2	tablespoons flour	½	cup toasted almonds, sliced
¼	teaspoon salt		

1. In a saucepan, cook broccoli and onions in boiling, salted water for about 10 minutes or until tender; drain.

2. In a saucepan, melt butter, blend in flour and salt. Add milk, all at once. Cook and stir until thickened and bubbly. Blend in cream cheese until smooth. Remove from heat; stir in wine. Fold in vegetables and pour into a 1½ quart greased casserole.

3. Bake, uncovered, in a preheated 350 degree oven for 30-35 minutes. Sprinkle with almonds.

Burgundy Beets

YIELDS: 4-6 servings

Wine and mandarin oranges compliment this beet recipe.

1	(11-ounce) can mandarin orange sections	1	(16-ounce) can beets (tiny-whole)
½	cup Burgundy wine	1	teaspoon lemon juice
4	teaspoons cornstarch		

1. Drain orange sections and reserve liquid.

2. In saucepan combine liquid, wine, and cornstarch. Bring to boil, stirring constantly. Add lemon juice, beets, and orange sections. Heat through, stirring gently.

ACCOMPANIMENTS ⚜

Butternut Squash and Apple Casserole

YIELDS: 6 servings

A great way to use fall squash and apples.

1	large butternut squash	¼	teaspoon cinnamon
3	cooking apples	⅛	teaspoon nutmeg
4	tablespoons margarine or butter		(or ½ teaspoon allspice instead of
⅓	cup brown sugar, packed		cinnamon and nutmeg)
1	tablespoon flour	1	teaspoon salt
½	teaspoon mace		

1. Wash, peel, and slice or cube squash (½ inch pieces). Wash, peel, and slice apples.

2. Layer squash and apples in a greased casserole. Cut up margarine and distribute evenly on apples and squash.

3. Mix together all remaining dry ingredients and sprinkle over apples and squash. Cover and bake in a preheated 325 degree oven for 1 hour, uncover last 15 minutes.

Lemon Crumb Vegetable Topping

A little zip for any vegetable.

3	tablespoons butter or margarine	⅛	teaspoon pepper
6	tablespoons fresh bread crumbs	1	teaspoon lemon rind, finely grated
⅛	teaspoon salt		

1. Melt butter in skillet. Add bread crumbs, salt, and pepper. Stir over low heat until lightly toasted. Stir in lemon rind, mixing well.

2. Sprinkle over hot, well drained, cooked vegetables.

Calico Baked Beans

YIELDS: 6-8 servings

Super for summer picnics.

½ pound bacon, cubed (optional)	1 teaspoon dry mustard
1 pound hamburger	2 tablespoons vinegar
1 medium onion, chopped	1 (16-ounce) can pork 'n beans
½ teaspoon salt	1 small can lima beans
½ cup catsup	1 (16-ounce) can kidney beans
¾ cup brown sugar, packed	

1. Brown bacon, hamburger, and onion together. Drain. Then add salt, catsup, brown sugar, mustard, and vinegar. Mix well and bring to a boil.

2. Add all beans (undrained) to the hamburger mixture and bring to a boil again. Then put into a 2 quart baking dish and bake, uncovered, in a preheated 350 degree oven for 1 hour.

MICROWAVE DIRECTIONS

1. Combine bacon, hamburger, and onion in 3 quart bowl. Cover with paper towel. Cook on full power 4-5 minutes, stop once to stir, until ground beef is brown and onion tender. If necessary, drain off excess grease.

2. Add seasoning ingredients. Stir together and cook on full power 2 minutes. Add beans (drain kidney beans only). Cook on full power 3 minutes or until it boils.

3. Turn into large casserole and microwave at 50% power for 30 minutes. Use shallow casserole and turn dish once or twice.

Helpful Hints: To rid hands of onion smell, rub them with dry mustard. Then wash them in warm water.

ACCOMPANIMENTS

Carrots ala Ann

YIELDS: 4-6 servings

8	carrots, peeled and cut into strips, not too thin	2	tablespoons sugar
	salt and pepper	2	egg yolks
¼	cup butter	½	cup cream
		2	tablespoons parsley
		2	tablespoons lemon juice

1. Place carrots in pan and cover with water. Boil for 3 minutes. Drain, reserve ½ cup of liquid.

2. Combine reserved liquid, salt, pepper, butter, and sugar to carrots and bring to a boil. Cover and simmer 10 minutes. Remove cover and boil the liquid down.

3. Beat egg yolks and cream with fork and add to carrots. Add parsley and lemon juice and serve.

May be prepared a day ahead and heated, being careful not to boil. Do not freeze. Easy.

Cheese Potatoes

YIELDS: 6 servings

As a side dish, they're great...add a salad and bread sticks for a full course.

6-8	potatoes	1	teaspoon salt
2	cups Cheddar cheese, shredded	¼	teaspoon pepper
1½	cups sour cream	½	cup butter or margarine, sliced into pats
½	cup green onions		paprika

1. Boil potatoes in the skin until just tender. Drain and cool. Peel skin and shred potatoes. Fold in cheese, sour cream, onions, salt, and pepper. Pour into a 2½ quart baking dish. Slide pats of butter down each side of casserole and into casserole from the top. Sprinkle with paprika and bake in a preheated 350 degree oven for 30 minutes or until heated through and cheese has melted.

May be prepared ahead. Freezes well.

⚜ ACCOMPANIMENTS

Cauliflower au Gratin

Even those who aren't fond of cauliflower enjoy this casserole.

1 head cauliflower, separated into florets	5 slices bread, made into crumbs
5 tablespoons butter, divided	¼ teaspoon garlic salt
4 tablespoons flour	3 tablespoons Parmesan cheese
1 cup milk	
8 ounces Old English cheese, cut into small pieces	

1. Cook cauliflower 20 minutes or until tender. Drain well; put in greased casserole dish.

2. In a saucepan, melt 3 tablespoons butter; add 4 tablespoons flour to make a paste. Add 1 cup of milk, slowly, and stir until thick. Turn off heat and add Old English cheese, stir. Pour over cauliflower.

3. In a skillet, melt 2 tablespoons of butter; add bread crumbs. Sprinkle with Parmesan cheese and garlic salt. Stir 4-5 minutes to brown. Sprinkle bread crumbs on top of the casserole. Bake in a preheated 350 degree oven for 15-20 minutes.

Sauce for Potatoes

½ cup sour cream	4 slices bacon, crumbled
¼ cup butter or margarine, softened	2 tablespoons green onions, chopped
1 cup sharp Cheddar cheese, grated	

1. Combine sour cream, butter, cheese, bacon, and onions. Mix well. Serve over hot baked potatoes.

Cheesy Vegetable Pie

YIELDS: 6 servings

Tasty as a main luncheon entree.

1 (8-ounce) package crescent rolls
1 (16-ounce) can asparagus, cut into fifths, drained
½ cup mayonnaise
1 cup Cheddar cheese, shredded
1 teaspoon lemon juice

1. Unroll and separate dough into 8 triangles. Place on an 8 or 9 inch pie plate. Press together to form crust, covering bottom and sides of plate.

2. Combine remaining ingredients, tossing lightly. Spread mixture in unbaked crust.

3. Bake in a preheated 350 degree oven for 35 minutes. Let set 10 to 15 minutes before serving.

Beer Batter

YIELDS: 6 servings

This batter stays crispy!

1 cup beer
1 cup flour
½ teaspoon salt

1. Combine beer, flour, and salt. Stir until well mixed. Cover and refrigerate at least 4 hours.

2. Dip bite size pieces of vegetables in batter, then deep fry until golden brown.

If batter seems thin, add a little flour. Suggested vegetables: onion, cauliflower, broccoli, zucchini, mushrooms. For a large amount, deep fry and keep warm in a 250 degree oven, on a large platter.

Batter must be prepared early in the day.

Corn Stuffed Tomatoes

YIELDS: 6 servings

A good choice for summer dinners.

6 large fresh tomatoes salt to taste	1 (16-ounce) can whole kernel corn, drained
2 tablespoons butter or margarine	1 cup Cheddar cheese, shredded
4 tablespoons onion, finely chopped	Parmesan cheese (optional)
½ cup cracker or potato chip crumbs	

1. Cut off top of tomatoes and hollow out pulp. Set tomatoes in a 8 x 11 inch glass baking dish.

2. In a skillet, saute onion in the butter. Add corn and crumbs and mix lightly. Stuff mixture into tomatoes. Top with Cheddar cheese and sprinkle with Parmesan cheese, if desired.

3. Bake in preheated 350 degree oven approximately 15 minutes until tender.

Variation: Fresh corn can be used. Cooking time should be extended, or semi-cook corn before stuffing.

Helpful Hints: Green tomatoes ripen quickly stored in a brown paper bag in a cool, dark location.

Creamed Spinach Ring

YIELDS: 6-8 servings

A very attractive presentation.

2	(10-ounce) packages frozen spinach, chopped		1	teaspoon salt
	Parmesan cheese, grated		¼	teaspoon pepper
4	tablespoons butter		¼	teaspoon nutmeg
½	cup onion, chopped		4	eggs
1	cup light cream or half and half		½	cup fresh bread crumbs (2 slices)
½	teaspoon sugar		⅓	cup Swiss cheese, grated

1. Cook spinach according to package directions. Drain well.

2. Grease a 4½ cup ring mold well and dust with grated Parmesan cheese.

3. In large saucepan, saute onion in butter until tender, about 5 minutes. Add spinach, cream, sugar, salt, pepper, and nutmeg; heat just to boiling. Remove from heat.

4. Beat eggs slightly; add bread crumbs and Swiss cheese; gradually stir in spinach mixture. Turn into prepared mold. Set mold in baking pan on oven rack and pour boiling water into baking pan to depth of 1½ inches. Place a piece of wax paper over top of mold. Bake in a preheated 350 degree oven 30 to 35 minutes or until knife inserted in center of spinach mixture comes out clean. Loosen mold around edge and invert onto heated serving plate.

Deviled Mushrooms on Broccoli or Asparagus

Yields: 6 servings

This is great with salmon cakes or any other fish.

2 tablespoons butter	½ teaspoon pimento, chopped
3 tablespoons flour	6 ounces mushrooms, sliced and undrained
2 cups non-dairy creamer, frozen	6 freshly cooked broccoli spears or 12 asparagus spears
2 teaspoons prepared mustard	6 slices toast, buttered
1½ teaspoons salt	
⅛ teaspoon chili powder	
2 teaspoons chives, chopped	

1. In large frying pan, melt the butter and blend in flour. Add the non-dairy creamer and stir until smooth and thick. Stir in mustard, salt, chili powder, chives, pimento, and mushrooms. Heat thoroughly, stirring constantly.

2. Arrange hot broccoli or asparagus spears on buttered slices of toast and top with mushroom mixture.

Note: Can be made into appetizers by cutting the toast into wedges, then topping with ½ spears and mushroom mixture.

Helpful Hints: Use an egg slicer for slicing raw mushrooms.

Dad's Favorite Asparagus

YIELDS: 4-6 servings

Mom's too!

1	pound fresh asparagus	⅛	teaspoon salt
2	tablespoons margarine	⅛	teaspoon pepper
2	tablespoons flour	½	cup pecans, chopped
1	cup milk		
1	cup Cheddar cheese, shredded		

1. Cut asparagus into 2 inch pieces. Set aside.

2. Melt margarine and add flour, cooking over medium heat for 2 minutes. Add milk, stirring constantly until thick. Take off of heat and add one half of the cheese. Add salt, pepper, and nuts. Stir to melt cheese and mix well.

3. Arrange asparagus in 1½ quart casserole dish and cover with cheese mixture. Top with remaining cheese and bake in a preheated 350 degree oven for 25 to 30 minutes or until tender.

Fresh Corn and Tomatoes

YIELDS: 5-6 servings

Substitute frozen corn in the winter, thaw and drain well.

8	to 10 ears fresh corn (4-5 cups)	4	slices crisp bacon
¼	cup butter or bacon drippings	1	teaspoon salt
		2	large tomatoes, peeled and sliced

1. Cut corn from cob. Melt butter or bacon drippings in skillet. Add corn and saute quickly, about 5 minutes.

2. Add crumbled bacon and salt. Arrange in a buttered casserole in alternate layers with sliced tomatoes.

3. Bake, uncovered, in a preheated 350 degree oven for 30 minutes or until corn is tender. Serve hot.

🌿 ACCOMPANIMENTS

Family Vegetable Casserole

An eye appealing combo of vegetable colors and shapes.

1 (16-ounce) can green beans, French style	½ cup sour cream
1 (16-ounce) can small green peas	¾ cup mild cheese, shredded
1 (12-ounce) can corn, white shoe peg	1 (4-ounce) package of round crackers, crumbled
1 can cream of celery soup or Cheddar cheese soup	1 (3-ounce) package almonds, sliced
½ cup onions, chopped	½ cup butter, melted

1. Drain all vegetables. Combine soup, onion, sour cream, and cheese. Mix gently with vegetables and pour into 2 quart casserole.

2. Spread crumbled crackers over top. Sprinkle almonds on top and pour melted butter over all.

3. Bake in a preheated 350 degree oven for 45 minutes or microwave at cook power 5 for 12 minutes, then full power for 6 to 8 minutes.

Helpful Hints: Keep a supply of 3 ounce paper cups on hand to hold small amounts of ingredients you have measured for a recipe. Helps organize the cooking process and saves clean-up time.

Pepper-Corn Casserole

YIELDS: 6 servings

- 2 eggs
- 2 tablespoons sugar
- 2 tablespoons flour
- salt and pepper to taste
- 2 tablespoons butter or margarine, melted
- ¼ cup onion, chopped
- 1 green pepper, chopped
- 4 ounces sharp Cheddar cheese, grated
- 1 (16 ½-ounce) can whole kernel corn
- paprika

1. Beat eggs. Add sugar, flour, salt, pepper, butter, onion, and green pepper. Stir in corn with juice. Pour into 1½ to 2 quart casserole. Bake in a preheated 350 degree oven for 30 minutes.

2. Remove from oven and sprinkle cheese and paprika on top. Return to oven until cheese melts.

Scalloped Pineapple

YIELDS: 4-6 servings

An enjoyable touch to your Sunday brunch or as a partner to the finest of Easter hams.

- ¾ cup sugar
- 2 eggs
- ¼ cup butter
- ¼ cup milk
- 1 (16-ounce) can crushed pineapple, drained
- 4 slices bread, cubed

1. Cream sugar, eggs, butter, and milk together. Add pineapple and cubed bread and place in a 1½ quart casserole.

2. Bake, uncovered, in a preheated 350 degree oven for 50 minutes. Let stand 5 minutes before serving.

May be prepared 2 days ahead. Freezes up to 3 months.

⚜ ACCOMPANIMENTS

Far East Celery

YIELDS: 8-10 servings

Exceptional company dish.

4 cups celery, cut into diagonal pieces	¼ cup pimento, diced
1 cup cream of chicken soup	1 can water chestnuts, sliced

1. Boil celery 8 minutes in salted water. Drain. Put in a medium bowl with soup. Mix well. Add pimento and water chestnuts. Mix again. Put mixture in a 2 quart casserole.

TOPPING

½ cup bread crumbs	¼ cup almonds, toasted and sliced
2 tablespoons butter	

1. Brown all topping ingredients in a frying pan. Sprinkle on top of celery mixture. Bake, uncovered, in a 350 degree oven for 35 minutes.

Note: May be made a day ahead and freezes well one to two weeks.

Buttery Cinnamon Skillet Apples

YIELDS: 4-6 servings

Pleasantly accents your favorite pork entree.

½ cup sweet butter	¼ to ½ teaspoon cinnamon
⅓ to ½ cup sugar	4 cooking apples, peeled, cored, and halved
2 tablespoons cornstarch	
1½ cups water	

1. Melt butter in skillet. Stir in sugar and cornstarch; mix well. Add water, cinnamon, and apples. Cover and cook over medium heat.

2. Spoon sauce over apples until they are fork tender and sauce is thick, about 12-15 minutes. Serve warm.

Easy.

Green Pea and Water Chestnut Casserole Supreme

YIELDS: 6-8 servings

Delightfully different!

1 package frozen green peas	1 (4-ounce) can mushrooms, whole or sliced, reserve juice
¼ cup butter or margarine	1 tablespoon flour
1 small onion, chopped	½ cup herb stuffing mix
2 ribs of celery, chopped	
1 can water chestnuts, sliced	

1. Cook peas slightly. Drain.

2. Saute onions and celery in butter. Add mushroom juice and flour. Stir until thickened. Mix all ingredients, except stuffing mix. Put in buttered casserole and sprinkle with herb stuffing mix. Dot with butter. Bake in a preheated 350 degree oven until hot.

Mediterranean Green Beans

YIELDS: 6-8 servings

Very appealing with either fresh or frozen green beans.

2 (10-ounce) packages frozen cut green beans or fresh green beans	6-8 ounces tomato sauce
2 tablespoons vegetable oil	1½ teaspoons oregano
2 tablespoons onion, chopped	¼ teaspoon salt, or to taste pepper to taste

1. Cook green beans until tender.

2. Saute onions in oil, until transparent. Add tomato sauce, oregano, salt, and pepper; stir until bubbly. Add green beans, heat until warm.

May be made ahead and kept warm on the stove for 30 minutes.

Lima Bean-Broccoli Casserole

YIELDS: 8-10 servings

A magic combination made even better by its crunchy topping.

1 small package frozen lima beans	1 envelope dry onion soup
1 small package frozen broccoli, chopped	1 small can water chestnuts, sliced, drained
1 cup sour cream	½ cup margarine
1 can cream of mushroom soup	3 cups Rice Krispies

1. Cook vegetables according to package directions. Drain.

2. Combine sour cream, mushroom soup, and dry onion soup. Mix vegetables with sour cream mixture and drained water chestnuts. Set aside.

3. Melt margarine in saucepan. Add Rice Krispies to margarine.

4. Pour vegetable mixture into a 9 x 13 inch casserole dish. Top with Rice Krispie mixture. Bake in a preheated 350 degree oven for 30 minutes.

May be prepared 1 day ahead. Freezes well.

Rice Mingle

YIELDS: 4 servings

Prepare ahead and bake just before serving.

1 cup long grain rice	1 can onion soup
1 can beef consomme soup	½ cup butter or margarine
1 (3-ounce) can mushrooms, undrained	

1. Mix all ingredients together. Pour into 1½ quart baking dish. Bake in a preheated 350 degree oven for 1 to 1½ hours.

2. Microwave instructions: Cook at full power for 10-15 minutes.

Mushroom Casserole

Great served with Black Tie Standing Rib Roast!

1 pound fresh mushrooms, washed and cut up	1 pound Cheddar cheese, grated
½ cup onion, chopped	salt and pepper to taste
½ cup celery, chopped	2 eggs, beaten
¼ pound butter	1½ cups milk
½ cup mayonnaise	8 slices buttered bread, cut in quarters
1 can cream of mushroom soup	

1. Saute mushrooms, onions, and celery in butter. Turn off heat. Add mayonnaise, soup, half of the cheese, and salt and pepper.

2. Put half of the bread into a 3 quart casserole. Add half of mushroom mixture. Repeat.

3. Beat eggs and combine with milk. Pour over mixture in casserole. Sprinkle rest of grated cheese on top. Refrigerate over night.

4. Bring to room temperature. Bake in a preheated 350 degree oven 60-70 minutes.

Must be made ahead 1 day.

Helpful Hints: Always use twice the amount of fresh herbs than dry ones.

⚜ ACCOMPANIMENTS

Polynesian Oven Baked Beans

YIELDS: 8 servings

Try this baked bean version at your next backyard barbeque. Boston, look out!

3	tablespoons onion, chopped	1	(4½-ounce) can deviled ham
3	tablespoons olive or vegetable oil	½	cup green pepper, chopped
2	(16-ounce) cans baked beans	¼	cup catsup
1	(12-ounce) can pineapple tidbits, well drained	½	teaspoon salt
1	(11-ounce) can mandarin oranges, drained (optional)	½	teaspoon Tabasco sauce
		2	tablespoons brown sugar

1. Saute onion in oil until transparent.

2. In a 2 quart casserole, mix together baked beans, onions, and all remaining ingredients. Bake, uncovered, in a preheated 375 degree oven for 30-35 minutes or until bubbly.

Pureed Carrots and Turnips

YIELDS: 4 servings

Compliments chicken or turkey.

4	large carrots, peeled and diced	½	cup water
2	medium turnips, peeled and sliced	1	tablespoon sugar
		2	tablespoons milk
		1	tablespoon butter

1. Boil carrots and turnips, covered, in water for 15 minutes. Drain. Add sugar, milk, and butter. Blend in blender until just pureed.

May be prepared ahead. Reheats well.

ACCOMPANIMENTS ⚜

Potatoes Romanoff

YIELDS: 6-8 servings

Bacon, horseradish, and three cheeses highlight this potato casserole.

3 slices bacon, cooked and crumbled	2 tablespoons fresh parsley, chopped
1 (8-ounce) package cream cheese, softened	1 teaspoon salt
1½ teaspoons horseradish	6 cups cubed potatoes, cooked
1½ cups cream style cottage cheese	paprika
½ cup sharp process American cheese, shredded	

1. Combine bacon, cream cheese, horseradish, cottage cheese, half the shredded cheese, parsley, and salt. Add potatoes. Toss gently to coat. Turn into 10 x 6 x 2 inch baking dish. Sprinkle with paprika.

2. Bake, uncovered, in a preheated 350 degree oven for 30-35 minutes or until heated through. Top with remaining cheese. Bake 3-4 minutes more or until cheese melts.

May assemble 1 day ahead and bake before serving.

Helpful Hints: Cut off ends of potatoes to speed cooking time when baking in oven.

Red Cabbage

YIELDS: 6-8 servings

1	firm medium head red cabbage	1	large onion
1	cup cold water	½	cup red vinegar (white may be substituted)
1	tablespoon shortening	2	tablespoons sugar
2-3	large cooking apples, peeled and sliced	1	small raw potato, peeled and grated
2	teaspoons salt		
½	teaspoon pepper		
4	cloves		

1. Wash, quarter, and finely shred cabbage. Put water, shortening, cabbage, apples, salt, and pepper into saucepan.

2. Stick the cloves into the onion and add to mixture in saucepan. Bring the ingredients to a boil and cook about 40 minutes or until cabbage is tender.

3. Heat vinegar to boiling and pour it over contents in saucepan. Stir well. Add sugar and stir. Add potato and stir. Boil for 7 minutes. If it should become too dry, add water. Remove onion with cloves before serving.

Helpful Hints: Rub lemon juice over your hands after handling strong smelling foods, like garlic, onion and fish. Odors rinse off with juice.

Roasted Peppers with Potatoes

YIELDS: 6 servings

Goes well with meat loaf or roast beef. Makes an attractive platter arranged around the sliced meat.

6	green bell peppers	½	cup water
6	red bell peppers	1	tablespoon vegetable oil
3	medium potatoes	2	tablespoons onion flakes
1	tablespoon soy sauce		or fresh onion, minced

1. Wash and core peppers. Cut in thin strips.

2. Peel and parboil potatoes, 5 minutes. Cut potatoes in half and then lengthwise in strips. Place peppers and potatoes in roasting pan. Sprinkle with remaining ingredients. Mix well.

3. Bake in a preheated 350 degree oven for 1¼ hours turning pieces occasionally.

Creamy Vegetable Sauce

YIELDS: 2 cups

Excellent chilled and used as a dip for fresh vegetables.

2	ounces sharp Cheddar cheese, grated grated rind and juice of 1 lemon	1	cup sour cream
		½	teaspoon prepared mustard
1	cup mayonnaise scattering of cayenne pepper	¼	cup milk

1. Melt cheese in milk at low heat stirring constantly. Remove from heat and add remaining ingredients. Refrigerated it will keep for several days.

2. Reheat gently, but do not boil, and spoon over fresh cooked vegetables.

Posh Potatoes

YIELDS: 4 servings

A new twist to serving mashed potatoes casserole style.

6-7 medium potatoes,
     peeled and diced
3 cloves garlic, peeled
¼ cup butter
½ cup sour cream
     salt and pepper, to
     taste

2 egg yolks, slighty beaten
1 (3-ounce) can mushroom
     pieces, well drained
     buttered fresh bread
     crumbs

1. Boil potatoes in salted water to which 3 cloves garlic have been added. When tender, remove from heat and drain. Return to heat until potatoes are dry. Discard garlic.

2. Mash potatoes with electric mixer. Add butter, sour cream, and salt and pepper. Beat until smooth. Add egg yolks and stir until smooth. Fold in mushrooms. Turn into buttered 2 quart casserole. Top with buttered bread crumbs. Bake in a preheated 350 degree oven for 30-40 minutes.

May be made ahead and refrigerated. Bring to room temperature before baking.

Spicy Whole Cranberries

YIELDS: 4-6 servings

Attractively served in a festive bowl, this will be a nice addition to your most traditional holiday dinner.

1 pound fresh cranberries
2 cups sugar
¼ cup orange juice
1 tablespoon orange
     rind, grated

2 cinnamon sticks, broken
12 cloves
½ teaspoon nutmeg
½ cup walnuts, chopped

1. Combine cranberries, sugar, orange juice, and rind in large saucepan.

2. Tie cinnamon sticks and cloves in cloth and add to pan with nutmeg. Bring mixture to boil, reduce heat, and simmer 5 minutes, stirring frequently. Cool 30 minutes, stirring occasionally. Stir in nuts.

Sensational Vegetable Medley

YIELDS: 6-8 servings

A great dish because it will have a vegetable everyone likes.

1	red bell pepper	2	tablespoons fresh lemon juice
6	small red skin potatoes		
1½	pounds asparagus, trimmed	2	cups sour cream
1	bunch broccoli, separated in florets	6	scallions, minced
1	head cauliflower, separated in florets	8	slices bacon, cooked and crumbled
¼	cup butter, melted		salt and pepper

1. Preheat oven to broil. Put pepper on rack and place 6 inches from heat. Broil 15 to 20 minutes, turning frequently. When skin is charred and blistered, it is done. Place pepper in paper bag until cool enough to handle. Peel skin and remove stem and seeds. Slice thin, lengthwise.

2. Steam potatoes 15 to 20 minutes (or microwave) until tender. Keep warm. Steam remaining vegetables separately for 4 to 5 minutes (or microwave) until they are tender, but still crunchy. Keep warm.

3. Combine butter and lemon juice in bowl. In another bowl combine sour cream and scallions.

4. Arrange vegetables in individual groups on platter. Season with salt and pepper. Spoon butter mixture on vegetables. Top with sour cream mixture. Place red pepper on top. Sprinkle with bacon.

Helpful Hints: To get more lemon, lime, or orange juice, microwave 30 seconds before squeezing.

Sherry's Zucchini

YIELDS: 8 servings

What to do with all those garden zucchini you planted?...Here's a good one!

2½ to 3 cups zucchini, cooked	1 (8-ounce) sour cream
1 medium onion, chopped	1 box stove top stuffing (chicken flavor or your choice)
1 can cream of chicken or cream of mushroom soup	½ cup butter or margarine, melted

1. Cut up zucchini and onion. Boil and cook until zucchini is done. Drain thoroughly and mash. Drain again after mashing.

2. Mix soup and sour cream together, mixing thoroughly; add mashed zucchini and onion.

3. Mix the herb packet and bread from the stuffing box together with the melted butter. Mixture should be crumbly. Sprinkle ⅔ mixture on bottom of 9 x 13 inch baking dish, reserving ⅓ for the top.

4. Pour zucchini mixture over stuffing. Garnish with remaining stuffing. Bake in a preheated 350 degree oven for 35 to 40 minutes or microwave on cook power for 10 minutes and full power 5 to 8 minutes.

Spinach Cheese Casserole

YIELDS: 8 servings

2 (10-ounce) packages frozen chopped spinach, drained dry	8 ounces sharp Cheddar cheese, grated
1 (16-ounce) sour cream	2 tablespoons butter Parmesan cheese cracker crumbs
1 small onion, chopped	
8 ounces Velveeta cheese, grated	

1. Cook spinach and drain very dry. Mix with sour cream, onion, Velveeta, and Cheddar cheeses. Pour into 2 quart casserole. Sprinkle with cracker crumbs and Parmesan cheese. Dot with butter. Bake in a preheated 350 degree oven for 30 to 35 minutes.

Spinach Madeline

YIELDS: 8 servings

A bubbly casserole finished with a nutty topping.

2 **(10-ounce) packages frozen spinach, chopped**	¾ **teaspoon salt**
4 **tablespoons butter**	½ **cup half and half**
2 **tablespoons onion, chopped**	½ **cup spinach liquid**
1 **rib celery, chopped**	1 **teaspoon Worcestershire sauce**
1 **clove garlic, minced**	6 **ounces Jalapeno cheese**
2 **tablespoons flour**	1 **(8-ounce) can water chestnuts, sliced**

1. Cook and drain spinach. Reserve ½ cup liquid.

2. Saute onion, celery, and garlic in melted butter. Blend in flour and salt. Stirring slowly, add half and half, spinach liquid, and Worcestershire sauce. Cook, stirring, until thick on low heat. Add Jalapeno cheese and stir until melted.

3. Mix cheese mixture with spinach and water chestnuts. Spoon into greased casserole and refrigerate overnight.

TOPPING

1 **cup soft bread crumbs**	2 **teaspoons sesame oil (optional)**
2 **tablespoons butter, melted**	
½ **cup slivered almonds, toasted**	

1. Mix together topping ingredients and spread over spinach. Bake in a preheated 350 degree oven for 20-30 minutes, until bubbly.

Must be prepared 1 day ahead.

Sweet Potato Crunch

YIELDS: 8-10 servings

2	cans sweet potatoes, mashed	½	cup margarine, melted
3	eggs	½	cup milk
1	cup sugar	2	teaspoons vanilla

1. Mix sweet potatoes, eggs, sugar, milk, margarine, and vanilla and put in a 2½ quart casserole dish.

TOPPING

1	cup brown sugar, packed	1	cup pecans, chopped
½	cup flour	½	cup margarine, melted

1. Mix brown sugar, flour, pecans, and margarine together. Put over sweet potatoes.

2. Bake in a preheated 350 degree oven for 1 hour.

Easy. May be prepared early in the day.

Potato-Tomato Scallop

YIELDS: 6-8 servings

An appetizing compliment to your favorite charcoaled beef recipe.

½	cup onion, chopped	1	(8-ounce) can tomatoes, cut in small pieces, use juice
2	tablespoons butter		
2	tablespoons flour		
1	teaspoon paprika	2	chicken bouillon cubes
½	teaspoon salt	5	cups raw potatoes, pared and sliced
⅛	teaspoon pepper		
1	cup water		

1. Cook onion in butter until just tender. Blend in flour, paprika, salt, and pepper. Add water, tomatoes, and bouillon cubes. Cook and stir over medium heat until mixture thickens and boils and bouillon cubes dissolve.

2. Place potato slices in greased 2 quart casserole, add sauce. Cover and bake in a preheated 400 degree oven 1 to 1¼ hours.

Sweeterkraut

Great with a pork roast.

1	small onion	1/3	bay leaf
1	tablespoon butter	3	tablespoons brown sugar
1	(32-ounce) jar or can sauerkraut	1	medium apple
2	peppercorns (pepper may be used instead)		

1. Peel the onion; chop it finely and saute it in the butter until it is nearly transparent. Drain the sauerkraut well and add to onion. Add the peppercorns or pepper, bay leaf, and brown sugar. (Increase brown sugar to 4 tablespoons for a sweeter taste.)

2. Dice apple and stir it into sauerkraut mixture. Mix well and add enough boiling water to cover. Cook over medium heat until tender, adding a little water if it starts to dry out.

May be prepared 2 or 3 days ahead. Reheat.

Swiss Creamed Peas

3	cups frozen peas	1	cup whipping cream
1	cup green onion, sliced	½	teaspoon lemon peel, finely shredded
2	tablespoons butter or margarine	¾	cup (3-ounces) Swiss cheese, shredded
1	tablespoon flour		
½	teaspoon salt		

1. Cook peas in saucepan according to package directions.

2. At same time, cook onion in butter until tender but not brown. Blend in the flour and salt. Add cream and lemon peel. Cook and stir until thickened and bubbly. Add cheese, cook and stir until cheese is melted. Do not boil.

3. Drain peas. Add to sauce, stir to coat.

Swiss Green Beans

YIELDS: 8-10 servings

2 (10-ounce) packages
frozen green beans
(whole or French style)
1 can water chestnuts,
sliced, drained
2 teaspoons onion, minced
2 tablespoons butter
2 tablespoons flour

1 teaspoon sugar
1 teaspoon salt
dash pepper
1 pint sour cream
6 slices Swiss cheese,
cut into strips
2 teaspoons paprika

1. Cook and drain green beans according to package directions. Place in buttered 9 x 13 inch casserole dish. Layer sliced water chestnuts over green beans.

2. Saute onion in butter. Add flour, sugar, salt, and pepper and blend over low heat. Stir in sour cream and heat. Do not boil.

3. Pour sauce over green beans and top with strips of cheese. Sprinkle with paprika. Bake in a preheated 325 degree oven for 45 minutes.

Cranberry-Orange Chutney

YIELDS: 5½ cups

A pleasant change from cranberry sauce, this may be presented in attractive canning jars for holiday giving.

1 cup fresh orange
sections
¼ cup orange juice
4 cups cranberries
2 cups sugar
1 cup apple, unpeeled
and chopped

½ cup raisins
¼ cup walnuts, chopped
1 tablespoon vinegar
½ teaspoon ginger
½ teaspoon cinnamon

1. Combine all ingredients in a large saucepan and bring to a boil. Reduce heat and simmer 5 minutes or until berries begin to burst.

2. Cool and serve. May be kept in refrigerator or poured into hot sterilized jars and sealed.

Swiss Potatoes

YIELDS: 6 servings

Make ahead and freeze.

5	tablespoons butter or margarine, divided
2	tablespoons flour
1½	teaspoons salt
½	teaspoon dry mustard
½	teaspoon Worcestershire sauce
⅛	teaspoon pepper
3	cups milk

1	cup Swiss cheese, shredded
6	cups potatoes, peeled and thinly sliced
1	(4-ounce) jar pimentos, chopped
¼	cup onion, finely chopped
1½	cups soft bread crumbs

1. In a saucepan, melt 3 tablespoons of the butter or margarine; blend in the flour, salt, mustard, Worcestershire sauce, and pepper. Add milk all at once. Cook and stir until thickened and bubbly.

2. Remove from heat. Add cheese; stir to melt. Stir in potatoes, pimento, and onion. Turn into a greased 2½ quart casserole.

3. Bake, uncovered, in a preheated 350 degree oven for 45 minutes. Melt remaining butter or margarine; toss with bread crumbs. Sprinkle over potatoes; bake, uncovered, 30 minutes more.

Helpful Hints: Use a pizza cutter to make small bread cubes to be toasted for croutons—faster and neater.

The Best Spinach Ever

YIELDS: 8-10 servings

4 (10-ounce) packages
   frozen spinach
1 (8-ounce) package
   cream cheese
½ cup butter
2 cans artichoke hearts,
   drained

1 can water chestnuts,
   sliced and drained
   bread crumbs
   Parmesan cheese

1. Cook spinach and drain.

2. Melt butter and cream cheese together. Whip.

3. Cut up artichoke hearts. Layer spinach, artichokes, and water chestnuts into a 9 x 11 inch casserole dish. Spread cream cheese mixture over the vegetables. Top with bread crumbs and Parmesan cheese. Bake in a preheated 350 degree oven for 30 minutes.

May be prepared 1 day ahead. Do not freeze.

Snow Peas and Mushrooms

YIELDS: 4 servings

An easy and attractive accompaniment.

½ pound fresh snow peas
¼ pound fresh mushrooms
2 tablespoons butter

1 teaspoon soy sauce
   (optional)
1 tablespoon slivered
   almonds, toasted
   (optional)

1. String ends of snow peas and slice mushrooms thinly.

2. Melt butter in a fry pan. When butter bubbles, add snow peas and mushrooms. Stir fry until tender crisp. Add soy sauce in the last minute of cooking, mix throughout snow peas. Sprinkle with almonds, if desired. Serve immediately.

Tomatoes with Spinach Rockefeller

YIELDS: 6 servings

A uniquely attractive side dish for beef or pork.

6	large tomatoes	½	cup fresh thyme
⅓	cup butter or margarine	½	scant teaspoon salt
½	cup onion, finely chopped	½	cup seasoned bread crumbs
	garlic salt	2	eggs, slightly beaten
1½	cups spinach, cooked and drained	½	cup Parmesan cheese, grated

1. Peel tomatoes, remove stem end, and scoop out seeds. Turn upside down to drain on paper towel.

2. Melt ¼ cup butter; add onions, garlic salt, and saute until tender. Add spinach, seasonings, and bread crumbs. Mix well. Add eggs and cook, stirring constantly, until eggs are firm.

3. Stuff tomatoes, sprinkle cheese on top, and dot with additional butter. Bake in a preheated 350 degree oven for 10 minutes or until slightly brown and heated through.

Helpful Hints: To tell which eggs are hard boiled in refrigerator add food coloring to water when boiling.

Tomatoes Tossed in Butter and Herbs

YIELDS: 4-6 servings

This dish compliments roasted meats.

40	red cherry tomatoes, firm	½	teaspoon dried tarragon
3	tablespoons butter		salt
2	tablespoons fresh parsley, minced		pepper
1	tablespoon chives, minced	¼	cup garlic croutons, crushed (preferably home made)

1. Drop tomatoes, a few at a time, into boiling water. Simmer 3-4 seconds, remove, and cool.

2. With a sharp knife, slip off skins and cut away stem.

3. Just before serving, heat butter in large skillet until foaming. Add tomatoes and herbs. Gently shake pan until tomatoes are coated with butter-herb mixture and are warmed through.

4. Sprinkle with crushed croutons and serve immediately.

Helpful Hints: Don't leave a spoon or other metal in a pot that you want to come to a boil quickly. The metal deflects the heat lengthening the time to reach the boiling point.

White Tie Asparagus

1 pound asparagus
6 ounces bowtie pasta
1 tablespoon plus
1 teaspoon olive
   oil, divided
2 cloves garlic, crushed
1 (14 ½-ounce) can
   whole tomatoes,
   drained and chopped

1 (3-ounce) jar pimento
   stuffed olives, rinsed,
   drained, sliced
¼ cup green onion, minced
1 tablespoon fresh basil,
   minced or ½ teaspoon
   dried
1 teaspoon salt
   freshly ground pepper

1. Rinse and trim asparagus. Peel, if necessary. Cook until just tender. Drain, cool, and cut into diagonal 1 inch pieces. Set aside.

2. Cook pasta according to package directions. Drain and transfer to a large bowl. Sprinkle 1 teaspoon olive oil over pasta and toss well. Add asparagus, tossing gently.

3. Heat remaining 1 tablespoon olive oil in a small skillet; add garlic and saute 1-2 minutes or until golden. Add next 4 ingredients; cover and cook over low heat until thoroughly heated. Pour hot tomato mixture over pasta. Toss and sprinkle with salt and pepper. Serve at room temperature or chilled.

Prepare early in the day.

Helpful Hints: Add salt to water when cooking fresh asparagus. Salt makes asparagus turn bright green.

Zucchini Souffle

YIELDS: 8 servings

A delicious recipe for a popular garden vegetable.

6 cups zucchini, grated	1½ teaspoons salt
3 cups Provolone cheese, grated	1½ cups seasoned bread crumbs
6 eggs	

1. Blend all ingredients together with fork and turn into greased 2½ quart casserole dish.

2. Refrigerate minimum of one hour. (May also be frozen at this point. After thawing, add one more egg before baking.)

3. Bake in a preheated 350 degree oven for 1¼ hours.

4. May make individual servings by heating 1 teaspoon oil in each section of muffin tin. Then spoon mixture in each section. Bake in a preheated 350 degree oven for 20 minutes.

Must be prepared ahead.

Helpful Hints: If an egg breaks on one end, crack the other end and you can boil it without the contents coming out of the shell.

Zesty Bean Casserole

3 (15-ounce) cans kidney beans, drained, and rinsed	1 cup celery, chopped
½ cup green pepper, chopped	½ cup onion, chopped
1 cup tomato, chopped	1 (4-ounce) can green chilies, chopped
2 teaspoons chili powder	2 cups Cheddar cheese, shredded
1 cup mayonnaise (not salad dressing)	1 teaspoon salt
	1 cup Tostado or Dorito chips, crushed

1. Combine everything except the crushed chips. Mix carefully, but thoroughly. Place in a lightly greased 13 x 9 inch baking dish and top with crushed chips. Bake in a preheated 350 degree oven, uncovered, for 40 minutes. Allow additional baking time if you have refrigerated before cooking.

May be prepared 1 day ahead. Put chips on just before baking.

Hot Bacon Dressing with Vegetables

This dressing may be used over any of your favorite vegetables.

6 slices bacon, fried and crumbled	2 tablespoons vinegar
2 tablespoons bacon drippings	1 tablespoon brown sugar
1 medium onion, diced	1 tablespoon sugar
3 tablespoons water	½ teaspoon salt

1. Combine all the above ingredients in medium saucepan and bring to boil. Let cool.

2. Pour over the following vegetables: 2 cups cherry tomatoes, 1 cup sliced mushrooms, 1 red onion cut in rings, and 2 cups each bite size cauliflower and broccoli cooked until crisp tender.

Variation: Pour dressing over 6 cups cooked fresh green beans.

Baked Tortellini

For a main dish simply add a crusty loaf of warm Italian bread.

1 (7-ounce) box tortellini (regular or spinach)	½ teaspoon salt
1 cup prosciutto or ham, diced	¼ teaspoon dry mustard
1 cup peas, cooked	¼ teaspoon ground white pepper
4 egg yolks, lightly beaten	¼ teaspoon paprika
1 cup milk	⅛ teaspoon ground nutmeg
1 cup whipping cream	3 tablespoons butter
1⅓ cups sharp Cheddar or Fontinella cheese, shredded	1 cup soft bread crumbs
	¼ cup Parmesan cheese, grated

1. Cook tortellini according to package directions, but remove from stove al dente. Drain well and place in buttered 1½ quart casserole. Add ham and peas to tortellini, just to combine evenly.

2. Mix egg yolks with ¼ cup milk and set aside.

3. Heat remaining milk and whipping cream until hot, do not boil.

4. Combine egg yolk mixture, shredded Cheddar, and all seasonings; add to hot milk. Toss with tortellini.

5. Melt butter and mix with bread crumbs and Parmesan cheese. Sprinkle over top of tortellini.

6. Bake, uncovered, in a preheated 350 degree oven for 35-40 minutes or until bread crumbs are brown. Let stand 15 minutes before serving.

Fettuccini and Spinach

YIELDS: 6-8 servings

This would be a nice accompaniment to a zippy, Italian sausage entree.

1 (8-ounce) package fettuccini
1 (10-ounce) package frozen chopped spinach, thawed
1 clove garlic, finely chopped (garlic powder may be substituted)
¼ cup vegetable oil
1 teaspoon instant chicken bouillon

½ cup water
½ teaspoon basil leaves
1 cup cottage cheese
½ teaspoon salt
¼ cup Parmesan or Romano cheese, grated
parsley

1. Cook fettuccini according to package directions and drain.

2. Drain thawed spinach well. In a large skillet, cook spinach and garlic in oil for 5 minutes, stirring frequently.

3. Dissolve bouillon in boiling water. Add bouillon, basil, cottage cheese, and salt to spinach. Stir over low heat until blended.

4. Toss spinach mixture, fettuccini, and grated cheese together. Serve in heated dish, garnished with parsley.

Leftovers may be refrigerated and reheated.

Marinated Cheese Noodles

YIELDS: 8-10 servings

An appealing accent to a baked ham.

6	cups water	1	small jar pimentos, minced
6	tablespoons chicken bouillon	¼	teaspoon Tabasco sauce
1	(8-ounce) package fine noodles	1	teaspoon Worcestershire sauce
1½	cups large curd cottage cheese	1	(10-ounce) package extra sharp Cracker Barrel cheese, grated
1½	cups sour cream		
1	clove garlic, minced		
2	tablespoons onion, minced		

1. Bring water to a boil and stir in bouillon. Add noodles and cook on low heat until all the liquid is absorbed into the noodles, 20-30 minutes.

2. Mix cottage cheese, sour cream, garlic, onion, pimentos, Tabasco sauce, and Worcestershire sauce together. Add noodles.

3. Place half of noodle mixture in a 3 quart casserole dish and top with half of the grated cheese. Add remaining noodle mixture and top with remaining cheese. Let marinate for 2 hours or overnight before baking.

4. Bake, covered, in a preheated 350 degree oven for 1 hour. Remove lid and bake 15 additional minutes.

Must start preparation a few hours in advance. Freezes well 2 to 3 weeks.

Helpful Hints: To cook pasta ahead, cook pasta in water with 1 teaspoon salt until "al dente." Drain and cool under cold running water. When cooled, toss with 1 tablespoon oil for 8 ounces dried pasta. Place in bowl, cover and chill.

Microwave Rice Casserole

YIELDS: 4-6 servings

This makes an attractive side dish for your favorite roast.

2 cups water	1 (2.5-ounce) jar mushrooms, sliced and drained
2 chicken bouillon cubes	½ (10-ounce) package frozen peas, uncooked
1 cup raw rice	
¼ cup margarine	¼ cup green onions, sliced
2 tablespoons fresh parsley, chopped, or	salt and pepper to taste
1 teaspoon parsley flakes	

1. Place water in a 2 quart casserole dish in the microwave on high for 5-6 minutes, until water boils.

2. Mix all remaining ingredients in casserole dish. Cover. Microwave on 50% power for 15 minutes or until rice is done.

May cook earlier. Reheat, covered, on high; no water added. Freezes well.

Mideastern Style Rice

YIELDS: 4 servings

Raisins and almonds add an appetizing touch to this side dish.

1 medium onion, chopped	¼ cup seedless raisins
¼ cup butter or margarine	½ cup slivered almonds, toasted
1⅓ cups Minute Rice, uncooked	
1⅓ cups beef bouillon (or 2 beef bouillon cubes dissolved in 1⅓ cups water)	2 tablespoons fresh parsley, chopped

1. Saute onion in butter in large skillet until tender, but not brown, approximately 5 minutes. Add rice and saute for 3 minutes. Pour in bouillon and add raisins. Bring to a boil. Remove from heat; cover and let stand 5 minutes.

2. Fluff with a fork and stir in almonds and parsley.

✿ ACCOMPANIMENTS

Parmesan Pasta with Fresh Tomatoes   YIELDS: 8-10 servings

Cheese it up according to your personal taste.

2 pounds tomatoes (6 medium)	1 teaspoon dried basil
1 pound thin spaghetti	1 teaspoon dried oregano
2 tablespoons vegetable or olive oil	¼ cup green onion, thinly sliced
1 large clove garlic, finely chopped	½ teaspoon salt
2 tablespoons margarine	½ teaspoon pepper
¼ cup parsley, chopped	⅓ cup Parmesan cheese (or more to taste)

1. Remove skin from tomatoes by placing in boiling water for 1-2 minutes. Cut tomatoes in half crosswise. Gently squeeze out seeds, and remove cores; discard. Cut tomatoes into ½ inch chunks; keep at room temperature. (The above may be done several hours ahead.)

2. Cook spaghetti following label directions until just barely tender.

3. Heat oil in small skillet over low heat. Saute garlic until softened but not colored, about 2 minutes; add the margarine and melt.

4. Transfer drained hot spaghetti to large bowl. Add margarine mixture, tomatoes, parsley, basil, oregano, green onion, salt, and pepper. Toss. Add Parmesan cheese and lightly toss. Serve immediately.

Helpful Hints: To keep pasta from boiling over, add a tablespoon of oil to the pot. This also helps keep it from sticking.

Apple-Maraschino Coffee Cake

YIELDS: 15 servings

1	cup butter or margarine	1	teaspoon salt
2	cups sugar	4	cups apples, peeled and diced
2	eggs		
2	cups flour	½	cup walnuts, chopped
2	teaspoons baking powder	½	cup maraschino cherries, diced
1	teaspoon cinnamon		

1. Cream butter, sugar, and eggs together.

2. Sift flour, baking powder, cinnamon, and salt together. Add to creamed mixture and blend well. Fold in apples, walnuts, and maraschino cherries.

3. Spoon batter into greased and floured 9 x 13 inch pan. Bake in a preheated 350 degree oven for 50-60 minutes.

Caramel Pecan Rolls

YIELDS: 8-10 servings

5	tablespoons butter or margarine	3	tablespoons butter or margarine, softened
¾	cup brown sugar, packed	¼	cup sugar
¼	cup water	2	teaspoons cinnamon
½	cup pecans, chopped		
2	(8-ounce) cans crescent rolls		

1. Preheat oven to 350 degrees. In ungreased 13 x 9 x 2 inch baking pan, melt 5 tablespoons butter in oven. Stir in brown sugar, water, and pecans.

2. Separate each can of rolls into 4 rectangles, press to seal. Spread 3 tablespoons softened butter over rolls. Combine cinnamon and sugar, and sprinkle over dough.

3. Starting at shorter side, roll up each rectangle. Cut each roll into 4 slices, forming 32 pieces. Place cut side down in pan. Bake 25-30 minutes. Invert immediately to remove and serve.

Cranberry Swirl Coffee Cake

YIELDS: 10-12 servings

A favorite at a brunch.

2	cups flour	1	cup sour cream
1	teaspoon baking soda	2	teaspoons vanilla or
1	teaspoon baking powder		almond flavoring
½	teaspoon salt	1	(7-ounce) can whole
½	cup shortening		cranberry sauce
1	cup sugar	⅓	cup nuts, chopped
2	eggs		

1. Sift together flour, baking soda, baking powder, and salt; set aside.

2. Cream shortening and sugar. Gradually add unbeaten eggs, one at a time, using mixer at medium speed. Reduce speed and add sifted dry ingredients, alternating with sour cream, ending with dry ingredients. Add flavoring.

3. Grease an 8 inch tube pan. Spoon layer of batter in pan. Swirl half of the cranberry sauce on batter. Add remaining batter and swirl remaining cranberry sauce on top. Sprinkle with nuts. Bake in a preheated 350 degree oven for 55 minutes. Cool cake in pan 5-10 minutes before removing.

ICING

¾	cup powdered sugar	1	tablespoon warm water
½	teaspoon vanilla or		
	almond flavoring		

1. Mix all ingredients and spread over top of cake. Let icing drizzle over sides.

Devil's River Sour Cream Cake

YIELDS: 16-20 slices

Made from a cake mix and layered with a crunchy cinnamon filling. You'll enjoy this easy to make recipe.

CAKE
1	Duncan Hines Butter Recipe Golden Cake Mix	¼	cup sugar
		4	eggs
⅔	cup oil	1	cup sour cream

1. Blend cake mix, oil, sugar, eggs, and sour cream. Beat at medium speed for 4 minutes.

STREUSEL
6	tablespoons brown sugar	1	cup nuts, chopped
2	teaspoons cinnamon		

1. Combine streusel ingredients. In the bottom of a greased bundt pan, sprinkle a layer of streusel mixture. Add ½ of cake batter, sprinkle with ½ remaining streusel mixture, add other ½ cake batter, and top with remaining streusel.

2. Bake in a preheated 350 degree oven for 45-55 minutes. Remove from pan immediately.

May be prepared 3 to 4 days ahead. Freezes well.

Helpful Hints: Cooling properly can also eliminate cracking. Cakes should be left in the pan in a switched off oven with the door slightly ajar until almost room temperature—several hours. Then refrigerate. Bring to room temperature to serve.

French Breakfast Puffs

YIELDS: 3 dozen small puffs

These pop-in-your-mouth goodies can become almost addictive.

⅓	cup butter	1½	teaspoons baking powder
½	cup sugar	½	teaspoon salt
1	egg	¼	teaspoon nutmeg
1½	cups flour	½	cup milk

1. Mix butter, sugar, and egg together; set aside. In a separate bowl, mix flour, baking powder, salt, and nutmeg.

2. Stir flour mixture into sugar mixture alternately with the milk until all are combined.

3. Spoon batter into greased 1½ inch muffin cups, filling cups ¾ full. Bake in a preheated 350 degree oven for 20-25 minutes. Turn out when done.

TOPPING

1	teaspoon cinnamon	½	cup melted butter
½	cup sugar		

1. Combine cinnamon and sugar. Immediately after baking, while puffs are still hot, roll puffs in melted butter and the sugar-cinnamon mixture.

Must use small muffin cups. May be prepared 1 day ahead. Freezes well.

Helpful Hints: Always sift dry ingredients onto creased waxed paper. Fewer bowls and easy to add while stirring.

Kolachi
(Czechoslovakian Nut Roll)

YIELDS: 4 nut rolls

A recipe passed through generations of love and served at baptisms, weddings, and most family gatherings.

4½ cups flour	1 cup milk
2 tablespoons sugar	2 cakes yeast, crumbled
1¾ cups margarine	(do not use dry yeast)
6 egg yolks, reserve whites for filling	

1. Combine flour and sugar; cut margarine into mixture as for pie crust. Mix well.

2. Whip yolks with milk and add crumbled cakes of yeast. Place this liquid mixture into flour and sugar mixture.

3. Work with hands and gently knead dough until smooth and elastic, about 8-10 minutes. Divide into 4 sections and wrap each in plastic wrap. Place in refrigerator several hours or overnight.

FILLING

6 egg whites	1 pound walnuts, ground
2 cups sugar	1 teaspoon vanilla

1. Whip egg whites until stiff. Sprinkle sugar into egg whites. Fold vanilla and walnuts into egg white mixture.

2. Roll chilled dough on lightly floured surface. Spread a thin layer of nut filling over entire surface of dough.

3. Gently roll into long roll, pinching each end closed. Place on baking sheet, cover with a soft cloth, and let rise for about an hour.

4. Bake in a preheated 350 degree oven for 40-45 minutes or until golden brown.

To serve, slice and sprinkle with a light dusting of powdered sugar.

May be frozen. Wrap in foil and place in a plastic bag until ready to serve.

New England Blueberry Tea Cake

YIELDS: 10-12 servings

2	cups sifted flour	¾	cup sugar
2	teaspoons baking powder	1	egg, unbeaten
½	teaspoon salt	½	cup milk
¼	cup butter	2	cups blueberries, fresh or frozen

1. Sift together flour, baking powder, and salt; set aside.

2. Cream butter and gradually beat in sugar. Add egg and milk, and beat until smooth. Add dry ingredients to creamed butter mixture and fold in blueberries.

3. Spread batter in a greased and floured 8 or 9 inch square pan.

TOPPING

½	cup sugar	½	teaspoon cinnamon
¼	cup flour	¼	cup butter or margarine

1. Mix together sugar, flour, and cinnamon. Cut in butter to make coarse crumbs. Sprinkle crumb topping over batter.

2. Bake in a preheated 375 degree oven for 40-45 minutes.

Easy to prepare and freezes well.

Helpful Hints: Never beat a muffin mixture, only stir ingredients for best results.

Norwegian Kringler

YIELDS: 12-15 servings

An irresistible cake laced with a pleasing almond flavor.

1	cup flour	½	cup butter or
2	tablespoons sugar		margarine
¼	teaspoon salt	2	tablespoons water, cold

1. Mix flour, sugar, and salt together. Cut in butter until the mixture has the appearance of cornmeal. Add the water and mix until it will hold together in a ball.

2. Press evenly into a 9 x 13 inch pan.

FILLING

1	cup water	4	eggs
½	cup butter or margarine	½	teaspoon almond extract
1	cup flour		

1. Heat butter and water in a pan until butter melts. Bring to a rolling boil. Add the flour, all at once, remove from heat immediately. Beat vigorously until you have a smooth paste. Stir in eggs, one at a time, and beat until batter is smooth and shiny. Add almond extract. Spread over pastry base.

2. Bake in a preheated 425 degree oven for 30 minutes until golden and puffy. Cool. The pastry will fall.

ICING

1	cup powdered sugar	½	teaspoon almond extract
1	tablespoon butter, melted	¾	cup toasted almonds, sliced
2-3	tablespoons milk		

1. Mix powdered sugar, butter, milk, and almond extract to a spreading consistency. Spread on pastry. Sprinkle with sliced toasted almonds.

Pumpkin Roll

YIELDS: 12-16 servings

This hearty cake may be served as a dessert or as a breakfast accompaniment.

3 egg yolks	¼ teaspoon salt
1 cup sugar	½ cup nuts, chopped
⅔ cup pumpkin	(optional)
¾ cup flour	powdered sugar
1 teaspoon baking soda	
½ teaspoon cinnamon	

1. Beat egg yolks 5 minutes, gradually adding sugar and pumpkin. Sift together dry ingredients and then mix with egg mixture.

2. Spread batter in a greased and floured 10 x 15 inch jelly roll pan. Bake in a preheated 375 degree oven for 15 minutes.

3. Invert hot cake onto dish towel, sprinkle with powdered sugar, and roll up jelly roll style in the dish towel to cool.

FILLING

1 cup powdered sugar	2 tablespoons butter
1 (8-ounce) package	¾ teaspoon vanilla
cream cheese	

1. Beat ingredients until smooth, about 5 to 10 minutes.

2. Unroll cake, spread with filling, and roll it back up.

May be prepared 2 days ahead.

Helpful Hints: To keep cakes from sticking, sprinkle the tins with equal parts of flour and fine sugar.

Sour Cream Coffee Cake

YIELDS: 10-12 servings

What a way to start a day!

¾ cup butter, softened	2 cups flour
2 cups sugar	1 teaspoon baking powder
1 cup sour cream	½ teaspoon salt
2 eggs, beaten	1 cup pecans, chopped
1 teaspoon vanilla	(optional)

1. Cream butter, sugar, and sour cream. Add eggs and vanilla. Combine dry ingredients and add to mixture. Chopped pecans may be added to the batter.

2. Thoroughly grease a 10 inch bundt pan.

FILLING

1 cup pecans, chopped	1 teaspoon ground cinnamon
3 tablespoons dark brown sugar	

1. Make filling by combining nuts, brown sugar, and cinnamon.

2. Pour half of cake batter in the pan and sprinkle with all of the filling. Add remainder of batter. Bake in a preheated 350 degree oven for 45 minutes or until done. Let cake cool before turning out.

GLAZE

1 cup powdered sugar	2-4 tablespoons condensed milk

1. Combine milk and powdered sugar. Mix well and drizzle over cake while still warm.

Helpful Hints: Never beat egg whites in an aluminum pan as it will darken them.

❦ ACCOMPANIMENTS

Bubble Bread

YIELDS: 1 loaf

1	loaf Rhodes frozen bread dough, white	½	teaspoon garlic powder
¼	cup butter or margarine, melted	1	teaspoon dried parsley flakes
1	egg, beaten	¼	teaspoon salt

1. Thaw and soften dough. Blend together cooled melted butter, egg, garlic powder, parsley, and salt.

2. Cut off pieces of softened dough about the size of small walnuts. Dip into butter mixture. Place pieces of dough in greased loaf pan until all dough is used. Cover, let rise until doubled in size, about 1 hour.

3. Bake in a preheated 375 degree oven for 30 minutes. After baking, brush with melted butter. Cool on wire rack.

Mom's Bread Sticks

YIELDS: 3 dozen

You may freeze these indefinitely and have them ready to serve when surprise guests arrive.

1	cake of yeast	¾	cup boiling water
¼	cup lukewarm water	1	egg
¼	cup sugar	3½	cups flour
1	teaspoon salt		your favorite vanilla frosting
1½	tablespoons Crisco shortening		

1. Crumble yeast in lukewarm water.

2. Combine sugar, salt, shortening, and boiling water. Cool to lukewarm. Add yeast mixture and beaten egg. Stir in flour, mix thoroughly, cover, and let rise until double in size, about 1 hour.

3. Knead well, about 8-10 minutes, and form into rolls or bread sticks. Deep fry at 375 degrees until golden brown. Cool and frost with your favorite vanilla frosting.

Cheese Topped French Bread

YIELDS: 1 loaf

May be made ahead and rewarmed in the microwave.

1 loaf French bread, cut in half lengthwise	½ teaspoon garlic powder
1½ cups mayonnaise	1 teaspoon Dijon style mustard
2 cups Cheddar cheese, shredded	½ cup bacon bits
1 medium onion, finely chopped	

1. Mix mayonnaise, cheese, onion, garlic powder, and mustard together until well blended. Spread half of mixture on each half of bread. Sprinkle bacon bits on both pieces.

2. Bake in a preheated 350 degree oven until hot and bubbly. Remove and let cool a few minutes. Cut in strips crosswise and serve warm.

Dill Casserole Bread

YIELDS: 1 round loaf

1 package dry yeast	2 tablespoons dill seed
¼ cup warm water	1 tablespoon butter, melted
1 cup creamed cottage cheese	1 egg, unbeaten
2 tablespoons sugar	2¼ to 2½ cups flour, sifted
1 tablespoon instant minced onion	1 teaspoon salt
	¼ teaspoon baking soda

1. Add yeast to warm water. When dissolved, add cottage cheese that has been heated to lukewarm. Stir in sugar, onion, dill, butter, and egg. Sift salt and baking soda with flour and gradually add to dough.

2. Knead for 10 minutes. Let rise in greased bowl in warm place until double in bulk, about 1 hour. Punch down and place in 1½ quart round, ovenproof casserole. Let rise again 30-40 minutes.

3. Bake in a preheated 350 degree oven for 40-45 minutes.

Coconut Bread

YIELDS: 1 loaf

Tied up in a cheery bow this makes a nice welcome for a new neighbor.

1¼ cups coconut, shredded, toasted, and cooled
2¾ cups flour
1 cup sugar
4 teaspoons baking powder
1 teaspoon salt

1½ cups milk
1 egg, beaten
2 tablespoons oil
1 teaspoon coconut extract

1. Toast coconut on cookie sheet in a preheated 350 degree oven for 5 minutes. Cool.

2. Mix together flour, sugar, baking powder, and salt. Add coconut to dry ingredients. Blend well.

3. In separate bowl, mix milk, egg, oil, and extract. Stir two mixtures together until moistened.

4. Pour into greased 9 x 5 inch loaf pan. Bake in a preheated 350 degree oven for 1 hour. Cool in pan 10 minutes.

Helpful Hints: To cut fresh bread easily, use a hot knife.

Oatmeal Tea Bread

YIELDS: 1 loaf

A moist, rich flavor.

1¼	cups flour, sifted	¼	teaspoon ginger
1	cup quick rolled oats	¼	teaspoon ground cloves
¾	cup sugar	2	eggs
1	teaspoon salt	1¼	cups applesauce
1	teaspoon baking powder	½	cups raisins (optional)
1	teaspoon baking soda	⅓	cup vegetable oil
1	teaspoon cinnamon	¼	cup milk

1. Mix together dry ingredients in large bowl; set aside.

2. Combine eggs, applesauce, raisins, oil, and milk in bowl. Stir applesauce mixture by hand into flour mixture until flour is moistened. Pour batter into a greased 9 x 5 x 3 inch loaf pan.

TOPPING

2	tablespoons brown sugar, packed	¼	teaspoon cinnamon
2	tablespoons pecans, chopped		

1. Mix brown sugar, pecans, and cinnamon together in a small bowl. Sprinkle on top of batter. Bake in a preheated 350 degree oven for 55-60 minutes, or until toothpick comes out clean. Cool in pan for 10 minutes. Remove from pan and cool on wire rack.

Helpful Hints: When bread is baking, a small dish of water in the oven will help to keep the crust from getting too hard.

Pear Bread

A unique fruit flavor.

½ cup butter or margarine	1 teaspoon baking powder
1 cup sugar	¼ cup yogurt or buttermilk
2 eggs	1 cup pears, chopped
2 cups flour	1 teaspoon vanilla
½ teaspoon baking soda	

1. Combine butter and sugar. Mix until creamed. Add eggs.

2. Combine all dry ingredients and add to mix. By hand, gently stir in buttermilk or yogurt, pears, and vanilla. Pour into a greased 9 x 5 x 3 inch loaf pan.

3. Bake in a preheated 350 degree oven for 50-60 minutes. Remove from pan after 10 minutes. Cool on cooling rack.

Pumpkin Bread in Clay Pots

An instant gift! Just add a pretty ribbon.

2 new 4 inch clay pots	1⅔ cups flour
1½ cups sugar	¼ teaspoon baking powder
2 beaten eggs	1 teaspoon baking soda
⅓ cup Crisco shortening	½ teaspoon pumpkin pie spice
1 cup canned pumpkin	½ teaspoon salt
¼ cup water	⅓ cup raisins

1. Season Pots: Bake pot, greased with oil, empty, in a preheated 425 degree oven for 30 minutes. Grease again and bake another 30 minutes. After seasoning, line bottom of pots with foil.

2. Mix sugar, eggs, shortening, pumpkin, and water. Combine dry ingredients and add slowly. Stir in raisins.

3. Fill pots ¾ full. Bake in a preheated 325 - 350 degree oven for 45-60 minutes or until toothpick comes out clean. Bread will mushroom out of pot. Cool and cover with plastic wrap.

Potato Rusks

YIELDS: 20 rolls

1 cup sugar	6 cups flour
1 cup mashed potatoes, warm	1 cup butter, melted
1 package dry yeast	2 tablespoons butter
1 cup lukewarm water	2 tablespoons shortening
4 eggs, beaten	2 tablespoons flour
1 teaspoon salt	sugar to sprinkle on top

1. Add sugar to the mashed potatoes and stir until smooth. In a large mixing bowl, add yeast to the warm water. Stir until yeast dissolves; add eggs and potato mixture to this. Stir in salt and 3 cups of flour. Add the melted butter, then the remaining 3 cups of flour.

2. Let dough rise until light, about 2 hours. Turn out onto a floured surface and roll out to ¾ inch thickness. Cut with 3 inch round biscuit cutter and place on greased cookie sheet. Let rise again until doubled in size, about 1 hour.

3. Cream together butter, shortening, and flour until it is very soft, almost liquid. With a pastry brush, delicately brush this mixture over the entire top of the rolls, being careful not to deflate the rolls. Sprinkle with sugar lightly.

4. Bake in a preheated 350 degree oven for 12-15 minutes or until pale golden in color.

5. To freeze, bake until very lightly baked, about 10-12 minutes. Remove from oven, cool, and freeze in plastic bags. To use, let thaw in bags 30 minutes. Place on baking sheet and bake in a preheated 350 degree oven for 10 minutes or until pale golden. Freezes well 2 to 3 months.

Helpful Hints: Run hot water over outside of cup when measuring shortening and it will slip right out.

⚜ ACCOMPANIMENTS

Bran Muffins

A make ahead batter that keeps well up to 6 weeks.

4	eggs	2½	cups sugar
1	quart buttermilk	5	teaspoons baking soda
1	cup oil	2	teaspoons salt
5	cups flour	1	(15-ounce) box Raisin Bran

1. Mix eggs, buttermilk, and oil. Add flour, sugar, baking soda, and salt; mix well. Stir in Raisin Bran.

2. Refrigerate 24 hours in an airtight container. Batter may be stored up to 6 weeks in airtight container in refrigerator.

3. Fill greased muffin cups ⅔ full. Bake in a preheated 400 degree oven for 15-20 minutes.

Batter must be prepared 1 day ahead.

Lemon Muffins

Try in place of shortcake with fresh strawberries.

2	cups flour	½	cup fresh lemon juice
1	cup sugar	3	eggs
2	tablespoons baking powder		finely grated peel of 1 lemon
1	teaspoon salt	2	tablespoons oil
1	cup butter	2	tablespoons sugar

1. In large bowl, combine flour, 1 cup sugar, baking powder, and salt. Blend well.

2. In saucepan, melt butter. Remove from heat and stir in lemon juice, eggs, lemon peel, and oil. Stir egg mixture into dry ingredients and blend with spoon until just moistened.

3. Spoon into buttered muffin cups and sprinkle top of batter with sugar. Bake in a preheated 400 degree oven for 15-20 minutes until lightly brown. For mini-muffins bake for 12 minutes.

ACCOMPANIMENTS

Cheese Filled Bacon Muffins

1½ cups Hungry Jack
    Buttermilk or Extra
    Light Pancake and
    Waffle Mix
1 cup milk
½ pound bacon, crisply
    cooked and crumbled
    (reserve ⅓ cup
    drippings)

1 egg
⅓ cup green pepper, chopped
⅓ cup onion, chopped
3 ounces Velveeta cheese,
    cut into 12 (½-inch)
    cubes

1. In large bowl, combine pancake mix, milk, reserved bacon drippings, and egg. Stir until blended. Add bacon, green pepper, and onion. Mix well.

2. Line with paper baking cups or grease 12 muffin cups; fill ⅔ full with mixture. Press a cheese cube in center of batter.

3. Bake in a preheated 400 degree oven for 15-20 minutes or until golden brown. Remove from pan immediately. Serve warm.

Herbed Bread Sticks

Delicious along side your favorite pasta dish.

1 loaf French or
    Italian bread
1 cup butter, melted

2 cloves garlic, crushed
¼ cup parsley, chopped

1. Cut loaf of bread into thirds. Cut each third in half, lengthwise.

2. Combine melted butter, garlic, and parsley. Brush on bread sections. Cut each section into ¾ inch slices. Wrap sticks in aluminum foil, securely. May refrigerate until serving.

3. Bake in a preheated 400 degree oven for 8-10 minutes or until heated through. Unwrap and bake 3-5 minutes longer or until golden.

Coffee Cake Muffins

YIELDS: 12 muffins

These small, individual coffee cakes are a big hit at buffets.

1½ cups flour, sifted	¼ cup brown sugar, packed
½ cup sugar	¼ cup walnuts or pecans,
2 teaspoons baking powder	chopped
½ teaspoon salt	1 tablespoon flour
¼ cup shortening	1 teaspoon cinnamon
1 egg, beaten	1 tablespoon butter,
½ cup milk	melted

1. Sift 1½ cups flour, sugar, baking powder, and salt into mixing bowl. Cut in shortening until mixture resembles coarse crumbs.

2. Mix egg and milk, add to flour mixture. Stir until just moistened.

3. Combine brown sugar, nuts, 1 tablespoon flour, cinnamon, and melted butter.

4. Spoon half of batter in greased muffin cups. Sprinkle nut mixture over batter, then top with the remaining batter, filling cups one-half full. Bake in a preheated 350 degree oven for 20 minutes.

Helpful Hints: Try using a single beater in your mixer when mixing stiff dough. It blends the dough very well and eliminates the problem of the beaters binding.

Orange Muffins

YIELDS: 36 small muffins

Delicious for breakfast or alongside a salad luncheon.

1	cup sugar	1	teaspoon baking soda
	juice of one orange	1	teaspoon salt
	(about ½ cup)	1	teaspoon orange rind,
½	cup butter, softened		grated
1	cup sugar	½	cup raisins
¾	cup sour cream	½	cup nuts, chopped
2	cups flour, sifted		

1. Mix sugar and orange juice. Set aside for dipping after muffins are cooked.

2. Cream butter and sugar; set aside. Sift dry ingredients together. Add sour cream alternately with the dry ingredients to creamed butter mixture. Fold in orange rind, raisins, and nuts. This is a stiff batter. Spoon batter into greased 1½ inch muffin cups, filling each cup completely full.

3. Bake in a preheated 375 degree oven for 12-15 minutes. While still warm, dip in sugar-orange juice mixture. Cool on a wire rack.

Helpful Hints: To remove the skin from oranges, place orange in boiling water for two minutes. Then place in cold water. The skin just slips off.

Sweet Potato Muffins

YIELDS: 24 small muffins

Served in a napkin lined basket along side a freshly brewed pot of coffee, you have an instant friendship warmer.

⅔	cup canned or cooked fresh sweet potatoes	½	teaspoon salt
4	tablespoons butter	½	teaspoon cinnamon
½	cup sugar	¼	teaspoon nutmeg
1	egg	½	cup milk
¾	cup flour	¼	cup pecans or walnuts, chopped
2	teaspoons baking powder	¼	cup raisins, chopped

1. Puree sweet potatoes in food processor or blender. Cream butter and sugar. Beat in egg and pureed sweet potatoes.

2. Sift flour with baking powder, salt, cinnamon, and nutmeg. Add the dry ingredients alternately by hand with the milk and nuts and raisins, mixing just until blended. Do not overmix.

3. Spoon into greased 1½ inch muffin cups, filling each cup completely full. Sprinkle a little cinnamon and sugar on top of each muffin.

4. Bake in a preheated 400 degree oven for 25 minutes.

Helpful Hints: Hard boiled eggs spin quickly and evenly. Raw eggs wobble slowly.

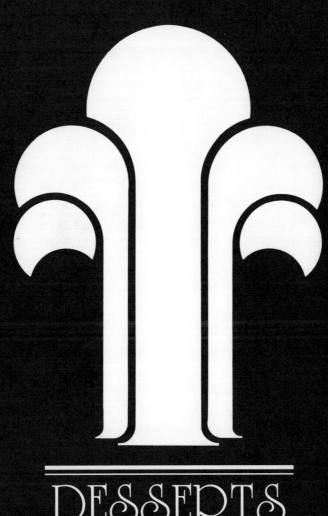

DESSERTS

 # DESSERTS

DESSERTS

Apple Brown Betty with Lemon Sauce   YIELDS: 4-6 servings

A traditional old-fashioned dessert that could add to the warmth of a winter fire.

APPLE BROWN BETTY

- 2 cups graham cracker crumbs
- 3 tablespoons butter, melted
- 3-4 medium apples, sliced
- ½ cup brown sugar, packed, (or granulated sugar or half of each)
- 1 tablespoon lemon juice
- ½ teaspoon grated lemon peel
- ⅓ cup hot water

1. Combine graham cracker crumbs and butter, stir over low heat until lightly browned. Pat ⅓ of graham cracker crumb mixture in greased 8 x 8 x 2 inch pan. Arrange half of sliced apples over crumbs.

2. Combine sugar, lemon juice, and peel. Sprinkle ½ of sugar mixture over apples.

3. Layer ⅓ more crumbs and remaining apples and sugar mixture. Sprinkle last ⅓ crumbs on top. Pour hot water over mixture. Bake in a preheated 375 degree oven for 30 to 40 minutes.

LEMON SAUCE

- 1 cup boiling water
- ½ cup sugar
- 1 tablespoon cornstarch
- dash of salt
- dash of nutmeg
- 2 tablespoons butter
- 1½ tablespoons lemon juice

1. Gradually add boiling water to sugar, cornstarch, salt, and nutmeg. Cook over low heat until clear. Add 2 tablespoons butter and 1½ tablespoons lemon juice. Drizzle sauce over each serving.

Apple Dumplings

YIELDS: 12 servings

Best served warm out of the oven.

CRUST

2⅔ cups flour
1 teaspoon salt

1 cup Crisco shortening
6-7 tablespoons cold water

1. Mix flour and salt together. Cut in shortening until consistency of meal. Sprinkle in water, 1 tablespoon at a time, stirring with a fork after each addition. Mix lightly until all flour is moistened and dough cleans side of bowl.

2. Form 2 balls of same size. Roll out 1 ball to form thin crust and line bottom of 9 x 12 inch baking dish with pastry. (Don't worry about taking dough up the sides.) Save other ball to form top crust.

FILLING

12 or more medium cooking apples (Jonathan's preferred)

¾ cup sugar
2 teaspoons cinnamon

1. Peel and slice apples. Spread into pan lined with pastry. Sprinkle with sugar and cinnamon. (Use more or less cinnamon to taste.)

2. Roll out top crust and place on top of apples. Do not put the crust together as a fluted pie. Instead, make sure top crust is pushed inside the edges of pan (allowing liquid sauce to run down in) and slit top.

SAUCE

½ cup brown sugar
½ cup sugar
1 tablespoon cinnamon
¼ teaspoon salt

½ teaspoon nutmeg
¼ cup margarine
¾ cup water

1. Combine sauce ingredients in saucepan. Bring to a boil over medium high heat. Pour over top of crust, making sure sauce goes inside evenly.

2. Bake in a preheated 400 degree oven for 10 minutes. Turn oven down to 375 degrees and bake an additional 40 minutes, or until nicely brown and apples are done.

Variation: Serve with whipping cream poured over the dumplings.

Black Bottoms

The chocolate chips sink to the bottom of these cupcakes with a rich creamy center.

FILLING

1	(8-ounce) package cream cheese, softened
1/3	cup sugar
1	egg

1/8	teaspoon salt
1	cup chocolate chips

1. Combine cream cheese, sugar, egg, and salt in a bowl. Beat until smooth. Mix in chocolate chips. Set aside.

CUPCAKES

1½	cups flour
1	cup sugar
1/3	cup cocoa
½	teaspoon salt
1	teaspoon baking soda

1/3	cup vegetable oil
1	cup water
1	tablespoon vinegar
1	teaspoon vanilla

1. Combine ingredients in order listed. Blend well on low speed of mixer. Fill 24 foil lined muffin cups ½ full with batter. Spoon approximately 1 tablespoon of cheese filling into each cupcake.

2. Bake in a preheated 350 degree oven for approximately 20 minutes or until cupcakes test done.

Note: Cupcakes may be made in mini muffin cups. Bake in a preheated 350 degree oven for approximately 15 minutes.

# DESSERTS

Baklava

YIELDS: 60 pieces

A sellout at Sugarplum Shoppe, our auxiliary fund raiser, every year!

SYRUP

5	cups sugar	1½	tablespoons light corn
2½	cups water		syrup
2	tablespoons fresh lemon	1	cinnamon stick
	juice (save rind)	4	cloves

1. Place ingredients in saucepan. Stir lightly. Add lemon rind. Bring to boil. Reduce to low and allow to simmer for 15 minutes (no longer). Remove spices and lemon rind.

2. Pour into glass container and allow to cool completely before pouring on pastry. (Syrup can be made in advance and stored for weeks in refrigerator, bring to room temperature.)

FILLING

1½	pounds English walnuts, ground fine	2	pounds butter, melted and clarified
1	cup sugar	2	pounds phyllo, cut
1½	teaspoons cinnamon		sheets in half
½	teaspoon allspice		

1. Mix walnuts, sugar, and spices. Set aside.

2. Butter a 17½ x 13½ x 1 inch pan with a pastry brush. Place 5 sheets of phyllo in pan, buttering generously between each sheet.

3. Sprinkle top sheet lightly with nut mixture. Cover with one sheet of phyllo. Butter this and cover with another sheet of phyllo and sprinkle with nut mixture. (Reserve 5 untorn sheets for final layer.)

4. Continue this process until all but the 5 reserved sheets are used. Place sheets on top, buttering generously between each one.

5. Make cuts horizontally across length of pan. Turn and cut diagonally to make diamond pattern.

6. Bake in a preheated 325 degree oven for 1 hour or until lightly browned. (Be certain phyllo is baked.)

continued

Baklava *continued*

7. Remove from oven and pour cooled syrup on pastry immediately. Let set in pan overnight so syrup will soak into pastry.

Hint: To keep phyllo from drying out, cover with plastic wrap and then dampened towel.

May be prepared ahead. Freezes well up to 3 months. Recipe may be halved and prepared in a 9 x 13 inch pan.

Banana Split Dessert

YIELDS: 12-16 servings

Go ahead - indulge!

2 cups graham cracker crumbs	4-5 bananas
½ cup margarine, melted	1 (8-ounce) Cool Whip garnish with cut-up cherries and nuts
½ cup soft margarine	
1½ cups powdered sugar	
2 eggs	
1 (17 to 20-ounce) can crushed pineapple, drained, reserve juice	

1. Mix graham cracker crumbs and melted margarine in 9 x 13 inch pan. Pat mixture on bottom of pan. Bake in a preheated 350 degree oven for 5 minutes. Cool.

2. Cream together ½ cup soft margarine and sugar. Add eggs, mix well for 10 minutes. Spread on graham cracker crust and refrigerate.

3. Drain crushed pineapple. Reserve juice in large bowl. Cut bananas in thick slices and place in pineapple juice.

4. Drain banana slices and arrange neatly on top of cream mixture. Sprinkle drained pineapple over banana slices. Frost with Cool Whip. Garnish top with cherries and nuts.

Easy. May be prepared ahead 1 day.

# DESSERTS

Bread Pudding with Irish Whiskey Sauce

YIELDS: 8 servings

A comforting dessert—but it can also be an elegant dinner party ending.

PUDDING

3 eggs	1 teaspoon vanilla
1 egg yolk	½ teaspoon cinnamon
2½ cups milk	3 cups French bread, diced
¾ cup sugar	and with crusts
¼ cup whipping cream	¼ cup dried currants
3 tablespoons Irish whiskey, divided	

1. Whisk eggs, yolk, milk, sugar, cream, 1 tablespoon whiskey, vanilla, and cinnamon in large bowl. Add bread; let soak at least 1 hour. Soak currants in remaining 2 tablespoons whiskey 1 hour.

2. Butter eight ¾-cup custard cups. Remove 1 tablespoon currants using slotted spoon; set aside.

3. Stir remaining 3 tablespoons undrained currants into bread mixture. Spoon into prepared cups.

4. Arrange in roasting pan. Add enough simmering water to pan to come half way up sides of cups. Bake in a preheated 350 degree oven until puddings are firm to touch, about 1 hour. Meanwhile prepare sauce.

continued

Bread Pudding with
Irish Whiskey Sauce *continued*

SAUCE

1 teaspoon cornstarch	3 egg yolks
1 cup milk, divided	3 tablespoons sugar
½ teaspoon vanilla	2 tablespoons Irish whiskey

1. Dissolve cornstarch in 2 tablespoons milk.

2. Scald remaining milk and vanilla in heavy small saucepan. Whisk cornstarch mixture into milk.

3. Whisk yolks and sugar in bowl until thick and pale. Gradually whisk in milk mixture. Whisk back into saucepan and stir over medium heat until sauce thickens enough to leave path on back of spoon when finger is drawn across. Do not boil. Remove from heat. Stir in whiskey.

4. Unmold puddings onto plates. Spoon sauce over. Sprinkle with reserved currants.

May prepare 1 day ahead. Store in molds. Reheat and unmold.

Brandied Coffee Velvet

YIELDS: 4 servings

A food processor makes this especially easy to prepare and a delightful after dinner touch.

2 tablespoons instant coffee	½ cup brandy
¼ cup warm water	1 quart vanilla ice cream
¼ cup chocolate syrup	whipped cream

1. Dissolve instant coffee in warm water. Add chocolate syrup, brandy, and vanilla ice cream.

2. Beat until smooth and well blended. Chill in freezer and take out about 30 minutes before serving. Pour into chilled glasses and top with whipped cream.

May be prepared 3 days ahead and frozen.

# DESSERTS

Chocolate Nut Bombe

YIELDS: 8-10 servings

Coffee ice cream is suggested but your choice of favorites can also be used.

1 quart coffee ice cream
½ cup walnuts, chopped
1 quart chocolate ice cream
1 pint vanilla ice cream
1 tablespoon brandy

2 (1-ounce) squares unsweetened chocolate, melted and cooled
¼ cup light corn syrup
1 egg
walnuts for garnish

1. Line a 2 quart mixing bowl with foil.

2. Soften coffee ice cream slightly; blend in walnuts. Pack over bottom and sides of bowl forming a shell. Freeze until firm.

3. Soften chocolate ice cream slightly. Pack over coffee nut layer to form second shell. Freeze.

4. Soften vanilla ice cream slightly. Blend in brandy. Pack in center of mold. Freeze 3 to 4 hours.

5. Turn mold out onto a cold tray. Peel off foil and return to freezer.

6. Combine cooled chocolate, corn syrup, and egg in a small bowl. Beat 3 to 4 minutes. Quickly frost mold.

7. Sprinkle top and sides with chopped walnuts. Freeze at least 4 hours. (A deep freeze works best.)

May be prepared ahead.

Danish Lemon Snow

YIELDS: 8-10 servings

Custom: When this dessert is served on Christmas Eve, whoever gets the nut, gets to open the first Christmas present.

3 **eggs, separated**	1 **teaspoon lemon rind**
1 **cup sugar**	1 **teaspoon orange rind**
1 **envelope Knox gelatin, unflavored**	2 **(8-ounce) containers whipping cream**
½ **cup water**	2 **teaspoons vanilla**
2 **tablespoons lemon juice**	**cherries, red and green (optional)**
½ **cup orange juice**	1 **nut (optional)**

1. Beat egg yolks and sugar until light lemon color. Set aside.

2. Soak the gelatin in ½ cup water. Melt over boiling water in double boiler or place gelatin in bowl and place in pan of hot water on stove.

3. Add gelatin to egg mixture, then add juices and grated lemon and orange rinds. Let stand in refrigerator until mixture begins to thicken, about 10 minutes.

4. Beat one container of whipping cream with one teaspoon of vanilla until peaks fold over. Beat egg whites until peaks fold over.

5. Fold whipping cream into gelatin mixture. Next fold in beaten egg whites.

6. Pour in glass bowl or souffle dish. Put one nut in mixture wherever you like. Refrigerate.

7. Beat remaining whipping cream and vanilla. Spread over lemon mixture. Garnish with cherries.

May prepare 1 day ahead.

DESSERTS

Easy Phyllo Dessert

YIELDS: 12 servings

SYRUP

2   cups sugar
1½ cups water

2   teaspoons lemon juice

1. Boil all ingredients slowly for 10 minutes. Cool.

PASTRY AND FILLING

1   pound phyllo
1½ cups butter,
    melted

12 ounces cream cheese,
    softened
1   pound Ricotta cheese

1. Remove phyllo from box, but do not spread out sheets. Cut the phyllo into shreds along the length of the pastry. Toss the entire amount of phyllo with all the melted butter.

2. Beat the cheeses together until well blended. Place ½ of the phyllo in a 13 x 9 inch pan. Distribute the phyllo evenly with your fingers. Pour in cheese filling and top with remaining phyllo. Press down lightly on the pastry.

3. Cover and bake in a preheated 350 degree oven for 30 minutes. Remove foil and bake an additional 30 minutes or until golden brown. Cut into squares and serve warm with syrup.

Butterscotch Dipper

YIELDS: 6-8 servings

½   cup butter or margarine
2   cups brown sugar, packed
1   cup light corn syrup
2   tablespoons water

1   (14-ounce) can Eagle Brand
    sweetened condensed milk
1   teaspoon vanilla
3-4 apples, cut in slices

1. In saucepan, melt butter. Stir in sugar, syrup, and water. Bring to a boil.

2. Stir in milk and continue stirring mixture until it reaches thread stage (230 degrees). Add vanilla. Pour into fondue pot to keep warm. Dip apple slices into it.

Frozen Banana Split

YIELDS: 8-12 servings

Great for teenage parties, picnics, and club meetings.

CRUST
½ cup butter, melted
1½ cups graham cracker
   crumbs

¼ cup sugar

1. Combine and pat in bottom of 9 x 13 inch pan.

FILLING
3-4 bananas
   chopped nuts

1 quart or more, ice cream
   of choice, softened

1. Slice bananas lengthwise over crust. Spread ice cream over bananas. Sprinkle with chopped nuts and freeze.

SAUCE
1 cup chocolate chips
½ cup butter
2 cups powdered sugar
1½ cups evaporated milk

1 teaspoon vanilla
1 (8-ounce) Cool Whip
   chopped nuts

1. Melt chocolate chips and butter. Add powdered sugar and evaporated milk. Cook until smooth and thick, up to ½ hour. Add vanilla. Cool completely and pour over dessert. Freeze.

2. Remove from freezer a few minutes before serving. Top with Cool Whip and chopped nuts.

Stores in freezer for up to 3 weeks.

 # DESSERTS

Karen's Cream Puffs

YIELDS: 8-10 puffs

You can make these puffs ahead and freeze if you add the filling later. The whipped cream makes the filling delicate and smooth.

CREAM PUFFS

1	cup water	1	cup flour
½	cup butter or margarine	4	eggs

1. Heat water and butter to rolling boil. Stir in flour. Stir vigorously over low heat until mixture forms a ball or leaves sides of pan. Remove from heat and beat in eggs thoroughly, one at a time. Beat until smooth.

2. Drop dough by ¼ cupfuls, 3 inches apart, onto ungreased baking sheet. Bake in a preheated 400 degree oven for 35-40 minutes until puffed, golden brown, and dry.

3. Cool. Cut off tops. Pull out soft dough.

FILLING

3	egg yolks	1	teaspoon vanilla
1½	cups milk	½	pint whipping cream
¾	cup sugar	3	tablespoons sugar
¼	cup flour		powdered sugar, to dust
½	teaspoon salt		

1. In medium pan, combine egg yolks, milk, ¾ cup sugar, flour, and salt. Bring to rolling boil, stirring constantly. Cook until thick. Remove from heat. Stir in vanilla. Refrigerate until cool.

2. Beat whipping cream until slightly thick. Gradually add 3 tablespoons sugar. Beat until thick. Fold into cooled cream filling.

3. Fill puffs with cream filling, replace tops, and dust with powdered sugar. Refrigerate.

Eclairs

YIELDS: 8-10 eclairs

Irresistible!

1. Prepare Karen's Cream Puff dough and filling.

2. Instead of dropping dough by ¼ cupfuls, form dough on cookie sheet into oblongs, 1 inch by 4 inch. Bake in a preheated 400 degree oven for 30-35 minutes. Cool.

3. To fill, either force filling into one end with pastry bag or cut in half lengthwise and spoon in.

CHOCOLATE GLAZE

1 square (1-ounce) unsweetened chocolate, melted	1 tablespoon cream
	2 teaspoons boiling water
	1 teaspoon butter
¾ cup powdered sugar	½ teaspoon vanilla extract
1 teaspoon dark corn syrup	

1. In heavy saucepan, combine all ingredients except vanilla extract. Place over low heat and stir constantly until butter melts.

2. Remove from heat and add vanilla. Cool slightly and spread over top of eclairs. Refrigerate until serving time. Cover lightly with plastic wrap.

May be made 1 day ahead.

 DESSERTS

Frozen Chocolate Almond Mousse

YIELDS: 8 servings

A beautiful presentation...a divine finish for an elegant dinner.

⅔ cup almonds, chopped	1 (6-ounce) package
½ cup graham cracker	semi-sweet chocolate chips
crumbs	2 eggs, separated
3 tablespoons sugar, divided	1 cup whipping cream
3 tablespoons butter,	3 tablespoons dark rum
melted	
1 pint chocolate chip	
ice cream, softened	

1. Toast almonds in a preheated 300 degree oven for 15 to 20 minutes; finely chop while warm.

2. Combine ⅓ cup chopped almonds with the graham cracker crumbs, 1 tablespoon sugar, and melted butter. Pack evenly in oiled 8 inch springform pan.

3. Bake in a preheated 350 degree oven for 10 minutes. Cool, then place in freezer until chilled.

4. Spoon softened ice cream over crumb crust evenly. Return to freezer.

5. Melt chocolate over hot water.

6. Beat egg whites to soft peaks. Beat in remaining 2 tablespoons of sugar, a tablespoon at a time.

7. With same beater, beat ½ cup whipping cream to soft peaks.

8. In separate bowl, beat egg yolks; then beat in warm melted chocolate and rum. Fold in egg whites; then beaten cream. Set aside 2 tablespoons almonds and fold remainder into the chocolate mixture.

9. Turn into the pan over ice cream. Sprinkle reserved almonds over the top. Return to freezer until frozen.

10. At serving time, beat remaining ½ cup whipping cream and decorate top of mousse. Cut into wedges.

Quick and easy to prepare. May be made ahead several days and stored in freezer.

Frozen Lemonade Cream

YIELDS: 8 servings

For an elegant touch, serve this in your best crystal with a slice of lemon tilted on the edge.

1 (6-ounce) can frozen lemonade concentrate, thawed	1 (8-ounce) container Cool Whip
1 (14-ounce) can Eagle Brand sweetened condensed milk	2 ounces Cool Whip, garnish mint leaves, garnish

1. In a large bowl, combine lemonade concentrate, sweetened condensed milk, and Cool Whip. Stir gently until well blended. Pour into 8 sherbet glasses or 8 scooped out lemon shells.

2. Freeze 8 hours or overnight. May stay in freezer up to 1 month. Do not thaw before serving. Garnish with a dab of Cool Whip and a mint leaf.

Variation for pie: Pour lemonade cream into a 9 inch graham cracker crust. Garnish top with Cool Whip and sprinkle with graham cracker crumbs.

Helpful Hints: To get best results when whipping cream use well chilled cream and use a bowl that has been in freezer for 1 hour.

# DESSERTS

Fruit Cioccolato

Orange liqueur adds a special touch to this dessert.

4 medium naval oranges, peeled, sliced then halved, drained	1 cup whipping cream, chilled
3 bananas, sliced	2 tablespoons sugar
1 cup strawberries, sliced and drained	1 tablespoon orange liqueur
	1 cup semi-sweet chocolate, grated

1. Arrange oranges, strawberries, and bananas in bottom of 8 x 8 inch dish or in individual souffle dishes.

2. Whip cream with sugar. Add orange liqueur and beat until stiff. Spread over fruit.

3. Sprinkle grated chocolate over cream making sure no cream remains exposed. Chocolate layer should be ¼ inch thick.

4. Preheat broiler. Place dish under broiler, 5 inches from heat source. Will burn so watch carefully. When chocolate is melted and whipped cream shows through creating a marbled look, remove from oven. Serve immediately.

Variation: Marinate oranges and strawberries in 3 tablespoons of orange liqueur for about 3 hours, drain. Put fruit in sherbet glass. Top with whipped cream. Drizzle melted chocolate over whipped cream.

Fruit Pizza

A fun twist for the use of summer fresh fruit. Easy and eye-catching!

ORANGE SAUCE

¼ cup sugar	dash of salt
1 tablespoon cornstarch	½ cup orange juice
¼ cup water	2 tablespoons lemon juice
½ teaspoon orange peel	

1. In saucepan, combine sugar, cornstarch, water, orange peel, salt, orange, and lemon juices. Bring to slow boil while stirring and cook 2 minutes. Chill.

DOUGH

1 (17-ounce) package
Pillsbury sugar cookie roll

1. Slice cookie dough into ¼ inch slices. Arrange on cookie sheet with slices touching. Make one large pizza or two smaller ones. Bake in a preheated 350 degree oven for 10 minutes. Cool a few minutes, then transfer dough to serving platter.

FILLING

1 (8-ounce) package cream cheese, softened	1 (4½-ounce) container Cool Whip
1 teaspoon vanilla	

1. Mix cream cheese, vanilla and cool whip until creamy. After cookie dough has cooled, spread cream cheese mixture on top.

FRUIT (your choice—fresh is best)

strawberries	kiwi
bananas	pineapple
blueberries	

1. Arrange fruit on top of cream cheese in circular rows. Spoon slightly thickened orange sauce over fruit to cover. Chill until serving time.

 # DESSERTS

Melt-In-Your-Mouth Meringues

YIELDS: 8-12 servings

Choose your favorite fruit to complete.

5	egg whites	1½	cups sugar
¼	teaspoon salt	½	pint whipped cream
½	teaspoon cream of tartar		fresh fruit, peaches, strawberries, etc.

1. Beat egg whites until foamy. Add salt and cream of tartar. Beat until stiff, but not dry. Slowly add sugar.

2. Pour into well greased 8 x 8 inch pan. Preheat oven to 450 degrees. Place 8 x 8 inch pan in oven and turn heat off. Leave pan in oven overnight.

3. Before serving, place whipped cream on top of meringue. Cover with fresh fruits. Cut into squares. Peaches and blueberries or peaches and strawberries make good combinations.

Variation: Place meringue mixture in pastry tube. Pipe individual circles (about 3 inches across) on a greased cookie sheet. Follow same baking directions. Top with whipped cream and fruit.

Must be prepared ahead 24 hours.

Whole Strawberries with French Cream

YIELDS: 6-8 servings

1	cup whipping cream	2	pints strawberries, rinsed and hulled
⅓	cup powdered sugar		grated dark, sweet, or
½	cup sour cream		milk chocolate (optional)
½	teaspoon orange peel, grated		

1. Beat whipping cream until stiff; fold in sugar, sour cream, and orange peel. Serve as topping for whole strawberries. Garnish with grated chocolate.

Old-Fashioned Raisin Rice Pudding

YIELDS: 8 servings

This recipe brings memories of family gatherings to mind. Easy.

4 eggs	1½ teaspoons vanilla
¾ cup sugar	1 tablespoon butter, melted
2 cups milk	1 teaspoon nutmeg
1⅓ cups cooked rice	⅔ cup seedless raisins
1½ teaspoons lemon juice	

1. Combine eggs, sugar, and milk and beat well. Fold in rice, lemon juice, vanilla, melted butter, nutmeg, and raisins.

2. Pour into greased 2 quart casserole and place dish in a pan of boiling water. Bake in a preheated 350 degree oven for approximately 45 minutes or until custard is set.

White Chocolate Sauce

YIELDS: 2 cups

Good over chocolate ice cream or fresh fruits.

1 cup whipping cream	½ cup Grand Marnier or
9 ounces white chocolate	Kahlua

1. Scald cream and remove from heat.

2. Cut white chocolate into pieces and add to cream. Process briefly in food processor until smooth. Add liqueur and serve.

 **DESSERTS**

Oranges with Sabayon

YIELDS: 4 servings

Grand Marnier is the elegant touch to this unusual dessert.

4	medium oranges (naval)	½	cup sugar
¼	cup plus 1 tablespoon Grand Marnier	½	cup dry white wine
4	egg yolks	¼	cup whipped cream (optional)

1. Cut peel and pith from oranges. Cut into sections, removing all membranes. Drain and transfer to medium bowl. Sprinkle with 1 tablespoon Grand Marnier. Refrigerate covered.

2. To make sabayon, whisk egg yolks and sugar in top of double boiler until light in color. Gradually beat in wine and Grand Marnier. Cook, whisking constantly, over hot, not boiling, water until thickened, about 5 minutes. Don't overcook or eggs will curdle. Immediately set top of double boiler in ice water. Continue whisking until cool.

3. Arrange orange sections in dessert dishes.

4. Fold whipped cream into sabayon.

5. Refrigerate oranges and sabayon separately until serving time. To serve, spoon some sabayon over oranges. Pass remaining sabayon.

Variation: Instead of the oranges and Grand Marnier, 1 pint of raspberries and raspberry brandy (Framboise) or 1 pint strawberries and Kirsch may be substituted.

May prepare oranges and sabayon 2 days ahead.

Oreo Cookies and Cream

YIELDS: 16 servings

CRUST

1 (16-ounce) package Oreo cookies, crushed, reserve 5 for garnish	⅔ cup butter, melted

1. Mix crushed Oreos and melted butter; press into a 9 x 13 inch buttered pan.

FIRST LAYER

½ gallon vanilla ice cream, softened

1. Spread softened ice cream over crust and place in freezer.

SECOND LAYER

4 (1-ounce) squares unsweetened chocolate	1 cup sugar
2 tablespoons butter	1 teaspoon vanilla
1⅓ cups evaporated milk (almost all of 12-ounce can)	1 (12-ounce) Cool Whip

1. Cook above ingredients, except Cool Whip, until thickened, stirring continuously. Cool chocolate sauce and spread on top of ice cream. Spread Cool Whip over chocolate sauce. Sprinkle 5 crushed Oreos on top for garnish. Freeze. Remove 5-10 minutes before serving.

 # DESSERTS

Raspberry Torte

CAKE

1⅓ cups flour	1 egg
1 teaspoon baking powder	¼ cup seedless black
⅓ cup sugar	raspberry jam
½ cup butter or margarine, softened	

1. Heat oven to 350 degrees. Grease a 9 inch springform pan.

2. In a medium size bowl, cut or process the butter into the dry ingredients. Mix in egg until moistened.

3. Press dough on the bottom and up sides of the pan. Spread jam over the dough and chill while making the filling.

FILLING

½ cup butter or margarine	1 cup almonds, ground
⅔ cup sugar	or chopped
½ teaspoon almond extract	¼ cup seedless black
2 eggs	raspberry jam

1. Cream butter and sugar. Add almond extract and eggs, beating after each addition. Stir in the almonds. Spoon filling over the cake layer. Bake for 50 minutes or until golden brown.

2. Carefully remove the sides from the springform pan. Spread remaining jam over the cooled cake.

GLAZE

½ cup powdered sugar	2 teaspoons lemon juice

1. In a small bowl, blend sugar and juice until smooth. Drizzle over torte.

May be frozen a week ahead of time. However, the jam bleeds into the cake when defrosted.

Red Fruit Pudding

YIELDS: 8-10 servings

The tangy combination of strawberries and raspberries is made even better when topped with the creamy vanilla sauce.

PUDDING

2 (10-ounce) packages sweetened frozen raspberries	½ cup water
	⅓ cup cornstarch
	1 tablespoon lemon juice
2 (10-ounce) packages sweetened frozen strawberries	2-3 tablespoons sugar

1. Combine raspberries and strawberries in saucepan. Cook until thawed. Puree in processor or blender. Press through fine mesh sieve to remove seeds.

2. Mix water and cornstarch. Stir into berry puree in large saucepan. Heat, stirring constantly, until it is thick and boils for 3 minutes. Remove from heat. Stir in lemon juice.

3. Spoon into heat-proof serving bowl. Sprinkle with sugar. Cover with plastic wrap. Refrigerate 6 hours or overnight.

VANILLA SAUCE

¼ cup sugar	2 egg yolks
1 tablespoon cornstarch	2 cups half and half
pinch of salt	1 teaspoon vanilla

1. In top of double boiler, combine sugar, cornstarch, and salt. Whisk in egg yolks and gradually stir in half and half. Cook, stirring constantly, until thick and it coats spoon, approximately 5 minutes. Immediately transfer to a bowl. Stir in 1 teaspoon vanilla. Cover with plastic wrap and refrigerate until well chilled.

GARNISH
⅓ cup slivered almonds

1. Serve for buffet by topping pudding with almonds and serving sauce separately. Serve individually by pouring pudding into dessert dishes, topping with almonds, and passing the sauce.

May be prepared 2 days ahead.

 **DESSERTS**

Strawberry Mousse with Raspberry Sauce

The perfect dinner finale!

2 pints fresh strawberries	juice of 1 lemon
2 envelopes unflavored gelatin	1 teaspoon vanilla
1 cup water	2 cups whipping cream
1 cup sugar	dash of salt

1. Wash strawberries and dry on paper towels. Hull berries and puree in blender.

2. Sprinkle gelatin over cold water in saucepan. Place over low heat and stir constantly until dissolved, about 5 minutes. Remove from heat. Stir in sugar.

3. Combine mixture with berries. Stir in lemon juice and vanilla. Chill in freezer or refrigerator until mixture forms a ball when dropped from a spoon.

4. Whip cream with salt until it forms stiff peaks. Fold berry mixture into cream. Pour into 6 cup mold and chill for 6 hours. Serve with sauce.

SAUCE

1 (10-ounce) package frozen raspberries or 1 pint fresh raspberries	1 tablespoon sugar
	1 tablespoon Kirsch (optional)

1. Wash berries. Puree berries and sugar in blender until smooth. Strain to remove seeds. Stir in Kirsch, if desired.

Must make ahead.

Swiss Trifle

A light ending to a heavy meal.

1 (3-ounce) package strawberry Jello

1 angel food cake

1 tablespoon sherry (optional) (Harvey's Bristol Creme preferred)

1 (16-ounce) package frozen strawberries, thawed (may substitute raspberries or peaches—if using fresh fruit, add sugar to make juice)

2 tablespoons Bird's custard powder

2 cups milk

2 tablespoons sugar (one 3-ounce vanilla pudding mix may be substituted for custard powder, milk, sugar; follow package directions)

1 (8-ounce) whipping cream

2 teaspoons sugar

1. Make Jello according to package directions. Leave in liquid form.

2. Slice cake in 1½ inch sections or cubes. Pack half the cake pieces in wide bottom bowl. Dribble sherry over cake. Pour ¼ cup fruit juice over cake. Pour ⅓ of Jello over this; cover cake completely with fruit. Cover fruit with rest of cake. Pour remaining Jello over cake and allow it to soak in.

3. Refrigerate and allow it to set.

4. Make custard according to package directions. Cover custard with plastic wrap so a skin won't form. Allow to cool. Pour custard over set cake. Refrigerate. (May make ahead this far the day before serving.)

5. A few hours before serving, whip whipping cream with 2 teaspoons of sugar until stiff peaks form. Spread whipped cream on top. Garnish with nuts, sliced almonds, or fruit.

May be made ahead 1 day.

DESSERTS

Fresh Apple Cake with Sterling Sauce

YIELDS: 12 servings

CAKE

4 cups apples, chopped	1 teaspoon nutmeg
lemon juice	2 teaspoons cinnamon
2 eggs	½ teaspoon salt
2 cups sugar	2 cups flour, sifted
1 cup oil	¾ cup dates, chopped
1 teaspoon baking soda	

1. Drizzle lemon juice over apples.

2. In a large bowl, cream eggs, sugar, and oil.

3. Sift dry ingredients together and add to the creamed mixture. Fold in apples and chopped dates. Pour batter into a greased 9 x 13 inch pan. Bake in a preheated 325 degree oven for 1 hour.

SAUCE

1 cup light brown sugar, packed	1 cup milk
1 tablespoon flour	¼ cup butter or margarine
2 teaspoons cornstarch	2 eggs, separated
¼ teaspoon salt	1 teaspoon vanilla
	½ pint whipping cream

1. In heavy saucepan, combine brown sugar, flour, cornstarch, and salt; blend. Add milk and butter. Cook over low heat until mixture coats spoon. Pour over slightly beaten egg yolks. Return to pan and continue to cook until it thickens, stirring constantly. Remove from stove. Add vanilla and cool. May be prepared ahead to this point.

2. When ready to serve, beat egg whites until stiff. Whip cream. Fold egg whites into cooled custard sauce; then fold in whipped cream.

Athenian Almond Cake

YIELDS: 10-12 servings

A dessert with a light and flavorful texture.

1 cup butter, softened	1 cup almonds, ground
½ cup sugar	(4 to 4½-ounces)
1 cup farina or cream of wheat	3 cups water
6 eggs	2 cups sugar
2 teaspoons vanilla	½ lemon, cut in 2 slices
1 cup cake flour (or ⅞ cup sifted all purpose flour)	whipped cream fresh strawberries, marinated in brandy
1 tablespoon baking powder	
½ cup milk	

1. Beat butter with sugar in large bowl until light and creamy. Gradually blend in farina, mixing well. Add eggs, one at a time, beating well after each addition. Blend in vanilla.

2. Sift flour with baking powder. Add flour mixture and milk alternately to batter, beginning and ending with dry ingredients. Stir in almonds and mix well. Pour batter into buttered 9 x 13 inch pan.

3. Bake in a preheated 350 degree oven about 35 to 40 minutes, until golden in color.

4. Meanwhile, combine water, 2 cups sugar, and lemon slices in a 2 quart sauce-pan and bring to boil over medium-high heat. Let boil 15 minutes. Remove from heat. Cool syrup slightly.

5. Prick cake in several places with sharp knife. Spoon slightly cooled syrup over top. Let cake cool completely. To serve, cut into diamond-shaped pieces. Pipe or spoon dollop of whipped cream over each and top with strawberry.

May be prepared up to 2 months ahead and frozen. Let stand at room temperature several hours to thaw.

 # DESSERTS

Apricot Nectar Cake

YIELDS: 10-12 servings

A flavor that's light and a dessert that's easy to make.

CAKE

1	lemon supreme cake mix	4	eggs
1	cup apricot nectar	½	cup sugar
½	cup Wesson oil		

1. Mix together cake ingredients and pour into a bundt pan. Bake in a preheated 325 degree oven for 1 hour. Glaze when cool.

GLAZE

1	cup powdered sugar	lemon juice

1. Thin powdered sugar with lemon juice until a glaze consistency is reached.

Easy. May be prepared ahead. Freezes well.

Cherry Pudding Cake

YIELDS: 6 servings

A quick and easy dessert that doesn't taste overly sweet.

1	cup flour	½	teaspoon vanilla
½	cup sugar	2	cups (number 2½ can)
¼	teaspoon salt		tart cherries, pitted
1	teaspoon baking powder		and drained
4	tablespoons shortening	½	cup sugar
½	cup milk	1	cup hot cherry juice
			(add water if necessary)

1. Sift flour, ½ cup sugar, salt, and baking powder together. Add shortening, milk, and vanilla.

2. Pour into greased 8 x 8 x 2 inch cake pan. Cover with cherries, then sprinkle ½ cup sugar over the top. Gently pour hot cherry juice over the top and bake in a preheated 375 degree oven for 40-45 minutes. Serve warm.

Easy. May be prepared 1 day ahead.

Black Bottom Cheesecake

YIELDS: 16 servings

CRUST

1½ cups chocolate wafer
    crumbs
1 cup slivered almonds,
    chopped

⅓ cup sugar
6 tablespoons butter,
    softened

1. Combine crust ingredients in food processor. Press crumb mixture onto bottom and sides of a buttered 10 inch springform pan.

FILLING

3 (8-ounce) packages
    cream cheese, softened
1 cup sugar
4 eggs

⅓ cup whipping cream
½ cup Amaretto
1 teaspoon vanilla

1. Cream together cream cheese and sugar. Add eggs, one at a time, beating well after each addition. Add cream, Amaretto, and vanilla, beating until light.

2. Pour over chocolate crust. Bake on middle rack in a preheated 375 degree oven for 30-40 minutes. Transfer cake to a wire rack and let set 5 minutes.

TOPPING

2 cups sour cream
1 teaspoon vanilla

1 tablespoon sugar
1 cup slivered almonds,
    toasted

1. Combine all topping ingredients except nuts. Spread evenly over cake. Bake for 5 more minutes. Cool on rack. Cover lightly with wax paper and chill overnight.

2. To serve, remove sides from pan. Break off crust above cheesecake and crumble around outer edge of top. Fill with toasted almonds.

 # DESSERTS

Apricot Rum Torte

YIELDS: 10 servings

A dessert that's worth the extra effort.

1	cup flour, sifted	1	tablespoon butter
1	teaspoon baking powder, sifted	2	eggs
¼	teaspoon salt, sifted	1	cup sugar
½	cup milk	1	teaspoon rum

1. Sift together flour, baking powder, and salt. Set aside.

2. In a small saucepan, heat milk and butter until melted.

3. Beat eggs in medium bowl with mixer until light and fluffy. Beat in sugar and rum until well blended. Stir in milk mixture, then fold in dry ingredients.

4. Generously grease and flour two 8 or 9 inch cake pans. Pour batter into pans, dividing evenly. Bake in a preheated 350 degree oven for 35 minutes or until top springs back.

5. Loosen cake around edges. Turn onto racks to cool slightly. Meanwhile, prepare Coffee Rum Syrup.

COFFEE RUM SYRUP

1	cup sugar	¼	cup rum
1	cup extra strong black coffee		

1. Combine sugar and coffee in a saucepan over low heat. Stir. Once sugar is dissolved, raise heat and bring to boil for 3 minutes. Add rum.

2. Spoon warm syrup slowly over tops of warm cakes until most is absorbed. (Put cakes on plates or wax paper as some syrup will gather under cakes.) Chill cakes and prepare Pastry Cream.

continued

Apricot Rum Torte *continued*

PASTRY CREAM

⅓ cup sugar	1 tablespoon rum
¼ cup flour	½ cup apricot preserves
⅛ teaspoon salt	1 cup whipping cream,
1 cup milk	whipped stiff
2 egg yolks	chopped pecans (optional)

1. Combine sugar, flour, and salt in small saucepan. Gradually stir in 1 cup milk. Cook, stirring constantly, over low heat until mixture thickens.

2. Lightly beat 2 egg yolks in a small bowl. Pour small amount of hot mixture into yolks, blend well; pour yolk mixture into saucepan with milk and flour mixture. Cook 3 minutes, stirring constantly. Add rum. Press a piece of wax paper over cream surface and chill thoroughly in refrigerator.

3. When cream mixture is chilled, split each cake layer in half horizontally. Makes 4 cake layers. Place layer on serving plate. Add layer of pastry cream and continue to alternate cake and cream ending with final cake layer.

4. Spread apricot preserves over top of cake. Frost sides with whipped cream and pipe a whipped cream lattice over top. Press chopped pecans on side, if desired. Chill well before serving.

May be prepared early in the day and assembled except for whipped cream topping. Refrigerate covered until time to frost.

Blueberry Cake with Lemon Filling

YIELDS: 12 servings

A pretty summer fruit cake.

3 eggs	¼ teaspoon salt
1½ cups sugar	1 cup walnuts, ground
1½ cups cake flour, sifted	1 cup fresh or frozen
2 teaspoons baking powder	blueberries, well
1½ cups whipping cream	drained
2 teaspoons vanilla	

1. Butter three 8 inch layer pans, line with wax paper, and butter again.

2. In large bowl, beat eggs until thickened. Beat in sugar, 2 tablespoons at a time, until mixture is light and fluffy.

3. Sift flour and baking powder together. Reserve.

4. Beat cream, vanilla, and salt in a chilled bowl to stiff peaks.

5. Fold whipped cream into egg mixture, alternating with flour mixture and nuts. Divide batter among pans. Sprinkle each layer with ⅓ cup blueberries.

6. Bake in a preheated 350 degree oven for 30-35 minutes. Cool 5 minutes on racks; remove from pans and cool.

LEMON FILLING

¾ cup butter, room temperature	1½ tablespoons lemon juice
3 cups powdered sugar	¾ teaspoon vanilla
	3 egg yolks

1. Beat together the butter, sugar, lemon juice, and vanilla until light and fluffy. Beat in yolks, one at a time, until well combined.

TO ASSEMBLE CAKE

1. Invert 1 cake layer on serving plate. Spread with ⅓ the lemon filling; add a second layer and spread with ⅓ filling.

2. Top with last layer. Frost sides with remaining filling; sprinkle top of cake with powdered sugar.

3. Garnish with fresh blueberries and lemon leaves.

Buttermilk Chocolate Cake

YIELDS: 12 servings

Old-fashioned enjoyment!

¼ to ½ cup cocoa	½ teaspoon salt
1 cup water	2 cups sugar
1 cup butter	½ cup buttermilk
2 cups flour	2 eggs
1 teaspoon baking soda	1 teaspoon vanilla

1. Combine cocoa, water, and butter in saucepan. Bring to boil and remove from heat and cool.

2. Using electric mixer, mix flour, soda, salt, and sugar to combine. Pour into the cooled chocolate mixture and combine. Add buttermilk, eggs, and vanilla and combine.

3. Pour into two greased and floured 8 or 9 inch pans. Bake in a preheated 375 degree oven for 25 minutes.

FROSTING

½ cup unsalted butter	1 teaspoon vanilla extract
¼ to ½ cup cocoa	1 pound powdered sugar
6 tablespoons buttermilk	

1. Melt butter with cocoa in saucepan. Bring to a light boil. Remove from stove. Add buttermilk and vanilla.

2. Place powdered sugar in mixing bowl and pour chocolate mixture over this and whip slowly. Scrape down sides of bowl and whip 5 to 10 minutes until smooth.

Cake may be prepared 1 day ahead or freeze cake and frost after thawed.

 **DESSERTS**

Charlie Brown's Birthday Cake

FILLING

2	tablespoons butter, softened	1	tablespoon cornstarch
1	(8-ounce) package cream cheese, softened	1	egg
		2	tablespoons milk
¼	cup sugar	½	teaspoon vanilla

1. Cream butter, cream cheese, sugar, and cornstarch. Add egg, milk, and vanilla. Beat until smooth. Set aside.

CAKE

2	cups flour	½	cup butter, softened
2	cups sugar	1⅓	cups milk, divided
1	teaspoon salt	2	eggs
1	teaspoon baking powder	4	envelopes Choco-Bake
½	teaspoon baking soda	1	teaspoon vanilla

1. Combine flour, sugar, salt, baking powder, baking soda, butter, and 1 cup milk. Blend, then beat 1½ minutes on low speed. Add ⅓ cup milk, eggs, Choco-Bake, and vanilla. Beat 1½ minutes.

2. Grease and flour 13 x 9 inch pan. Spread ½ chocolate batter in pan. Carefully spoon cream cheese filling over chocolate batter, do not pour. Spread remaining chocolate batter on top.

3. Bake in a preheated 350 degree oven for 40 to 45 minutes or until toothpick comes out clean. Cool and frost.

FROSTING

¼	cup milk	2½	cups powdered sugar, sifted
¼	cup butter		
2	envelopes Choco-Bake	1	teaspoon vanilla

1. Bring milk and butter to boil. Remove from heat. Blend in Choco-Bake. Stir in vanilla and powdered sugar until spreading consistency. (May use more or less sugar.)

Easy. May be made ahead 2 days.

Coca Cola Cake

YIELDS: 12-15 servings

Simply addictive.

CAKE

1 cup Coca Cola	2 cups sugar
½ cup butter	1 teaspoon baking soda
½ cup Wesson oil	½ cup buttermilk
¼ cup cocoa	2 eggs, beaten
1½ cups miniature marshmallows	1 tablespoon vanilla
2 cups flour	

1. Mix and bring to a boil the cola, butter, oil, and cocoa. Remove from heat and add marshmallows. Let melt.

2. Mix together the flour, sugar, and baking soda. Set side. Combine buttermilk, eggs, and vanilla; add to dry ingredients and mix well; fold in chocolate mixture. Pour in a greased and floured 9 x 13 inch pan and bake in a preheated 350 degree oven for 1 hour.

FROSTING

½ cup butter	1 pound powdered sugar
¼ cup cocoa	1 cup nuts, chopped
6 tablespoons Coca Cola	1 teaspoon vanilla

1. In a saucepan, combine butter, cocoa, and cola. Bring to a boil. Remove from heat. Add powdered sugar, nuts, and vanilla.

May be prepared ahead and frozen.

Coconut Cake

A crazy over coconut delight!

CAKE
1   white cake mix
1   cup coconut

1   tablespoon coconut
    flavoring

1. Mix cake mix according to package directions. Add coconut and coconut flavoring.

2. Pour batter into greased and floured 13 x 9 inch pan, and bake as directed on the cake mix box.

3. Cool 15 minutes, then punch holes with ice pick all over top of cake.

GLAZE
1   (5-ounce) can
    evaporated milk
1   tablespoon coconut
    flavoring

1   tablespoon vanilla
¼   cup powdered sugar
1   (8-ounce) Cool Whip
½   cup coconut, flaked

1. Measure evaporated milk, coconut flavoring, and vanilla into 1 cup measure; add enough water to equal 1 cup. Add powdered sugar and mix well. Pour glaze over top of the cake.

2. When cake is cool, top with Cool Whip and sprinkle with coconut. Refrigerate.

May be prepared ahead 2 days.

Eggnog Cake

This is easily made ahead and would be a wonderful gift.

CAKE
1   10 inch angel food cake

1. Cut cake into 4 layers.

FILLING

½ cup butter or margarine	⅓ cup rum, brandy, or
3 cups powdered sugar or	sherry
more	1 teaspoon vanilla
3 egg yolks	nutmeg to taste
	⅔ cup almonds, toasted

1. Combine butter and powdered sugar. Beat until fluffy.

2. Beat egg yolks and add one at a time to mixture. Add rum, brandy, or sherry. Add 1 teaspoon of vanilla and a dash of nutmeg. Fold in almonds. More powdered sugar may have to be added to get spreading consistency. Spread eggnog filling between each layer of cake.

FROSTING

½ pint whipping cream	almonds for garnish
or 1 (8-ounce) Cool	cherries (optional)
Whip	red or green sugar
2 teaspoons rum flavoring	(optional)

1. If using whipping cream, whip until stiff and sweeten to taste. Add rum to whipped cream or Cool Whip. Mix.

2. Frost top and sides of cake. Sprinkle with almonds and chill. Decorate for the holidays with cherries or red and green sugars.

Easy. May be prepared ahead.

Italian Almond Cheesecake

YIELDS: 16-20 servings

Exceedingly rich!

CRUST

7	ounces amaretti cookies, finely ground	1	ounce unsweetened chocolate
2	tablespoons sugar	5	tablespoons unsalted butter

1. Place crumbs in a bowl and add sugar. Melt chocolate and butter. Add to the crumb mixture and stir. Butter sides only of a 9 inch springform pan and press crumb mixture into the bottom of the pan.

FILLING

6	ounces semi-sweet chocolate	½	cup sugar
4	ounces almond paste, cut into small pieces	4	eggs
⅓	cup Amaretto liqueur	½	cup whipping cream
3	(8-ounce) packages cream cheese, softened	8	ounces amaretti cookies, coarsely broken
			white chocolate (garnish)
			strawberries (garnish)

1. To make filling, melt chocolate in the top of a double boiler. Set aside to cool slightly. Place almond paste pieces in a mixer and, on low speed, gradually add the Amaretto. Beat until thoroughly mixed. Set aside.

2. In a large bowl, beat cream cheese until smooth. Add sugar and beat again until smooth. Add the almond paste mixture and mix well. Add melted chocolate and beat. On low speed, add the eggs, one at a time, and beat only until they are incorporated. Add cream and beat only until smooth. Do not overbeat. Gently stir in the broken cookies.

continued

Italian Almond Cheesecake *continued*

3. Pour batter into prepared pan. Rotate the pan gently to spread batter evenly. Bake in a preheated 350 degree oven for 45 minutes in the bottom third of the oven. Do not bake any longer, it will firm as it chills. Cool to room temperature. Remove sides of the pan. Refrigerate for several hours or overnight.

4. To remove from pan, insert and rotate sharp knife to release crust. Mound white chocolate shavings on top and encircle cheesecake with fresh, perfect strawberries topped with whipped cream.

Freezes well.

Grasshopper Cake

YIELDS: 12-15 servings

Great for St. Patrick's Day or a pretty and cool dessert for a hot summer evening.

1	package Duncan Hines white cake mix with pudding	1	(12-ounce) jar hot fudge ice cream topping, chilled
3	tablespoons green Creme de Menthe	1	(8-ounce) Cool Whip
		1	tablespoon green Creme de Menthe

1. Prepare cake mix according to directions substituting 3 tablespoons green Creme de Menthe for 3 tablespoons of water. Bake in a 9 x 13 inch pan following cake mix package directions. Cool and store in refrigerator overnight.

2. Mix Cool Whip with 1 tablespoon of green Creme de Menthe. Cover and refrigerate.

3. Just before serving, cut cake into squares and place on plates. Spread top with hot fudge sauce and then spread with Cool Whip mixture and serve.

Easy. Must be prepared 1 day ahead.

Imogene's Perfect Sponge Cake

YIELDS: 16 servings

Don't let the length of this recipe scare you away. It's perfectly wonderful.

CAKE

1¼ cups cake flour, sifted
(do not substitute)
¼ teaspoon baking powder
6 eggs, separated
¾ teaspoon cream of tartar

1½ cups sugar
⅓ cup cold orange juice
¼ teaspoon salt
1 teaspoon vanilla

1. Sift cake flour with baking powder.

2. Put egg whites in large bowl. Beat whites at high speed until frothy, then sprinkle in cream of tartar and continue beating until whites stand in peaks but still cling to side of bowl, about 3 minutes. Add ½ cup sugar gradually, still beating at high speed until you have a smooth satiny meringue. Set aside.

3. Put yolks in bowl and beat at high speed for 2 minutes. Pour in orange juice and continue beating for 1 more minute on high speed. Add remaining sugar gradually to yolks. Add salt and vanilla and continue beating until mixture looks light and smooth.

4. Fold flour into egg yolk mixture until batter is smooth. Do not beat. Pour yolk and flour mixture into meringue and fold very gently until all patches of egg white disappear. Pour into ungreased 12 inch tube pan and bake in a preheated 300 degree oven for 1¼ hours. (If top browns too quickly, cover loosely with foil.)

5. Cool upside down on a rack for 1 hour and then pull cake carefully away from pan with your hands. When cool, cover with powdered sugar or pineapple glaze. Glaze no earlier than 2 hours before serving.

continued

Imogene's Perfect Sponge Cake *continued*

PINEAPPLE GLAZE

2   tablespoons butter, melted
1   egg yolk
3   tablespoons crushed pineapple, drained, reserve juice
2   tablespoons pineapple juice
1¼ cups powdered sugar rind of ½ small lemon, grated

1. Beat egg yolk 1 minute at high speed. At low speed, blend in butter, crushed pineapple, juice, lemon rind, and powdered sugar. Beat 2 minutes. Spoon this thin glaze over top of sponge cake, allowing some of it to drizzle over sides.

Italian Creme Cake

YIELDS: 4 layer, 8 inch cake

CAKE

2   cups flour
2   cups sugar
1   teaspoon vanilla extract
½   cup butter
½   cup Crisco
5   egg yolks (reserve whites)
1   (3½-ounce) can coconut
1   teaspoon baking soda
1   cup pecans, chopped
1   cup buttermilk

1. Mix all ingredients, except egg whites. Beat egg whites and fold into batter. Pour batter into 4 greased and floured, 8 inch cake pans.

2. Bake in a preheated 350 degree oven for 25-30 minutes or until tops turn brown or toothpick comes out clean. Cool.

FROSTING

12 ounces cream cheese (or 1 large soft tub)
½   cup nuts
1   pound powdered sugar
½   cup butter
1   teaspoon vanilla

1. Mix all ingredients in medium size bowl with mixer. Spread between cake layers and on top.

May prepare ahead 2 days. In warm weather, refrigerate.

Milky Way Cake

YIELDS: 20 servings

CAKE

6 (2.10-ounce) or 13 (fun size) Milky Way candy bars
1 cup butter, divided
2 cups sugar
4 eggs

2½ cups flour
1 cup buttermilk
½ teaspoon baking soda
2 teaspoons vanilla
½ to 1 cup pecans, chopped

1. Melt candy bars and ½ cup butter in microwave or double boiler. Set aside.

2. Cream ½ cup butter and sugar together. Add eggs, one at a time. Mix thoroughly. Add flour and baking soda alternately with buttermilk to creamed mixture. Add melted candy. Mix well. Stir in vanilla and nuts.

3. Pour batter into greased tube or jelly roll pan. Bake in a preheated 350 degree oven for 1 hour or until top springs back when lightly touched. (May take less time in jelly roll pan.)

FROSTING

2 (2.10-ounce) Milky Way candy bars
½ cup butter
2 cups powdered sugar

2 teaspoons vanilla
buttermilk

1. Melt Milky Way bars and butter in microwave or double boiler. Remove from heat. Stir in powdered sugar and vanilla. Add enough buttermilk to make it spreadable. Frost cooled cake.

Peanut Butter Fudge Cake

YIELDS: 12-15 servings

Who put the peanut butter in my chocolate?

CAKE

1 cup butter	2 cups sugar
¼ cup cocoa	2 cups flour
1 cup water	1 teaspoon baking soda
½ cup buttermilk	1 teaspoon vanilla
2 eggs, well beaten	

1. Combine butter, cocoa, water, buttermilk, and eggs in a saucepan. Stir constantly over low heat until mixture boils. Remove from heat.

2. In a large bowl, combine sugar, flour, and baking soda. Add to hot mixture. Stir in vanilla. Pour batter into a greased and floured 9 x 13 inch pan.

3. Bake in a preheated 350 degree oven for 40 minutes or until firm to the touch. Cool completely in pan.

FILLING

1 cup creamy peanut butter	1 tablespoon vegetable oil

1. Combine filling ingredients. Spread over cake.

FROSTING

½ cup butter	1 pound powdered sugar
¼ cup cocoa	1 teaspoon vanilla
6 tablespoons buttermilk	

1. In saucepan, combine butter, cocoa, and buttermilk. Bring to a boil.

2. Remove from heat and add powdered sugar and vanilla. Spread frosting on top of peanut butter filling.

Pear Upside Down Cake

YIELDS: 9 servings

A beautiful dessert with a lightly spiced flavor. Be sure to serve it warm.

3 tablespoons butter or margarine	1 teaspoon baking soda
¾ cup brown sugar, packed, divided	1 teaspoon cinnamon
5 canned pear halves	1 teaspoon ground ginger
5 maraschino cherries	¼ teaspoon ground cloves
⅓ cup Crisco	¼ teaspoon salt
1 egg	½ cup light molasses
1¼ cups flour	½ cup boiling water
	whipped topping

1. In an 8 x 8 inch baking pan, melt butter. Add ¼ cup of the brown sugar; blend.

2. In the hollow of each pear half, place a maraschino cherry. Invert pear halves in pan to form a 5 pointed star.

3. Cream Crisco and remaining ½ cup brown sugar. Add egg; beat well.

4. Sift together flour, baking soda, cinnamon, ginger, cloves, and salt.

5. Combine molasses and water; add alternately with dry ingredients to creamed mixture. Pour carefully over fruit.

6. Bake in a preheated 350 degree oven for 45-50 minutes or until done. Let stand 5 minutes on cake rack. Invert over serving plate; remove pan. Serve warm with whipped topping.

Polish Pound Cake

Ethnic, old world goodness!

½ cup Crisco
1 cup butter or margarine, softened
3 cups sugar
5 large eggs
3 cups flour
¼ teaspoon salt
2 tablespoons vanilla butternut flavoring (by Durkee)

1 (5-ounce) can evaporated milk, add water to make 1 cup
1 cup nuts, chopped
1 (10-ounce) jar maraschino cherries, cut up and dried on paper towel

1. Do not use mixer. Cream Criso and butter together. Add sugar, gradually; then eggs, one at a time. Beat well.

2. Combine flavoring with milk. Combine salt with flour. Add milk and flour mixtures alternately to creamed mixture. Mix well. Stir in nuts and cherries. Pour into greased and floured tube pan.

3. Place in cold oven on lower shelf. Turn heat to 300 degrees and bake 1¾ to 2 hours. Cake is moist. Let cool ½ hour before removing from pan. Needs no icing.

May prepare ahead 3 to 4 days. Freezes well.

 **DESSERTS**

Praline Cheesecake

YIELDS: 10-12 servings

A richly rewarding southern treat.

CRUST

1 cup graham cracker crumbs	3 tablespoons margarine, melted
3 tablespoons sugar	

1. Combine crumbs, sugar, and margarine. Press into bottom of a 9 inch springform pan.

2. Bake in a preheated 350 degree oven for 10 minutes. Remove pan to cool and increase oven to 450 degrees.

FILLING

3 (8-ounce) packages cream cheese, softened	1½ teaspoons vanilla
1¼ cups dark brown sugar, packed	½ cup pecans, finely chopped pecan halves and maple syrup for garnish
2 tablespoons flour	
3 eggs	

1. Combine cream cheese, sugar, and flour, mixing at medium speed until well blended. Add eggs, one at a time, mixing well after each. Blend in vanilla and chopped nuts. Pour over crust.

2. Bake in a preheated 450 degree oven for 10 minutes, then reduce oven to 250 degrees, and continue baking for 30 minutes.

3. Loosen cake from rim and remove side of pan. Garnish with pecans around edge and drizzle syrup over top. Chill. May add more syrup before serving.

May be prepared 1 to 2 days ahead.

Helpful Hints: The texture of a cheesecake should be creamy and smooth. To achieve this, it is crucial to incorporate each ingredient thoroughly before the next is added.

White Chocolate Cake

YIELDS: 3 layer cake

An especially rich dessert for that special occasion.

CAKE

¼ pound white chocolate (plain or with almonds)
½ cup boiling water
1 cup butter
1¾ cups sugar
2½ cups flour, sifted
1 teaspoon baking soda

4 eggs, well beaten
1 cup buttermilk
1 cup coconut
1 cup pecans, floured lightly
1 teaspoon vanilla

1. Melt chocolate in boiling water. Cool.

2. Cream butter and sugar. Add to chocolate mixture.

3. Mix flour and baking soda. Add alternately with eggs and buttermilk to the chocolate mixture. Beat well after each addition. Add coconut, pecans, and vanilla. Blend thoroughly. Pour batter into 3 greased and floured 8 or 9 inch round cake pans.

4. Bake in a preheated 350 degree oven for 30 minutes. Cool, remove from pans, and frost.

FROSTING

½ cup butter, softened
1 (8-ounce) package cream cheese, softened
3 cups powdered sugar

1 teaspoon vanilla
½ cup coconut
pecan halves

1. Cream butter and cream cheese. Add sugar and vanilla. Frost and sprinkle with coconut between layers and on top. Decorate top with pecan halves.

Must prepare one day ahead.

# DESSERTS

Strawberry Orange Cream Cake

YIELDS: 8-10 servings

A light and creamy dessert great for those lazy days of summer.

CAKE

6 eggs, separated room temperature	1 cup flour
1 teaspoon fresh lemon juice	¾ cup orange juice, divided
1 teaspoon cream of tartar	1 teaspoon baking powder
1¼ cups sugar, divided	½ teaspoon salt
	⅓ cup water

1. In large bowl, beat egg whites, cream of tartar, and lemon juice at high speed until soft peaks form. Continue beating at high speed, gradually adding ½ cup of sugar until whites stand in stiff peaks. Set aside.

2. In large bowl, beat egg yolks until thick and lemon colored. Continue beating, gradually sprinkling ½ cup of the sugar into the yolks, until mixture is pale yellow. Reduce to low speed, add flour, ¼ cup orange juice, baking powder, and salt until well mixed.

3. Fold egg white mixture into the egg yolk mixture until just blended. Pour batter into 2 wax paper lined 8 or 9 inch round cake pans. Do not grease.

4. Bake in a preheated 325 degree oven for 30 to 40 minutes or until test done. Cool in pans on wire racks for 10 minutes. Remove from pans and cool completely. Split each layer horizontally into two layers.

5. In small saucepan, over medium heat, boil water and remaining ¼ cup sugar for 3 minutes to make a light syrup. Stir in remaining orange juice. Drizzle evenly over layers and let stand 30 minutes.

continued

Strawberry Orange Cream Cake *continued*

FILLING AND FROSTING

2   cups whipping cream
3   tablespoons powdered
     sugar
2   tablespoons orange
     peel, grated

1   pint strawberries, sliced
     whole strawberries for
     garnish

1. Whip cream with powdered sugar until soft peaks form. Fold in orange peel.

TO ASSEMBLE

1. Place one cake layer on platter. Spread with about ⅓ cup whipped cream. Place ⅓ sliced berries on top. Repeat with remaining layers. Frost top only with remaining whipped cream. Garnish with whole strawberries and grated orange peel. Refrigerate until ready to serve.

May be prepared ahead and assembled day to be served.

Brownie Pie

YIELDS: 6-8 servings

Definitely for chocolate lovers!

3   egg whites
     dash of salt
¾   cup sugar
¾   to 1 cup Archway Dutch
     Cocoa cookies, crumbled

½   cup pecans, chopped
½   teaspoon vanilla
1   (8-ounce) container
     Cool Whip

1. Beat egg whites and salt until soft peaks form. Add sugar, gradually, until whites are stiff. Fold in cookie crumbs, nuts, and vanilla. Spread in a buttered 9 inch pie pan.

2. Bake in a preheated 325 degree oven for 35 minutes. Cool. Top with Cool Whip and chill 3 to 4 hours. Slice and serve.

Easy. Best made the same day.

Wine Country Cheesecake

YIELDS: 10-12 servings

CRUST

1½ cups vanilla wafer crumbs (34 wafers)

3 tablespoons sugar
⅓ cup butter, softened

1. Combine vanilla wafers, sugar, and butter.

2. Press onto bottom and part way up the sides of an ungreased 9 inch springform pan.

3. Bake in a preheated 350 degree oven for 10 minutes. Cool.

FILLING

3 (8-ounce) packages cream cheese, softened
¼ cup semi-dry Rose or white wine

½ teaspoon salt
1 cup sugar
4 eggs

1. Combine cream cheese, wine, and salt. Gradually mix in the sugar.

2. Add eggs, one at a time, beating well after each addition. Pour into baked crust.

3. Bake in a preheated 300 degree oven for 60-80 minutes. Cool completely. Run knife around sides of cake and remove from pan.

GLAZE

1 (1 pound) can apricot halves
½ cup sugar
4 teaspoons cornstarch

½ cup semi-dry Rose or white wine
3-4 drops red food coloring
¼ cup seedless grapes

1. Drain apricots, reserving ½ cup of syrup.

2. Combine sugar and cornstarch in a small saucepan. Gradually add syrup and wine, stirring constantly. Cook over medium heat, stirring until mixture comes to a boil and thickens. Add food coloring.

continued

Wine Country Cheesecake *continued*

3. Cool glaze to room temperature.

4. Arrange apricots and grapes on top of cheesecake. Spoon glaze over fruit, letting it drip down sides of the cake. Chill.

Igloo Cake

YIELDS: 10-12 servings

A fun to make ahead cake.

2 **Sara Lee frozen pound cakes, thawed**	2 **eggs, separated**
1 **(12-ounce) package chocolate chips**	1½ **cups water**
	1 **(8-ounce) carton whipping cream, whipped**

1. Slice thawed cakes lengthwise as thin as possible.

2. Make frosting by combining chocolate chips, water, and a pinch of salt in a double boiler. Cook until chocolate melts. Add egg yolks. Cool to room temperature. Fold in beaten egg whites (mixture will be runny).

3. In a medium mixing bowl, layer slices of cake, alternating one slice of cake and then icing, until all is used.

4. Chill in refrigerator overnight. Turn cake out upside down (slip knife around edge). Frost cake with a thin layer of whipped cream. Refrigerate until served.

Must be prepared ahead 1 day.

# DESSERTS

Coconut Meringue Pie

YIELDS: 6-8 servings

1	9 inch baked pie shell
2½	cups (20-ounces) evaporated milk
¾	cup sugar
½	cup flour
¼	teaspoon salt
3	eggs, separated

2	tablespoons butter
1	teaspoon vanilla
¾	cup coconut, shredded
6	tablespoons sugar
¼	teaspoon cream of tartar

1. Heat 1½ cups milk in double boiler.

2. In large mixing bowl, mix ¾ cup sugar, flour, and salt.

3. In another bowl, beat egg yolks well and add remaining milk. Add this gradually to the sugar mixture and stir until smooth. Add the hot milk slowly.

4. Return the mixture to the double boiler and cook over boiling water until very thick, approximately 10 minutes.

5. Remove from heat and add butter, vanilla, and coconut. Let cool.

6. Beat 3 egg whites until stiff peaks form, gradually adding 6 tablespoons sugar and cream of tartar.

7. Pour cream mixture into pie shell and top with meringue, sprinkling some coconut on top.

8. Bake in a preheated 350 degree oven until meringue peaks are brown, approximately 10 minutes.

Frozen Lemon Pie

YIELDS: 6-8 servings

A lemon-y light touch to that special dinner.

CRUST
½ cup butter, melted
¼ cup sugar
1½ cups graham cracker crumbs

1. Mix butter, sugar, and graham cracker crumbs. Pat into a 9 inch pie pan.

2. Bake in a preheated 325 degree oven for 8 minutes.

FILLING
3 eggs, separated
1 cup sugar
⅛ teaspoon salt
¼ cup fresh lemon juice
½ teaspoon grated lemon rind
½ pint whipping cream

1. Combine 3 well beaten egg yolks with sugar, salt, lemon juice, and rind. Cook in double boiler over simmering water until it begins to thicken. Stir frequently. Remove from heat and chill in pan of ice.

2. Whip ½ pint whipping cream.

3. Beat 3 egg whites until stiff, fold into whipped cream. Fold all into cooled lemon mixture. Pour into prepared crust. Freeze. Remove from freezer 5 to 10 minutes before serving.

Garnish with mint leaves, lemon slices, or whipped cream.

May be prepared 2 days ahead and frozen. Easy.

 # DESSERTS

Harvest Pumpkin Ice Cream Pie

YIELDS: 6-8 servings

You'll want to serve this pie more often than in the fall.

1 baked 9 inch pie shell	¾ teaspoon pumpkin pie spice
1 quart vanilla ice cream, softened	½ teaspoon salt
1 cup canned pumpkin	1 cup whipping cream
¾ cup sugar	

1. Spread ice cream in cooled pie shell. Place in freezer until thoroughly hardened.

2. Blend together pumpkin, sugar, salt, and spice.

3. Whip cream until stiff and fold into pumpkin mixture. Spoon mixture into frozen pie shell over the ice cream. Return to freezer until ready to use. Serve with additional whipped cream.

May be prepared 1 week ahead and frozen.

Peanut Butter Pie

YIELDS: 8 servings

P-nutty good!

¾ cup powdered sugar	1 (3-ounce) package instant French vanilla pudding
½ cup peanut butter	1 (8-ounce) Cool Whip
1 9 inch baked pie shell or graham cracker pie shell	

1. Mix powdered sugar and peanut butter until crumbly. Reserve 3 tablespoons for topping.

2. Fill bottom of pie shell with crumbly mixture.

3. Prepare instant pudding from package instructions. Pour pudding on top of crumbly peanut butter mixture. Chill in refrigerator until pudding sets.

4. Top with Cool Whip and sprinkle remaining peanut butter mixture on top.

Hula Moon Pie

YIELDS: 8 servings

Greet your guests with Hawaiian leis and treat them to this taste of the islands.

½ cup sugar	1 large banana, mashed
2 tablespoons cornstarch	2 egg yolks, well beaten
¼ teaspoon salt	1 tablespoon butter
1⅓ cups crushed pineapple, drained, reserve syrup	2 egg whites
	2 tablespoons sugar
¾ cup pineapple syrup	1 9 inch graham cracker crust
1 tablespoon lemon juice	

1. Combine sugar, cornstarch, salt, syrup, and lemon juice and cook in a double boiler until thick and transparent.

2. Combine the mashed banana and egg yolks and stir into the cooked mixture. Add the pineapple and butter and cook for an additional 5 minutes, stirring occasionally.

3. Make meringue by beating 2 egg whites until stiff. Add 2 heaping tablespoons sugar. Fold together.

4. Turn pineapple mixture into an uncooked graham cracker crust. Cover with meringue. Sprinkle with a few graham cracker crumbs. Bake in a preheated 325 degree oven for 20 minutes. Cool and refrigerate. Serve cold.

May be prepared 1 day ahead.

# DESSERTS

Nut-Butter Ice Cream Pie

YIELDS: 12-15 servings

This "sinful" pie must be prepared and frozen at least 2 days ahead.

12 ounces chocolate wafer crumbs	1 cup clover honey
¼ cup sugar	1 cup toasted cashews, chopped
¼ cup butter, melted	2 cups chocolate fudge sauce, heated
½ gallon vanilla ice cream, softened	2 cups whipped cream
2 cups creamy peanut butter	

1. Lightly grease 9 inch springform pan.

2. Blend chocolate crumbs, sugar, and melted butter in medium bowl. Press onto bottom and up sides of prepared pan. Bake in a preheated 350 degree oven for 5 minutes. Cool.

3. Mix ice cream, peanut butter, honey, and cashews in large bowl. Spoon into prepared crust. Freeze at least 2 days.

4. To serve, place pie in shallow pan of hot water 10 seconds. Remove pie from pan and top each serving with sauce and whipped cream.

Peaches and Cream Pie

YIELDS: 8 servings

A cake-like crust adds an interesting texture to this popular dessert.

CRUST

¾ cup flour
1 teaspoon baking powder
½ teaspoon salt
1 (3-ounce) package vanilla pudding (not instant)

3 tablespoons margarine, softened
1 egg
½ cup milk

1. Combine all ingredients and beat with mixer for 2 minutes. Pour into greased 9 inch pie plate. Set aside.

FILLING

1 (29-ounce) can peaches, sliced and drained, reserve juice
1 (8-ounce) package cream cheese, softened

½ cup sugar
3 tablespoons peach juice

1. Place peaches over crust.

2. Combine all filling ingredients and spoon over top of fruit to within 1 inch of edge of dish.

TOPPING

1 tablespoon sugar

½ teaspoon cinnamon

1. Mix topping ingredients together and sprinkle over pie.

2. Bake in a preheated 350 degree oven for 35-40 minutes. Refrigerate and serve cold.

Must be prepared several hours ahead.

Italian Easter Pie

YIELDS: 8-10 servings

Ricotta cheese and a touch of chocolate give this dessert that special holiday flair. It's worth the extra effort in preparation.

CRUST (cake-like)
¾   cup Crisco
2   cups flour
2   tablespoons sugar
1   teaspoon baking powder

½   teaspoon salt
1   egg plus enough milk to
    equal ¼ cup

1. In a deep bowl cut flour, sugar, baking powder, and salt into Crisco until the size of small peas. Sprinkle egg and milk mixture over flour until dough holds together. Probably will not use entire ¼ cup.

2. Chill about ½ hour, then roll out, and place in a 10 inch pie pan or casserole. Save dough trimmings to make lattice crust for top. Flute a high rim to prevent spillovers.

RICOTTA FILLING
1   pound moist Ricotta
    cheese
4   eggs, separated
1   teaspoon vanilla
½   teaspoon cinnamon

2   tablespoons candied fruits
½   cup powdered sugar
½   cup chocolate chips,
    sweet or semi-sweet

1. Place Ricotta, 4 egg yolks, vanilla, cinnamon, fruit, and sugar in a large bowl. Stir together.

2. Whip egg whites into soft peaks. Fold into Ricotta mixture. Stir in chocolate chips.

CREAM FILLING
2   tablespoons butter
¾   cup sugar
¼   cup cornstarch
½   teaspoon salt

2   cups milk
2   egg yolks
1   teaspoon vanilla

1. In quart saucepan, melt butter. Stir in sugar, cornstarch, and salt. Over low to medium heat, stir in milk and bring to a boil. Boil 2 minutes. Remove from heat.

continued

Italian Easter Pie *continued*

2. Beat egg yolks slightly, stir in 1 cup hot mixture. Return to pan, cook and stir 2 minutes more. Stir in vanilla. Let cool.

ASSEMBLY

1. Line bottom of crust with half the Ricotta mixture, then half the cream filling, last half Ricotta, and top with last of cream filling. Lattice strips of crust on top. Brush top with mixture of 1 egg yolk and 1 tablespoon water.

2. Bake in a preheated 350 degree oven (325 degrees if using glass dish) for 50 minutes or until knife comes out clean.

Mom's Yummy Chocolate Almond Pie   YIELDS: 6-8 servings

The almonds add a nice surprise.

FILLING

20 large marshmallows	¼ teaspoon salt
6 Hershey chocolate almond candy bars	1 teaspoon vanilla
	2 cups Cool Whip
½ cup milk	1 9 inch pie shell, baked or crumb crust

1. Melt marshmallows, candy bars, milk, salt, and vanilla in double boiler over medium high heat. Cool mixture. Fold in Cool Whip.

2. Place mixture in pie shell and chill 4 hours. Garnish with additional Cool Whip, if desired, before serving.

CRUMB CRUST

1½ cups cookie crumbs (chocolate, vanilla, or graham)	½ cup butter, melted
	½ cup powdered sugar (only if crumbs are not sweet enough)

1. Mix together and press into 9 inch pie pan. Bake in a preheated 350 degree oven for 8-10 minutes.

May be prepared 3 days in advance.

Peanut Brittle Pie

YIELDS: 6-8 servings

If you like peanut brittle, you'll love this pie!

CRUST

3	egg whites	½	cup flour
1	cup sugar	½	teaspoon almond extract
2	cups coconut, shredded	¼	cup butter or margarine, melted

1. In a small mixing bowl, beat egg whites until soft peaks form. Slowly add sugar. Continue beating until stiff peaks form.

2. Fold in coconut, flour, and almond extract. Gently fold in butter.

3. Spread mixture in a 9 inch pie pan. (To keep crust soft—first line pie pan with wax paper before pouring in mixture.)

4. Bake in a preheated 275 degree oven for 40-45 minutes. Cool completely. Top with filling.

If wax paper method is used; remove pie crust from wax paper and return crust to pan.

FILLING

½	cup peanut brittle, crushed	2	cups whipped topping
½	cup crushed pineapple, drained		peanut brittle for garnish

1. Gently fold peanut brittle, pineapple, and whipped topping together. Pour into pie crust. Garnish with peanut brittle. Freeze until firm. Let stand at room temperature 30 minutes before serving.

May prepare ahead 1 week.

Panache Chocolate Pie

YIELDS: 8 servings

Fantastically delicious!

½ cup butter	¼ cup flour
2 ounces unsweetened	½ teaspoon vanilla
pure chocolate	¼ cup pecans, chopped
2 eggs	(optional)
1 cup sugar	

1. Melt butter and chocolate in a double boiler. Set aside.

2. Beat eggs with sugar and add flour. Stir in the chocolate mixture, vanilla, and pecans. Pour into a heavily greased pie pan.

3. Bake in a preheated 325 degree oven for 30 minutes. Remove from oven and cover with foil to keep warm.

4. Serve warm or at room temperature with ice cream and fudge sauce.

Easy. May be prepared early in the day.

Perfect Pie Crust

YIELDS: 1 bottom plus a lattice top

This turns out right every time! The oil makes it delicate.

2¼ cups flour	⅔ cup Wesson oil
1 teaspoon salt	¼ cup water

1. Mix all ingredients. Roll out between wax paper.

2. Have filling ready before crust is made. Do not let set out. Bake immediately according to specific pie recipe.

Southern Nut Pie

YIELDS: 8-10 servings

Tastes better the next day!

1 cup soda crackers, coarsely crushed	dash of salt
	1½ teaspoons vanilla
1 cup pecans or English walnuts, coarsely chopped	1⅓ cups sugar
	1½ cups whipping cream, whipped or 1 (8-ounce)
1½ teaspoons baking powder	container LaCreme whipped topping
4 egg whites	extra nuts for garnish

1. Combine crackers, nuts, and baking powder. Set aside.

2. Beat egg whites until stiff peaks form. Slowly add salt, then vanilla. Slowly add sugar to egg whites while beating. Fold dry ingredients into egg whites. Line a buttered 10 inch pie plate with mixture.

3. Bake in a preheated 325 degree oven for 40 minutes. Cool completely. (It will fall in center). Spoon whipped cream into pie shell. Sprinkle with nuts. Refrigerate at least 2 hours.

The pie shell may also be filled with ice cream...peppermint is very good at Christmas.

May be prepared ahead 1 day.

Strawberry Short Pie

YIELDS: 8 servings

A dessert to celebrate the strawberry season.

CRUST

¾ cup flour
6 tablespoons margarine,
   melted

⅓ cup pecans, finely
   chopped (optional)
3 tablespoons brown sugar

1. Combine flour, margarine, pecans, and brown sugar. Mix until crumbly.

2. Press mixture firmly against sides and bottom of a 9 inch pie plate. Place an 8 inch pie plate firmly inside crust.

3. Bake in a preheated 425 degree oven for 15 minutes. Remove top pie plate. Cool.

FILLING

1 cup whipping cream
1 tablespoon sugar
1 cup cold milk
1 (3-ounce) package
   instant vanilla pudding

2 cups fresh strawberries,
   sliced, plus 6 to 8
   strawberries for garnish

1. Whip cream and sugar until soft peaks form. Set aside.

2. Pour milk into bowl with pudding. Beat until well blended, about 1 minute.

3. Immediately fold in whipped cream mixture and strawberries. Pour into pie shell. Chill until firm. Quarter large strawberries and place them all around the edge of the pie for garnish.

May be made ahead 1 or 2 days.

 # DESSERTS

After Dinner Menthes

YIELDS: 96 squares

More like a candy, this layered dessert is a nice touch to any meal.

1¼ cups butter or
   margarine, divided
½ cup unsweetened cocoa
3½ cups powdered sugar,
   sifted, divided
1 egg, beaten

1 teaspoon vanilla
2 cups graham cracker crumbs
⅓ cup green Creme de Menthe
1½ cups semi-sweet
   chocolate chips

BOTTOM LAYER

1. In saucepan, combine ½ cup of butter and cocoa powder. Heat and stir until well blended. Remove from heat; add ½ cup powdered sugar, egg, and vanilla. Stir in graham cracker crumbs. Mix well. Press into bottom of an ungreased 13 x 9 x 2 inch baking pan.

MIDDLE LAYER

1. Melt another ½ cup of butter. In small bowl, combine melted butter and Creme de Menthe. At low speed of electric mixer, beat in remaining 3 cups powdered sugar until smooth. Spread over the chocolate layer. Chill 1 hour.

TOP LAYER

1. In small saucepan, combine the remaining ¼ cup butter and chocolate chips. Cook and stir over low heat until melted. Melt chocolate just enough to spread. Spread over mint layer. Chill 1-2 hours. Cut in small squares. Store in refrigerator.

Prepare ahead. Keeps several weeks in refrigerator.

Apple Walnut Squares

YIELDS: 16-20 squares

Go for a day of fall apple picking and then serve these as a scout troop or classroom treat.

2 cups flour	¼ teaspoon salt
1 pound light brown sugar	1 egg, beaten
½ cup butter, softened	1 cup sour cream
1½ cups walnuts, chopped	1 teaspoon vanilla
1 teaspoon cinnamon	2-3 cups tart apples, peeled
1 teaspoon baking soda	and finely chopped

1. Combine flour, brown sugar, and butter in medium bowl and mix until finely crumbled. Stir in nuts.

2. Press 2 cups of mix evenly in bottom of a greased 9 x 13 inch pan.

3. Add cinnamon, baking soda, and salt to remaining mix and blend well. Beat in egg, sour cream, and vanilla. Gently stir in apples. Spoon evenly into dish.

4. Bake in a preheated 350 degree oven until cake begins to pull away from sides of dish and tester comes out clean, 35 to 40 minutes. Cool completely in dish and cut in squares.

Baby Ruth Bars

YIELDS: 3 dozen

If you enjoy the famous candy bar, you'll love these!

1 cup light Karo syrup	4-5 cups Rice Krispies
1 cup sugar	1 (12-ounce) package
12 ounces (1½ cups)	chocolate chips
chunky peanut butter	½ bar paraffin

1. Bring Karo syrup and sugar to a full boil. Remove from heat and add peanut butter and Rice Krispies. Form into logs, about 2 to 3 inches long.

2. Melt together chocolate chips and paraffin. Dip logs into this mixture. Logs will dry almost immediately.

# DESSERTS

Fudge Cheesecake Bars

YIELDS: 3 dozen

This combination of chocolate frosting and cream cheese is surprisingly wonderful... and it's easy to prepare.

CRUST

2 cups flour
1½ cups butter or
margarine, cut up

⅔ cup brown sugar,
packed

1. Mix flour and brown sugar. Cut in butter until it becomes a crumb-like mixture. Press into a 9 x 13 inch pan. Bake in a preheated 350 degree oven for 10 to 12 minutes.

FILLING

1 (14.3-ounce) package
creamy chocolate or
fudge frosting mix
1 (8-ounce) package
cream cheese, softened

2 eggs
¾ cup slivered almonds

1. Combine frosting mix and cream cheese. Add eggs and beat until smooth. Spread over crust and sprinkle with almonds.

2. Bake in a preheated 350 degree oven for 30 minutes. Cool. Store in refrigerator.

May be prepared ahead 1 day and stored in refrigerator.

Garbo Schnitte Bars

YIELDS: 7 dozen

A fun-to-make German cookie. A surprisingly easy dough to work with.

DOUGH

4 cups flour	2 packages dry yeast
1 cup butter	½ cup warm water
3 tablespoons sugar	3 egg yolks
6 tablespoons sour cream	

1. Mix flour and butter until crumbly. Add sugar and sour cream.

2. Dissolve yeast in warm water (105-115 degrees).

3. Add egg yolks and yeast mixture to flour mixture. Work with hands until dough leaves side of bowl. Divide dough into 3 equal parts. Roll one part out on counter until it measures 10 x 15 inches. After rolling it out, fold ends to center and sides to center to form a smaller rectangle for ease in lifting to pan.

4. Lay dough in bottom of an ungreased jelly roll pan. Dough is easy to work with. Fit sides and corners of dough to sides of pan.

FILLING

½ pound nuts, finely ground	1 (12-ounce) jar apricot preserves (Smuckers preferred)
1 cup sugar	

1. Combine nuts and sugar.

2. Spread half of preserves over dough. Sprinkle with half of the nut and sugar mixture.

3. Roll out second layer of dough. Repeat filling procedure.

4. Top with third layer of dough. Let stand in pan 1 hour. Bake in a preheated 350 degree oven for approximately 40 minutes or until golden brown. Cool.

ICING

1½ cups powdered sugar	2 tablespoons cocoa milk (enough to make icing smooth)
2 tablespoons margarine	

1. Combine icing ingredients. Beat until smooth. Frost entire pan when cool. Cut into small squares.

May be prepared ahead and frozen.

 # DESSERTS

Graham Brickle Bites

YIELDS: 64 bars

Rich toffee goodness.

FILLING

1 cup margarine	½ cup graham cracker crumbs
1 cup sugar	½ cup Bits o' Brickle
1 egg, slightly beaten	½ cup pecans, chopped
¼ cup milk	whole graham crackers

1. Melt margarine in pan. Add sugar, egg, and milk. Bring to boil, stirring constantly.

2. Remove from heat and cool to room temperature. Add remaining ingredients except whole graham crackers.

3. Line 9 x 13 inch pan with whole graham crackers. Pour filling over; top with another layer of whole graham crackers.

4. Frost and garnish with more Bits o' Brickle.

FROSTING

2 cups powdered sugar	milk
¼ cup margarine, melted	

1. Combine powdered sugar and margarine. Add enough milk to reach desired spreading consistency. Frost 9 x 13 inch pan. Cover and refrigerate overnight. Cut into small squares. This is very rich.

Must be prepared 1 day ahead.

Maple Raisin Nut Bars

YIELDS: 18-24 bars

A chewy snack especially good accompanied by a hearty mug of tea.

BARS

2	eggs	½	teaspoon nutmeg
1	cup sugar	½	teaspoon cinnamon
⅔	cup salad oil	¼	teaspoon allspice
1	cup flour	2	cups walnuts, chopped
½	teaspoon salt	1	cup raisins
½	teaspoon baking powder	2	teaspoons maple flavoring

1. Beat eggs, sugar, and oil together.

2. Sift flour, salt, and baking powder together. Mix in nutmeg, cinnamon, and allspice. Add this mixture to eggs, sugar, and oil. Add walnuts, raisins, and maple flavoring. Mix.

3. Spread in a greased 9 x 13 inch pan. Bake in a preheated 350 degree oven for 30 minutes. Cool. Drizzle frosting over bars. Cut into bars.

FROSTING

6	tablespoons milk	⅛	teaspoon salt
6	tablespoons brown sugar, packed	¼	teaspoon maple flavoring
2	tablespoons butter	½	pound powdered sugar

1. Combine milk and brown sugar in saucepan. Bring just to a boil, stirring constantly. Pour mixture over butter in a bowl and beat. Add salt and maple flavoring. Gradually add powdered sugar until frosting is a pouring consistency. (If frosting becomes too stiff, add a little milk.)

May be prepared ahead 2 days or frozen for longer periods.

 DESSERTS

Milk Chocolate Pecan Bars

YIELDS: 4½ dozen

These bars will disappear fast! Easy to prepare and may be made ahead 2 days.

COOKIE BASE

1	cup unsifted flour	¼	teaspoon salt
½	cup brown sugar, packed	½	cup butter, softened
½	teaspoon baking soda		

1. Combine flour, brown sugar, baking soda, and salt. Cut in butter until mixture resembles fine crumbs. Press evenly into a greased 13 x 9 x 2 inch baking pan. Bake in a preheated 350 degree oven for 10 minutes.

TOPPING

1	(12-ounce) package milk chocolate chips	1	teaspoon vanilla extract
2	eggs	¼	teaspoon salt
¼	cup brown sugar, packed	1	cup pecans, chopped (divided into two ½ cups)

1. Melt chocolate chips over hot (not boiling) water. Remove from heat.

2. In a small bowl, combine eggs, brown sugar, vanilla, and salt. Beat 2 minutes at high speed with an electric mixer. Add melted chocolate and mix well. Stir in ½ cup pecans.

3. Pour topping over cookie base. Sprinkle with remaining pecans. Return to 350 degree oven and bake 17 to 19 minutes. Cool completely. Cut into 2 x 1 inch bars.

Mound Bars

YIELDS: 36 bars

2 cups graham cracker crumbs
1/3 cup sugar
1/2 cup melted butter
7 ounces flaked coconut

1 (14-ounce) can Eagle Brand sweetened condensed milk
1 (12-ounce) package chocolate chips
1/2 to 1 cup slivered almonds (optional)

1. Mix graham cracker crumbs, sugar, and butter. Press into a 9 x 13 inch pan. Sprinkle coconut on top. Pour on sweetened condensed milk.

2. Bake in a preheated 350 degree oven for 15 to 20 minutes. Remove from oven. Sprinkle on the chocolate chips and spread over top when melted. Sprinkle with slivered almonds, if desired. Cool completely. Cut into small bars.

May be prepared ahead. Freezes well.

Nutty Goody Bars

YIELDS: 4-5 dozen

1 (12-ounce) package semi-sweet chocolate chips
1½ cups margarine
2 cups creamy peanut butter
1 cup margarine, melted
1/2 cup evaporated milk

1 (3-ounce) package vanilla pudding (not instant)
2 pounds powdered sugar
1 teaspoon vanilla extract
1 pound salted peanuts

1. Melt together chocolate chips, margarine, and peanut butter. Pour half of mixture into jelly roll pan. Refrigerate until firm.

2. Mix melted margarine, pudding, and evaporated milk in saucepan. Cook over low heat for 1 minute. Add powdered sugar and vanilla and beat until smooth. Spread over chilled chocolate layer. Refrigerate for 30 minutes.

3. Add peanuts to remaining chocolate mixture. Spread on top. Keep in refrigerator.

May prepare ahead.

 # DESSERTS

Chocolaty Chocolate Brownies

YIELDS: 18 squares

½ cup margarine
½ cup butter
4 squares unsweetened chocolate
2 cups sugar

1 teaspoon vanilla
1 teaspoon baking powder
1¾ cups flour
4 eggs
1 (12-ounce) package chocolate chips

1. Melt butter, margarine, and chocolate. Remove from heat. Add sugar and vanilla to butter mixture.

2. Add baking powder and flour to chocolate mixture. Add 4 eggs, one at a time, beating after each addition. Fold in chocolate chips. Pour into a greased and floured 13 x 9 x 2 inch baking dish. Bake in a preheated 350 degree oven for 20-25 minutes.

Peanut Butter Dream Bars

YIELDS: 32 bars

2 cups quick oats, uncooked
1½ cups flour
1 cup peanuts, chopped
1 cup brown sugar, packed
1 teaspoon baking soda
¾ teaspoon salt

1 cup margarine, melted
1 (14-ounce) can Eagle Brand sweetened condensed milk
⅓ cup peanut butter
1 cup M&M's plain chocolate candies

1. Combine oats, flour, peanuts, sugar, soda, and salt. Mix well. Add margarine. Mix until dry ingredients are thoroughly moistened and mixture resembles coarse crumbs.

2. Reserve 1½ cups crumb mixture. Press remaining mixture onto bottom of greased 15½ x 10½ inch jelly roll pan. Bake in a preheated 375 degree oven for 12 minutes.

3. Combine sweetened condensed milk and peanut butter in small bowl. Mix until well blended. Spread over partially baked crust to within ¼ inch from edge. Combine reserved crumb mixture and candy. Sprinkle evenly over condensed milk mixture. Press in lightly. Continue baking for 20-22 minutes or until golden brown. Cool thoroughly before cutting.

Pumpkin Cheesecake Bars

YIELDS: 48 bars

1   package Betty Crocker golden pound cake mix
3   eggs, divided
2   tablespoons margarine, melted
4   teaspoons pumpkin pie spice, divided
1   (8-ounce) package cream cheese, softened

1   (14-ounce) can Eagle Brand sweetened condensed milk
1   (16-ounce) can pumpkin
½   teaspoon salt
1   cup nuts, chopped

1. In large mixing bowl, combine cake mix, 1 egg, margarine, and 2 teaspoons pumpkin pie spice. Beat at low speed until crumbly. Press into bottom of jelly roll pan. Set aside.

2. In another mixing bowl, beat cheese until fluffy. Gradually beat in condensed milk. Add remaining eggs, pumpkin, pumpkin pie spice, and salt. Mix well.

3. Pour over crust. Sprinkle with nuts. Bake in a preheated 350 degree oven for 30-35 minutes or until set.

4. Cool. Chill and cut into bars. Store in refrigerator.

May be frozen.

Helpful Hints: Freeze chocolate and then use a potato peeler to make chocolate curls for top of desserts.

 # DESSERTS

Rum Fudge Brownies

YIELDS: 25-36

Gourmet! Gooey! Good!

½ cup butter
4 ounces unsweetened chocolate
4 eggs
½ teaspoon salt
2 cups sugar
1 teaspoon vanilla

1 cup flour, sifted
1 cup walnuts, coarsely chopped
2 tablespoons light rum or milk
¼ cup powdered sugar

1. Melt butter and chocolate in double boiler or microwave. Allow to cool; set aside.

2. In another bowl, beat eggs with salt until foamy. Add sugar to egg and salt mixture, 1 tablespoon at a time. Add vanilla while beating.

3. Fold chocolate mixture gently into eggs, then slowly fold in flour and nuts. Pour into a well greased 9 x 9 inch pan.

4. Bake in a preheated 350 degree oven for 25 minutes or until done. Pour rum over warm brownies. When cool, sift powdered sugar over top. Cut into small brownies.

Note: This recipe contains no leavening agent, therefore, it is important to gently fold the egg mixture and then the flour into the batter. This is a light but delectable gourmet brownie.

Salted Nut Bars

YIELDS: 48 bars

For the nut fanatic!

CRUST

3 cups flour	1 cup margarine, softened
1½ cups brown sugar, packed	1 teaspoon salt

1. Lightly spoon flour into measuring cup. In large bowl combine flour, brown sugar, margarine, and salt. Blend well.

2. Press into ungreased 15 x 10 inch jelly roll pan. Bake in a preheated 350 degree oven for 10 minutes.

FILLING

2 cups mixed salted nuts	1 tablespoon water
½ cup corn syrup	1 (6-ounce) package butterscotch chips
2 tablespoons margarine	

1. Sprinkle nuts over partially baked crust.

2. In small saucepan, combine corn syrup, margarine, water, and butterscotch chips. Boil 2 minutes, stirring constantly. Pour cooked mixture over nuts.

3. Return to oven and bake an additional 8 to 10 minutes or until golden brown. Do not overbake. Cool. Cut into bars.

May be prepared ahead and frozen.

 DESSERTS

Sesame Crunch Bars

YIELDS: 24 bars

To develop a rich toffee texture, store these in a tightly covered tin for 3 days.

1 cup butter, softened	2 cups flour
1 cup sugar	½ teaspoon tarragon
1 egg, separated	¼ cup toasted sesame seeds
1 teaspoon vanilla	

1. Cream butter, sugar, egg yolk, and vanilla.

2. Combine flour and tarragon together; mix with creamed mixture. Spread on a well greased jelly roll pan. Dough will be stiff to spread.

3. Beat egg white until foamy. Spread over top with pastry brush. Sprinkle sesame seeds on top.

4. Bake in a preheated 275 degree oven for 1 hour until golden brown. Cut into bars and remove from pan to cool.

Helpful Hints: When making cupcakes for lunch boxes, split cakes in half and put frosting on inside. This prevents messes.

Sugar Cream Bars X X

YIELDS: 2 dozen

If there are any leftovers, be sure to store in refrigerator.

BOTTOM LAYER

1 box chocolate cake mix	½ cup margarine, softened
1 egg, slightly beaten	

1. Combine chocolate cake mix, egg, and margarine. Pat into a greased and floured 9 x 13 inch pan.

TOP LAYER

2 eggs	1 teaspoon vanilla
1 (8-ounce) package cream cheese, softened	4 cups powdered sugar

1. Combine eggs, cream cheese, vanilla, and powdered sugar. Blend until smooth. Pour over bottom layer. Sprinkle with powdered sugar, if desired.

2. Bake in a preheated 350 degree oven for 35 to 40 minutes.

May be prepared ahead 2 days.

Soft Caramels

YIELDS: 2 pounds

Irrestible chewy goodness.

½ pound butter	1 cup light Karo syrup
1 pound light brown sugar	1 (14-ounce) can Eagle Brand sweetened condensed milk

1. Melt butter in heavy saucepan over medium-high heat. Add brown sugar until sugar dissolves. Add 1 cup of Karo syrup and can of Eagle Brand milk. Stir constantly until candy reaches 238 degrees on a candy thermometer.

2. Pour on a greased cookie sheet and cool. Cut into 1 inch squares and wrap in wax paper. Keep refrigerated.

Turtle Bars

YIELDS: 3-4 dozen

These will remind you of the popular candy.

1 (14-ounce) package caramels	1 cup pecans, chopped
⅔ cup evaporated milk, divided	¾ cup margarine, softened
1 German chocolate cake mix	1 (12-ounce) package semi-sweet chocolate chips

1. Melt caramels with ⅓ cup evaporated milk in double boiler over hot water or in microwave.

2. Mix cake mix, pecans, margarine, and other ⅓ cup evaporated milk together. Put half of the dough in a 9 x 13 inch pan, pat it down. (It requires a lot of pushing and pressing to cover pan.)

3. Bake in a preheated 350 degree oven for 6 minutes. Sprinkle chocolate chips over the top. Drizzle melted caramel over the chips. Crumble remaining dough over the top. Bake at 350 degrees for an additional 15-25 minutes. Cool slightly, cut into squares.

May freeze after baking.

Anisplatzchen
(Anise Drops with Hats)

YIELDS: 7½ dozen 1½ inch cookies

A hint of licorice enhances these cookies.

3 eggs, room temperature	½ teaspoon salt
1 cup plus 2 tablespoons sugar	1 tablespoon anise seed or
1¾ cups flour, sifted	1 teaspoon anise extract
½ teaspoon baking powder	

1. Sift together flour, baking powder, and salt. Set aside.

2. Beat eggs in electric mixer at high speed until fluffy. Gradually add sugar beating constantly. Continue to beat for 15-20 minutes more.

3. Reduce mixer speed. Add flour mixture. Beat 3 minutes. Add anise seed.

4. Grease and flour cookie sheets. Drop by heaping teaspoonfuls onto cookie sheets. Let stand in cool place, uncovered, 8 hours to dry or preferably overnight.

5. Bake in a preheated 325 oven for 10 minutes or until golden on bottom. Cool and store in airtight containers.

Easy. May be made ahead 1 week.

Chewy Caramels

YIELDS: 1 pound

2 cups sugar	1¾ cups light Karo syrup
2 cups evaporated milk, divided	1 cup butter
	nuts or coconut (optional)

1. Combine sugar, 1 cup of milk, syrup, and butter in a deep heavy pan over medium heat and boil 30 minutes, stirring often. Add remaining milk, stirring constantly as it boils briskly. Cook until it forms a very firm ball in cold water. Be certain it is cooked enough to develop a good "chew", 250 degrees on a candy thermometer.

2. Pour into buttered shallow 9 x 13 inch pan or cookie sheet. Allow to cool, then cut into long strips an inch wide, then cut to desired size. Wrap in wax paper.

# DESSERTS

Applejacks

YIELDS: 4 dozen

Nutritiously moist and chewy.

1	cup light brown sugar, packed	1	teaspoon nutmeg
½	cup margarine	½	cup oatmeal
1	egg	1	cup unpeeled apples
2	cups flour		(Jonathans, not
½	teaspoon baking soda		Delicious), finely
½	teaspoon salt		chopped
		½	cup raisins

1. Cream sugar and margarine together and add egg.

2. Sift together flour, baking soda, salt, and nutmeg. Add oatmeal.

3. Stir dry mixture into creamed mixture. Fold in apples and raisins by hand. Drop by teaspoon onto greased cookie sheet.

4. Bake in a preheated 375 degree oven for 12 minutes.

Easy. May be made ahead several days and will get more moist in container.

Chocolate Covered Pretzels

YIELDS: 60

Delightfully easy...delightfully yummy.

1	(6-ounce) package semi-sweet chocolate chips or (6-ounces) white chocolate	1	tablespoon vegetable oil shortening
		60	small pretzels

1. Melt chocolate with shortening in a small bowl over simmering water. Remove from heat, but keep pan over the hot water.

2. Drop pretzels, one at a time, into chocolate. Lift out with a fork, lightly tapping fork against side of bowl to let excess chocolate drip into bowl. Place pretzels on a wire rack to dry.

Cherry Date Drops

YIELDS: 7 dozen

A nice addition to your holiday baking selections. Stores well in airtight container for a month.

2 cups dates, cut	1 cup brown sugar, packed
½ cup sugar	3 eggs
½ cup water	1 teaspoon vanilla
4 cups flour	1 cup English walnuts, chopped
1 teaspoon baking soda	
1 teaspoon salt	1 cup candied cherries, chopped
1 cup butter or margarine	
1 cup sugar	

1. Cook dates, sugar, and water over medium heat until thickened. Allow to cool.

2. Sift flour, baking soda, and salt. Set aside.

3. Cream butter and sugars. Blend in eggs and vanilla and beat well. Gradually add sifted dry ingredients and mix thoroughly. Stir in date mixture, nuts, and cherries.

4. Drop by rounded teaspoon onto greased cookie sheet. Bake in a preheated 375 degree oven for 12 to 15 minutes.

Peanut Butter Pinwheels

YIELDS: 2 pounds

Yes, a potato is really used in this fun to eat and make recipe!

1 small potato (2-2½ inches in diameter)	1 teaspoon vanilla
1½ to 2 pounds powdered sugar	peanut butter

1. Cook potato. While still warm, mash and add powdered sugar. (Use enough powdered sugar to handle like pie dough.) Add vanilla.

2. Coat rolling surface with powdered sugar. Roll out potato sugar dough.

3. Spread peanut butter in a thin layer and roll like jelly roll. Slice and eat.

 **DESSERTS**

Chocolate Cherry Sugarplums

YIELDS: 3-4 dozen

Featured at our Auxiliary's famous Sugarplum Shoppe Bazaar.

COOKIE

1 cup margarine, softened	½ teaspoon salt
2 cups sugar	½ teaspoon baking powder
2 eggs	1 cup cocoa
3 teaspoons vanilla	maraschino cherries,
3 cups flour	halved
½ teaspoon baking soda	

1. Cream margarine, sugar, eggs, and vanilla.

2. Mix dry ingredients together and add to creamed mixture. Dough will be stiff. Roll into 1 inch balls and place on ungreased cookie sheet. Bake in a preheated 350 degree oven for 12 minutes.

3. Press half a maraschino cherry on cookie immediately upon removal from oven. Frost while warm.

FROSTING

1 (14-ounce) can Eagle Brand sweetened condensed milk	3 teaspoons maraschino cherry juice
2 cups chocolate chips	

1. Mix all ingredients in double boiler until chocolate melts.

The frosting makes enough extra for a little dab of fudge!

Chocolate Chocolate Chip Cookies

YIELDS: 4 dozen

Double, chocolaty good!

1 cup butter or butter flavored Crisco	1½ cups flour
1½ cups sugar	2 teaspoons baking powder
2 eggs	½ teaspoon salt
2 teaspoons vanilla	3 cups rolled oats
2 ounces unsweetened chocolate, liquid or melted	1 cup chocolate chips (preferably mini chips)
	½ cup nuts, chopped (optional)

1. In large bowl, cream butter and sugar until light and fluffy. Beat in eggs, vanilla, and chocolate.

2. Stir together flour, baking powder, and salt; stir into creamed mixture. Add oats, chocolate chips, and nuts. Mix well.

3. Drop from teaspoon onto ungreased cookie sheet. Bake in a preheated 350 degree oven for 12 to 15 minutes.

May be prepared 1 week ahead. Freezes well.

Double Dutch Pizza Cookies

YIELDS: 8-12

A great children's party idea. Teens might enjoy this at their slumber parties. Use icing in decorator tubes to add a special message.

¾ cup butter, softened	¼ teaspoon salt
1 cup sugar	¾ cup plain M&M's, divided
1 egg	⅔ cup nuts, chopped, divided
1 teaspoon vanilla	¾ to 1 cup miniature
1½ cups flour	marshmallows
¼ cup cocoa	¼ cup coconut, flaked
½ teaspoon baking soda	

1. Cream butter and sugar until light and fluffy. Beat in egg and vanilla.

2. In separate bowl, combine flour, cocoa, baking soda, and salt. Slowly add to creamed mixture, mixing very well. Fold in ½ cup of M&M's and ⅓ cup of the nuts.

3. Lightly grease a 12 or 13 inch round pizza pan, then line with kitchen parchment paper. Spread dough on pan to within ½ inch from the edge.

4. Sprinkle with remaining candy and nuts. Sprinkle marshmallows evenly over dough.

5. Bake in a preheated 350 degree oven for 15 to 18 minutes until edges are set. (Do not overbake.) As soon as it is out of the oven sprinkle with coconut. Cool 10 minutes in pan. Gently remove cookie with liner to wire rack to cool thoroughly. Cut into wedges.

Filled Sandwich Cookies

YIELDS: 12

A nice addition to your youngster's lunch box.

FILLING

1 cup ground nuts	4 tablespoons flour
2 cups combined ground dates, figs, raisins	2 cups sugar
2 teaspoons vanilla	1 cup water

1. Combine all filling ingredients in saucepan and cook until mixture is clear.

DOUGH

2 cups sugar	5½ cups flour
1 cup Crisco shortening	3 teaspoons baking powder
2 eggs, beaten	
1 cup sour milk (or buttermilk with 1 teaspoon soda)	

1. Cream sugar and shortening together. Add beaten eggs and sour milk. Mix flour and baking powder together; fold into sugar and egg mixture.

2. Knead dough mixture with more flour when rolling dough. Cut dough using a round cookie cutter. Place filling in center of bottom circle and top with circle of the same size. Pinch sides together. Bake in a preheated 350 degree oven for 10 to 12 minutes.

Easy. May prepare ahead 1 week. Freezes well.

Frosted Sugar Cookies

YIELDS: 3-4 dozen

COOKIE

1½ cups powdered sugar	½ teaspoon almond extract
1 cup unsalted butter, softened	2½ cups flour, sifted
1 egg	1 teaspoon baking soda
1 teaspoon vanilla extract	1 teaspoon cream of tartar

1. Beat sugar and butter until well blended. Add egg, vanilla, and almond extract. Beat until light and fluffy.

2. Combine dry ingredients and stir into batter. Divide dough into two balls. Roll each ball between wax paper to flatten. Refrigerate overnight.

3. Roll dough on lightly floured surface to ⅛ inch thick. Cut shapes with cookie cutter.

4. Place on lightly greased cookie sheet. Bake in a preheated 375 degree oven for 5-7 minutes. Watch carefully.

FROSTING

2 cups powdered sugar	¼ cup milk or more
½ teaspoon almond extract	food coloring
1 teaspoon oil	

1. Combine sugar, flavoring, and oil. Beat well. Add milk to desired consistency. Add food coloring. Frost cookies.

Stores in airtight container for 1 week. Freezes well.

Grandma's Molasses Cookies

YIELDS: 3-4 dozen

Serve with a mug of hot spiced wine and you have a holiday memory that won't be forgotten.

1	cup butter, softened	1	teaspoon salt
1	cup sugar	1	teaspoon baking soda
3	eggs	1	tablespoon hot water
1	cup molasses	1	tablespoon apple
1	teaspoon cinnamon		cider vinegar
1	teaspoon ground cloves	5½	cups flour

1. Cream together the butter, sugar, eggs, and molasses. Mix in cinnamon, cloves, and salt.

2. In a small cup, combine baking soda, hot water, and vinegar and add to cookie mixture. Stir in flour, cup by cup. Cover bowl and refrigerate overnight.

3. The next day, roll dough about ¼ inch thick and cut with cookie cutters. Bake in a preheated 375 degree oven for 8 to 10 minutes and cool on cookie rack.

Decorate with candies, currants, and icing after baking. If icing is not desired, decorate with red hots before baking.

Must start preparing 1 day ahead.

Grandma's Peanut Brittle

YIELDS: 1 pound

2	cups sugar	1	pound raw peanuts
½	cup water	1½	teaspoons baking soda
1	cup light Karo syrup		

1. Mix sugar, water, and Karo syrup in heavy saucepan. Cook to between soft and hard ball stage. Add warmed, raw peanuts. Cook to 1 point under 325 degrees. Take off and stir in baking soda, quickly, and pour into a buttered sheet cake pan. When cool, break into small pieces.

DESSERTS

Krispie Krunchies

YIELDS: 5 dozen

1 cup butter or margarine
¾ cup brown sugar, packed
¾ cup sugar
2 eggs
2 teaspoons vanilla
1 teaspoon baking soda
½ teaspoon baking powder

½ teaspoon salt
2 cups flour
1 cup coconut
1 (12-ounce) package chocolate chips
2¼ cups Rice Krispies
1 cup nuts, chopped

1. Cream together butter and sugars.

2. Beat eggs with vanilla into butter mixture.

3. Combine soda, baking powder, salt, and flour. Add to butter mixture. Blend in remaining ingredients.

4. Drop by teaspoonful onto greased cookie sheets. Bake in a preheated 375 degree oven for 10 minutes.

Easy. May be made ahead 4 days. Freezes well.

Glazed Nuts

YIELDS: 2½ cups

Consider giving this in pretty clear glass candy jars accented with a holiday ribbon.

1½ cups sugar
1 tablespoon light corn syrup

½ cup strong coffee, leftover
2½ cups mixed nuts

1. Combine sugar, corn syrup, and coffee in large pan. Cook to 240 degrees or softball stage. Remove from heat and add nuts. Stir until syrup becomes creamy.

2. Turn out onto greased baking sheet. Working quickly, separate nut meats with two forks. Cool.

Melt-In-Your-Mouth Cookies

YIELDS: 4 dozen

These are butter cookies that will simply melt in your mouth.

PASTRY

1 cup butter, softened	2 cups flour
⅓ cup whipping cream	½ cup sugar

1. Mix pastry ingredients thoroughly. Separate dough into thirds and chill.

2. Use ⅓ of dough at a time and roll out ⅛ inch thick. Using a 1½ inch round cookie cutter, cut circles in dough, then coat with granulated sugar.

3. Place on ungreased cookie sheet and prick each cookie with a fork. Bake in a preheated 375 degree oven 7 to 9 minutes, but do not let them brown.

FILLING

¼ cup butter, softened	1 teaspoon vanilla
¾ cup powdered sugar	

1. Mix together filling ingredients until spreading consistency. Spread 1 teaspoon of filling mixture on one cookie. Press another cookie on top. Repeat until all cookies are sandwiched.

May prepare ahead and freeze 1 month.

 # DESSERTS

Nothing Better Sugar Cookies

YIELDS: 5 dozen

A sugar cookie that truly stays soft. A goodie to eat plain or iced. Easy!

½ cup butter or margarine	1 teaspoon salt
1½ cups sugar	½ teaspoon baking powder
2 eggs	½ teaspoon baking soda
1 teaspoon vanilla extract	1 cup sour cream
3 cups flour	

1. Cream butter and sugar. Add eggs, one at a time, beating after each addition. Stir in vanilla and beat until light and fluffy.

2. Mix flour, salt, baking powder, and soda. Add to creamed mixture alternately with sour cream.

3. Drop by heaped teaspoon, 2 inches apart, onto well greased cookie sheet. Bake in a preheated 375 degree oven for 8 minutes. Frost with desired frosting.

Crazy Crunch

YIELDS: 2 pounds

A handy gift or a fun treat for your Superbowl Sunday party.

2 quarts popped corn	1 cup margarine
2 cups mixed nuts	½ cup light corn syrup
1⅓ cups sugar	1 teaspoon vanilla

1. Mix popped corn and nuts on cookie sheet or broiler pan.

2. Combine sugar, margarine, and corn syrup in saucepan and bring to boil over medium heat, stirring constantly. Continue boiling, stirring occasionally, 10 to 15 minutes or until mixture turns a light caramel color, then remove from heat. Stir in vanilla.

3. Pour over popped corn and nuts and mix to coat well. Spread out to dry. Break apart and store in tightly covered container.

Note: More popped corn may be added to spread out the toffee mixture.

Orange Cookies

1   cup Crisco shortening
2   cups sugar
2   eggs
4½ cups flour
2   teaspoons baking soda
1   teaspoon baking powder

½   teaspoon salt
1   orange (juice and rind)
    or about ½ cup orange
    juice
1   cup buttermilk

1. Cream shortening and sugar until smooth. Mix in eggs. Add orange juice and rind.

2. Combine dry ingredients. Add to egg mixture alternately with buttermilk. Drop by spoonful onto greased cookie sheet and bake in a preheated 350 degree oven for 10 minutes. Cool.

ORANGE GLAZE

4   cups powdered sugar
6   tablespoons butter,
    melted

4   tablespoons frozen orange
    juice concentrate

1. Mix ingredients together. If necessary, add more orange juice concentrate to make a soft glaze. Glaze cooled cookies.

Freezes well.

Pineapple Drop Cookies

YIELDS: 7 dozen

A fun tropical treat.

COOKIE

1 cup margarine, softened	4 cups flour
2 cups brown sugar, packed	1 teaspoon baking powder
2 eggs	1 cup nuts, chopped
1 (15¼-ounce) can crushed pineapple, drained, reserve juice for frosting	2 teaspoons vanilla

1. Cream margarine, brown sugar, and eggs. Add pineapple; mix. Add remaining ingredients; mix.

2. Drop by teaspoon on greased cookie sheet. Bake in a preheated 350 degree oven for 12 to 15 minutes. Cool cookies slightly, then frost.

FROSTING

2 cups powdered sugar	2-3 tablespoons pineapple juice
1 tablespoon margarine	3-4 drops green food coloring

1. Mix ingredients together using enough pineapple juice for spreading consistency.

Store in cool place up to 2 weeks.

Surprise Cookies

YIELDS: 5 dozen

There's a little kiss in every bite!

1	cup peanut butter	1	cup flour
½	cup butter	1	teaspoon baking powder
1	cup brown sugar, packed	1	(16-ounce) bag Hershey
2	eggs		**Kisses**
1	teaspoon cinnamon		**powdered sugar**

1. Cream peanut butter, butter, and sugar in a bowl. Beat in eggs. In a separate bowl, combine cinnamon, flour, and baking powder. Gradually add dry ingredients to the peanut butter mixture until well blended. Chill dough for at least 30 minutes for ease in handling.

2. Wrap about 1 level teaspoon of dough around each Hershey Kiss. Place on an ungreased cookie sheet.

3. Bake in a preheated 350 degree oven for 10 to 12 minutes. Remove and cool slightly. Roll in powdered sugar and let cool completely.

Ohio Buckeyes

YIELDS: 5 dozen

Even Michigan fans have to admit these are winners!

1	pound margarine	1	(12-ounce) package
2	pounds peanut butter		chocolate chips
3	pounds powdered sugar	½	chunk paraffin, grated or you may use prepared chocolate

1. Combine first 3 ingredients. Shape into balls the size of walnut or smaller. Place on cookie sheet and put in refrigerator.

2. Melt chocolate and paraffin in double boiler. Dip balls into chocolate mixture. Place on wax paper to set.

 **DESSERTS**

Yule Crispies

A grandmother's recipe that is a holiday must.

¾	cup butter	2	teaspoons baking
1	cup sugar		powder
4	egg yolks	½	teaspoon salt
1	teaspoon vanilla	2	teaspoons cinnamon
1½	cups flour	¾	cup pecans, chopped
		24	candied cherries, red or green

1. Cream butter and sugar until light and fluffy. Add egg yolks and vanilla. Beat until creamy.

2. Combine flour, baking powder, and salt. Add to creamed mixture. Place in refrigerator a few minutes so dough is workable.

3. Form dough into 1 inch balls. Mix cinnamon and pecans. Roll balls in this mixture. Place on ungreased cookie sheet. Flatten with bottom of glass dipped in sugar. Place ½ candied cherry in center of each cookie.

4. Bake in a preheated 350 degree oven for 8 to 10 minutes until lightly browned.

Easy. May be prepared ahead 1 week, store in airtight container. Freezes well.

Coconut Bon Bons

YIELDS: 2½ dozen

It will be hard to wait the three days as these candies ripen to their best flavor.

¾   cup mashed potatoes,
    chilled
1   pound coconut, flaked

1   pound powdered sugar
1   teaspoon almond extract

1. Combine above ingredients and mix well. Cover and refrigerate.

2. When completely cold, remove coconut mixture from refrigerator and form into ¾ inch balls. Place on cookie sheets and put in freezer.

CHOCOLATE COATING
1   (6-ounce) package milk
    chocolate chips
4   (1-ounce) squares baking
    chocolate (or semi-sweet)

⅓   bar paraffin

1. Melt chocolate and paraffin in top of double boiler, making sure water is hot, but not boiling.

2. When coconut balls are very cold, dip into the chocolate, and place on wax paper to set. After candy is set, store in airtight container.

3. In about 3 days, coconut filling will be partially liquified and then they are ready to enjoy.

Must be prepared 3 days ahead.

English Toffee

YIELDS: 50-60 pieces

If you enjoy the popular Heath bars—this toffee will become addictive.

1 cup butter (do not substitute margarine)	½ cup walnuts, chopped
1 cup sugar	4 ounces dipping chocolate (from candy craft store)
1 tablespoon light corn syrup	½ cup walnuts, chopped
2 tablespoons water	

1. Lightly butter a cookie sheet and set aside.

2. In a 2 quart saucepan, melt butter. Add sugar, water, and corn syrup and cook over low heat, stirring occasionally, until mixture reaches 290 degrees on a candy thermometer. Remove from heat.

3. Quickly add ½ cup chopped nuts. Spread about ¼ inch thick on cookie sheet and cool.

4. Melt chocolate and cool slightly, then spread over cooled candy. Sprinkle with nuts. When chocolate is firm, break into small pieces.

Keeps well in plastic or tin for several weeks.

Frosted Nuts

YIELDS: 1 pound

Unusual and delicious. Great gift idea!

1½ cups sugar	1½ teaspoons vanilla
½ cup sour cream	1 pound walnuts

1. Mix sugar and sour cream and boil for 5 minutes. Remove from heat and add vanilla and nuts. Stir until mixture gets sugary.

2. Pour on wax paper. Separate and cool. Store in airtight container.

May be made ahead and stored in refrigerator for 3 months.

Grand Marnier Truffles

YIELDS: 2 pounds candy

Sinfully delicious! A real crowd pleaser.

1²/₃ cups whipping cream
7 tablespoons unsalted butter, softened
16 ounces semi-sweet chocolate mini chips

2 tablespoons Grand Marnier
cocoa powder for coating (may use ground nuts, coconut, or chocolate to coat truffle mixture)

1. In heavy saucepan, heat cream and butter over medium heat until butter melts. Increase heat until mixture boils, stirring constantly. Remove pan from heat.

2. Add chocolate mini chips and stir until smooth, cool, and thick. Add Grand Marnier and blend well. Cover mixture with plastic wrap to keep the top from drying. Refrigerate for approximately 8 hours, stirring often.

3. When ready to form truffles, put approximately ½ cup cocoa powder into bowl. Make a rough ball of the truffle mixture, then coat with cocoa. Store in the refrigerator.

Must be prepared ahead.

Million Dollar Fudge

YIELDS: 100 pieces

4½ cups sugar
1 (12-ounce) can evaporated milk
1 (8-ounce) Hershey bar
1 (12-ounce) package Nestle chocolate chips

1 (13-ounce) jar Kraft marshmallow creme
1 teaspoon vanilla
2 cups walnuts, chopped (optional)

1. Bring sugar and milk to boil over medium heat using Dutch oven. Boil for 7 minutes and remove from heat.

2. Add Hershey bar, chocolate chips, and marshmallow creme. Beat by hand until well mixed. Add vanilla and fold in nuts. Pour into 9 x 13 inch pan. Let set at room temperature.

Freezes 4 to 6 weeks.

# DESSERTS

Microwave 2-Minute Fudge

YIELDS: 60 (1 inch) pieces

Grandma's best recipe updated by the modern microwave.

1	pound powdered sugar	¼	cup milk
½	cup cocoa	1	tablespoon vanilla extract
¼	teaspoon salt	½	cup butter or margarine
		1	cup nuts, chopped

1. In 1½ quart casserole, stir sugar, cocoa, salt, milk, and vanilla together until partially blended (mixture is too stiff to thoroughly blend in all ingredients). Put butter over top in center of dish. Microwave at high 2 minutes or until milk feels warm. Stir vigorously until smooth. If all butter has not melted in cooking, it will when mixture is stirred. Blend in nuts.

2. Pour into wax paper lined 8 inch square dish. Chill 15 minutes in freezer or 30 minutes in refrigerator.

Microwave Peanut Brittle

YIELDS: 20-24 pieces

Super simple and great for holiday gift giving.

1	cup sugar	1	teaspoon butter
½	cup light corn syrup	1	teaspoon vanilla
1	cup peanuts	½	teaspoon baking soda

1. Mix sugar and corn syrup well and microwave on high for 4 minutes.

2. Add peanuts to mixture and microwave on high for 4 minutes.

3. Add butter and vanilla to mixture and microwave on high for 1½ minutes. Stir in baking soda. Quickly pour on buttered foil.

4. Crack into pieces when cooled. Store in covered tin in a cool place.

Strawberry Dates

Crunchy date candies shaped like small strawberries—so pretty in your silver candy dish.

½ cup margarine	½ cup nuts, chopped
1 egg, beaten	½ cup coconut (optional)
1 cup sugar	2 small jars red crystal
1 cup dates	sugar
1 teaspoon vanilla	decorative stems
2 cups Rice Krispies	(purchase at cake
	decorating store)

1. Melt margarine; add egg and sugar. Stir until well mixed. Add dates and vanilla. Cook on low 6 to 7 minutes, then remove from heat.

2. Gently add Rice Krispies, nuts, and coconut. Put into a bowl and cool until mixture can be handled.

3. With moist hands, roll into 1 inch balls and then mold each ball into the shape of a strawberry. Roll in red crystal sugar. Top each one with a decorative green strawberry stem. Keep in airtight container.

Variation: Shape into 1 inch balls and roll in powdered sugar.

KID'S KORNER

KID'S KORNER

Berry Mallow Yam Bake

YIELDS: 6 servings

½	cup flour
½	cup brown sugar, packed
½	cup old fashioned or quick oats, uncooked
1	teaspoon cinnamon
⅓	cup margarine

2	(17-ounce) cans yams, drained, cut in half
1	(16-ounce) can whole cranberry sauce or 2 cups fresh cranberries
1½	cups miniature marshmallows

1. Combine flour, sugar, oats, and cinnamon; cut in margarine until mixture resembles coarse crumbs.

2. Lightly toss 1 cup crumb mixture with yams and cranberries. Arrange in a 2 or 3 quart casserole. Sprinkle with remaining crumb mixture. Bake in a preheated 350 degree oven for 35 minutes.

3. Sprinkle marshmallows over top. Broil until lightly browned.

Cheesy Potato Sticks

YIELDS: 6 servings

Try this as a nice accompaniment to your favorite grilled burger recipe.

3	tablespoons butter or margarine
3	tablespoons flour
½	teaspoon salt pepper to taste

1½	cups milk
2	cups cheese, shredded
1	(16-ounce) package frozen french fries

1. Melt butter over low heat. Blend in flour, salt, and pepper. Add milk, all at once. Cook quickly, stirring constantly until thickened and bubbling. Add 1 cup of cheese and stir until cheese melts.

2. Place potatoes in greased 10 x 6 x 1½ inch dish. Top with cheese sauce. Sprinkle with remaining 1 cup of cheese.

3. Bake, covered, in a preheated 350 degree oven for 15 minutes; uncover, and bake for 25 more minutes.

Cheeseburger Pie

YIELDS: 5 servings

The ease of a one-dish dinner.

1	9-inch pie shell, unbaked	½	cup dry bread crumbs
¾	pound ground beef	¾	cup tomato sauce
¾	teaspoon salt	⅛	cup onion, chopped
½	teaspoon oregano	⅛	cup green pepper, chopped
	pinch of pepper		

1. In skillet, cook and stir meat until brown. Drain off fat. Stir in salt, oregano, pepper, bread crumbs, tomato sauce, onion, and green pepper. Put in pastry lined pan.

CHEESE TOPPING

1	egg	½	teaspoon pepper sauce
3	tablespoons milk	¾	cup Cheddar cheese, shredded
½	teaspoon salt		
½	teaspoon dry mustard	½	cup chili sauce

1. Beat egg and milk; stir in seasonings, chili sauce, and cheese. Spread the cheese topping over filling.

2. Bake in a preheated 425 degree oven for 30 minutes. Cut and serve warm.

Coke Chops

YIELDS: 4-6 servings

Coke makes the "poke" delicious!

6	(¾ inch) pork chops	1	cup Coca-Cola
3	tablespoons oil	1	tablespoon Worcestershire sauce
½	cup catsup		

1. Heat oil in skillet until hot. Brown chops on both sides.

2. Mix catsup, cola, and Worcestershire sauce in bowl. Pour over chops. Cover and simmer until chops are tender, about 1½ hours. Sauce thickens into a barbecue sauce.

Chili Coin Casserole

YIELDS: 4-6 servings

This recipe was created by a 9 year old and adult taste testers rated it a winner.

1 pound Kielbasa or smoked sausage	2½ cups elbow macaroni, cooked
1 (16-ounce) can green beans, drained	3 teaspoons chili powder
1 (30-ounce) can Caliente-style chili beans	½ cup Parmesan cheese, grated extra Parmesan cheese

1. Cut sausage into ¼ inch coins and put into medium casserole. Add green beans, chili beans, macaroni, chili powder, and ½ cup Parmesan cheese. Mix well. Top with more Parmesan cheese and cover casserole.

2. Bake in a preheated 350 degree oven for 30 minutes or in a microwave oven for 12 minutes on high.

Corn Fritters

YIELDS: 1½ dozen

Kids rate these the greatest!

1 (14½-ounce) can cream style corn	2 teaspoons baking powder
1 egg, slightly beaten	1½ cups flour
1 teaspoon salt	vegetable shortening
2 teaspoons sugar	syrup

1. Mix all ingredients except shortening. Heat shortening in french fryer or skillet until hot. Drop fritter mixture from a large spoon into hot shortening and fry until brown. Serve with warm syrup.

KID'S KORNER

Hot Doggies

YIELDS: 8 hot dogs

Kids love these!

8	hot dogs	1	can crescent rolls
4	teaspoons prepared mustard	2	tablespoons barbecue sauce

1. Cut hot dogs in half, lengthwise. Spread with mustard; put back together.

2. Unroll dough; separate into 8 triangles. Place hot dogs on wide end of triangle and roll up. Place on ungreased cookie sheet. Brush with barbecue sauce. Bake in a preheated 375 degree oven for 15-20 minutes.

Variation: Use 4 slices of American cheese in place of mustard and barbecue sauce. Fold a half piece of cheese in half lengthwise and place in split hot dog. Wrap in crescents and bake.

Mom's Easy Goulash

YIELDS: 6 servings

Your family will vote on having this dish again and again.

1	pound ground beef	1	large can whole tomatoes
1/3	cup onion, chopped		
1	small garlic clove, minced	1	(15-ounce) can tomato sauce
1/2	teaspoon basil	1	(17-ounce) can kernel corn
1/2	teaspoon salt		
1/4	teaspoon pepper	3	cups macaroni, cooked
		1	cup Colby cheese, shredded

1. Brown ground beef with onion, garlic, and seasonings.

2. Break up whole tomatoes by hand, or if you prefer, a large spoon. Add tomatoes, tomato sauce, and corn to ground beef mixture. Let cook on low for 20 minutes. Add macaroni. Pour into 2½ quart casserole dish. Sprinkle with cheese. Bake in a preheated 350 degree oven for 30 minutes.

458

Macaroni and Cheese

YIELDS: 10 servings

A family favorite.

½ pound macaroni	pepper
¼ cup butter	10 ounces Velveeta cheese,
¼ cup flour	grated
pinch of salt	5 ounces Colby cheese,
1 pint milk	grated

1. Cook macaroni in boiling water, according to package directions.

2. Combine butter, flour, salt, milk, and pepper to taste and cook until thickened (use part of actual amount of milk to mix with flour to thicken).

3. Add grated Velveeta cheese and heat until cheese is melted. Pour cheese sauce over macaroni and mix.

4. Sprinkle Colby cheese on top of casserole. Bake in a preheated 350 degree oven for 30 minutes or until casserole bubbles.

Honey Crunch Baked Apples

YIELDS: 6 servings

Choose a good baking apple such as Rome Beauty, Pippin, or Golden Delicious.

6 large apples	2 teaspoons lemon juice
1/3 cup granola	1/3 cup honey, divided
1/3 cup dates, chopped	3 tablespoons butter or
¼ cup walnuts or	margarine, melted
almonds, chopped	¾ cup apple juice or water
½ teaspoon cinnamon	half and half (light cream)
¼ teaspoon nutmeg	

1. Peel apples, if desired, and core; stand upright in a 9 inch round cake pan.

2. To make filling, combine granola, dates, walnuts, cinnamon, nutmeg, lemon juice, and 3 tablespoons of the honey. Spoon equal amounts of filling into center of each apple (pack filling in lightly). Combine the remaining honey with butter and apple juice; pour over apples.

3. Cover and bake in a preheated 350 degree oven for 30 minutes. Remove cover and bake, basting with pan juices several times, until apples are tender when pierced, about 35 minutes longer. Serve warm or cooled. At the table, pass a pitcher of cream to pour over each apple.

KID'S KORNER

Monkey Bread

Mom's favorite monkies can prepare this one.

½ cup sugar	½ cup margarine
2 teaspoons cinnamon	½ cup brown sugar,
3 packages Hungry Jack buttermilk biscuits	packed

1. Combine sugar and cinnamon. Use scissors to cut each biscuit into four pieces.

2. Roll each piece of biscuit in cinnamon-sugar mixture and put into a 10 inch tube pan.

3. Melt margarine in a small saucepan; add brown sugar and bring to a full boil. Pour over biscuits. Sprinkle remaining sugar on top.

4. Bake in a preheated 350 degree oven for 30 minutes. Cool and pull apart to serve.

Pink Cheese

Yes, pink! And there's a magical way to make other colors too.

1 (15-ounce) container cottage cheese, small curd	1 (20-ounce) can pineapple tidbits or
1 (12-ounce) container frozen whipped topping	1 (11-ounce) can mandarin oranges
1 (3-ounce) package orange Jello	

1. Drain fruit. Mix all ingredients together. Refrigerate until served.

Other fruit and Jello flavors may be used to suit your preference. For instance, "green cheese" is good with lime Jello and pineapple.

May be prepared 1 day ahead.

Orange Granola

¼	cup frozen orange juice concentrate (undiluted and thawed)	1	cup wheat germ
½	teaspoon vanilla	½	cup coconut
½	cup light brown sugar, packed	¾	cup raisins
⅓	cup salad oil	½	cup dates, chopped
2	cups rolled oats	2	tablespoons sesame seeds
		½	cup almonds, chopped
		½	teaspoon salt

1. Combine orange juice, vanilla, sugar, and oil; mix well. Place the remaining ingredients in a large mixing bowl and stir well to combine.

2. Add the juice mixture and dry mixture together and stir until the dry ingredients are well coated.

3. Turn the mixture into a shallow baking dish (or cookie sheet) and bake in a preheated 275 degree oven for 30 minutes, stirring occasionally. Cool and store in an airtight container.

Other dried fruits may be added or substituted to individual taste.

Orange Cooler

YIELDS: 2 servings

Kids' size summer citrus cooler.

⅓	cup frozen orange juice concentrate	¼	cup sugar
½	cup milk	½	teaspoon vanilla
½	cup cold water	6	ice cubes

1. Combine all the ingredients in a blender. Blend until ice is chopped and drink is frothy.

May be prepared by children and is nutritious.

🝫 KID'S KORNER

Quick Fruit Cobbler

YIELDS: 4-6 servings

A great hit with the men in your life - both young and old.

2 **tablespoons margarine**	½ **cup milk**
½ **cup self-rising flour**	1 **(20-ounce) can peaches,**
½ **cup sugar**	**blueberries, or cherries**

1. Melt margarine in 1 quart baking dish.

2. Mix flour, sugar, and milk. Pour slowly into baking dish. Carefully pour fruit over flour mixture. Bake in a preheated 350 degree oven for 30 minutes or until lightly browned.

If using fresh fruit, sprinkle 2 cups fruit with sugar and let set for 30 minutes to form a syrup.

May be made early in the day.

Sloppy Joes

YIELDS: 4 servings

1 **pound hamburger**	1 **teaspoon**
¾ **cup onion, finely**	**Worcestershire sauce**
chopped	¾ **cup catsup**
1 **teaspoon salt**	½ **teaspoon pepper**
½ **teaspoon chili powder**	2 **tablespoons flour**
7 **ounces Sprite**	

1. Brown the hamburger and onion together until meat is tender and cooked. Drain fat off meat.

2. Mix other ingredients together and add to hamburger and onion mix. Cook over low heat until mixture is the thickness you desire, about 15-20 minutes.

May be prepared ahead. Freezes well.

Souper Macaroni

YIELDS: 4 servings

Twenty years of family approved testing makes this souper-duper macaroni a sure bet!

½ cup cooked ham, finely chopped	1 cup sharp or mild Cheddar cheese, shredded
¼ cup onion, chopped	2 cups macaroni, cooked (about 4 ounces uncooked)
2 tablespoons margarine	1 tablespoon margarine
1 can cream of mushroom soup	¼ cup bread crumbs
½ cup milk or water	

1. Lightly brown ham and onion in margarine in large skillet. Stir in soup, milk, and ¾ cup cheese. Heat until cheese melts, stirring often.

2. Pour sauce over macaroni and mix. Pour into buttered 1½ quart casserole.

3. Melt 1 tablespoon margarine and add bread crumbs. Stir, but do not brown. Sprinkle remaining ¼ cup cheese and bread crumbs over macaroni. Bake in a preheated 350 degree oven for 30 minutes or until browned and bubbling.

Tuna Torpedoes

YIELDS: 2 servings

1 small can tuna, water packed, drained	3 tablespoons Miracle Whip salad dressing
1 green onion, chopped (optional)	1 stalk celery, chopped
	1 cucumber

1. Mix first four ingredients well.

2. Slice cucumber lengthwise and hollow out. Place mixture in cucumber boats (torpedoes).

Serve with crackers. For extra eye appeal, serve on a bed of lettuce.

Stone Soup

YIELDS: varies according to ingredients

Mystify a nursery school or brownie troop by requiring each child to bring in a stone to enhance the flavor.

1   copy of Stone Soup (by Marcia
    Brown, in children's section of
    library)

broth or tomato juice   cooked beef or
onions, cut up   pork, cut up
potatoes, cut up   stones, 1 per person
carrots, cut up
celery, cut up

1. Read the story. Have the children find small smooth stones. Wash the stones.

2. Use your own vegetable soup recipe or follow the guidelines in the story.

3. When it's soup, remove the stones and serve with crackers or bread.

You may substitute a can of Veg-All.

Vegetable Medley au Gratin

YIELDS: 8-10 servings

A great way to get kids to eat veggies!

1   can cream of mushroom   1   (10-ounce) package broccoli
    soup   spears, frozen
1   small jar Cheez Whiz   1   (10-ounce) package Brussels
2   (10-ounce) packages   sprouts, frozen
    cauliflower, frozen

1. Combine soup and cheese. Combine vegetables in large baking dish. Pour soup and cheese mixture over vegetables. Bake, uncovered, in a preheated 325 degree oven for 1½ hours.

Yogurt Pie

Kids can surprise you with a presentation of their own elegant dessert making.

1   (12-ounce) Cool Whip
2   containers Dannon strawberry or raspberry yogurt

1   ready-made graham cracker crust

1. Mix together Cool Whip and yogurt. Pour into pie shell. Put pie in freezer for a couple hours. Store in refrigerator.

Any flavor of yogurt could be used.

Apple Wheels

A great lunch box surprise!

apples
peanut butter

lemon juice

1. Core an apple. Pack the apple with peanut butter. Slice the filled apple into 5 or 6 slices. Brush the slices with lemon juice to keep from turning brown. Reassemble apple until serving.

Banana Balls

5-6 bananas
1   cup peanut butter
¾   cup powdered milk

½   cup nuts, chopped
½   cup raisins
    graham cracker crumbs

1. Cut bananas into ¾ inch chunks.

2. Combine all other ingredients. Roll banana chunks in mixture to form balls; then roll in graham cracker crumbs.

Banana Peanut Logs

YIELDS: 4 servings

A no-mess snack that children can make.

1 banana	salted peanuts, chopped
mayonnaise	

1. Halve banana lengthwise; then cut across making 4 pieces. Spread each piece with mayonnaise and dip in finely chopped peanuts.

Celery Cars

A fun lunch box treat!

celery	raisins
carrot	toothpicks
peanut butter	

1. Clean and cut celery into 3 inch lengths.

2. Peel and cut carrot into ¼ inch round slices.

3. Fill each piece of celery with peanut butter. Press a few raisins into the peanut butter. Attach 4 carrot slices to the celery car with 2 toothpicks to represent the wheels.

Variation: Omit carrots and call the treat "ants on a log".

Aggression Cookies

YIELDS: 85 cookies

Kids will love beating up this recipe—look out Mom!

3 cups oatmeal	1½ cups butter
1½ cups brown sugar, packed	1½ teaspoons baking powder
1½ cups flour	

1. Combine all ingredients in a large bowl. Mash it! Knead it! Pound it! The longer and harder you mix it, the better it tastes. (Beat at least 5 minutes if using a mixer.)

2. Roll dough into small balls. Place on cookie sheet. Bake in a preheated 350 degree oven for 10 to 12 minutes.

Banana Whole Wheat Bars

YIELDS: 18 bars

1⅔ cups whole wheat flour	2 eggs
1 teaspoon baking powder	1 teaspoon vanilla
½ teaspoon baking soda	1 cup mashed ripe bananas
½ teaspoon salt	(3 medium)
¼ cup brown sugar, packed	¼ cup milk
½ cup honey	1 cup walnuts, chopped
½ cup oil	

1. Combine flour, baking soda, baking powder, and salt. Set aside.

2. Beat together sugar, honey, oil, eggs, vanilla, and bananas. Stir in flour mixture, milk, and walnuts.

3. Spread in greased and lightly floured 13 x 9 x 2 inch pan. Bake in a preheated 350 degree oven for 30 minutes. Cut into bars.

Coconut Macaroons

YIELDS: 24

1 (7-ounce) package coconut, shredded	1 (14-ounce) can Eagle Brand sweetened condensed milk
⅓ cup flour	1 teaspoon vanilla
⅛ teaspoon salt	

1. Mix coconut, flour, and salt in a bowl. Stir in milk and vanilla until ingredients are moistened.

2. On a greased cookie sheet, drop by teaspoonful, about one inch apart. Bake in a preheated 250 degree oven for 35 minutes or until golden brown. Remove to wire rack to cool.

Crumbless Teething Biscuits

YIELDS: 12

A special treat for the smallest family member and big brother or sister could help prepare them.

2 eggs	2 to 2½ cups flour (white, wheat, or combination)
1 cup sugar	

1. Beat eggs in a bowl until creamy. Add sugar and stir. Gradually add enough flour to make a stiff dough. Roll out between two sheets of lightly floured wax paper to a ¾ inch thickness.

2. Cut in round shapes with rim of glass (a doughnut cutter may be used to make it easier for toddlers to grasp). Place on a lightly greased cookie sheet. Let stand overnight. Bake in a preheated 325 degree oven until browned and hard, about 25 minutes.

Gold Medal Chips

4 ounces Cheddar cheese	½ cup butter, chilled
1 cup whole wheat flour	½ cup sesame seeds

1. Grate cheese and add butter. Mix in flour and sesame seeds until you have produced a dough mixture.

2. Form 2 or 3 rolls. Refrigerate about 45 minutes. Slice into ½ inch rounds. Bake in a preheated 350 degree oven until they turn pale gold.

Granola Bars

YIELDS: 24 bars

Great for kids' lunch boxes or a nutritious snack!

2½ cups oatmeal	½ cup brown sugar, packed
½ cup coconut	½ cup margarine
½ cup pecans, chopped	½ cup peanut butter
¼ cup wheat germ	½ cup honey

1. Mix oatmeal, coconut, pecans, wheat germ, and brown sugar in a 9 x 13 inch pan. Brown in a preheated 400 degree oven, stirring frequently for 20 minutes. Watch closely to avoid burning. Transfer to large bowl.

2. Melt margarine. Stir in peanut butter and honey. Pour over oatmeal mixture and mix well. Press into 8 x 8 inch buttered pan. Chill. Cut into bars.

Granola Cheese Crispies

YIELDS: 24 cookies

¾ cup flour, sifted
½ teaspoon baking soda
½ teaspoon salt
½ cup margarine, softened
½ cup sugar

1 egg
1 teaspoon vanilla
2 cups raisin and date granola cereal
1 cup (4-ounces) Cheddar cheese, shredded

1. Combine flour, baking soda, and salt; set aside.

2. Beat together margarine and sugar in large bowl. Beat in egg and vanilla. Stir in flour mixture until well blended. Stir in granola and cheese.

3. Drop batter by well-rounded teaspoons, 2½ inches apart, onto ungreased cookie sheet. Bake in a preheated 350 degree oven for 12-13 minutes or until golden brown around edges. Remove cookies to wire racks to cool completely.

Note: To make 12 jumbo cookies use 2 tablespoons batter for each cookie and bake 14-15 minutes.

Halloween Tortilla Cookies

Great for Halloween party treats!

½ cup sugar
1½ teaspoons cinnamon

salad oil
10 (8 inch) tortillas

1. Combine sugar and cinnamon to make cinnamon sugar.

2. Cut face in flour tortillas. Fry tortillas, one at a time, in one-half inch hot salad oil until golden and puffy (350 degrees for about 30 seconds per side). Set on paper towel to drain.

3. While hot, sprinkle one side of the tortilla with cinnamon sugar. Cool. Place in plastic bags. Store at room temperature.

Peanut Butter Bars

YIELDS: 8 servings

For convenience, individually wrap and store in freezer.

¾ cup whole wheat flour
½ teaspoon baking soda
¾ cup chunky style
   peanut butter
½ cup butter or margarine
½ cup sugar
1 teaspoon vanilla

2 eggs
½ cup chunky style
   applesauce
1¼ cups quick cooking rolled
   oats, uncooked
¼ cup toasted wheat germ

1. In small bowl, combine whole wheat flour and baking soda.

2. In mixing bowl, beat peanut butter and butter on medium speed, about 30 seconds. Add the sugar and vanilla. Beat well. Add eggs, one at a time, beating for 1 minute after each addition. Stir in applesauce and flour mixture. Mix well. Add rolled oats and toasted wheat germ.

3. Pour into a greased and floured 13 x 9 x 2 inch baking pan. Bake in a preheated 350 degree oven for 25 minutes. Cool completely before cutting into bars.

Bewitching Balls

YIELDS: 1-3 dozen depending on size

Enjoy … if you dare!

1 ½ cups ghost dandruff
   (oatmeal)
1 cup Dracula butter
   (peanut butter)
¾ cup snake eyes
   (carob chips)

½ cup ground bones
   (chopped pecans)
1 teaspoon Vampire blood
   (vanilla)
½ cup witch's cream
   (honey)

1. In a large bowl combine all of the ingredients. Stir well. Roll into balls and place on wax paper.

May be prepared 5 days ahead. Easy for children to make.

 KID'S KORNER

Rangers

YIELDS: 4-5 dozen

Freeze a batch or two of these and save for an after school treat or for those summer "Kool-Aid" days.

1	cup margarine	1	teaspoon baking soda
1	cup sugar	½	teaspoon baking powder
1	cup brown sugar, packed	½	teaspoon salt
1	tablespoon milk	2	cups quick cooking
2	eggs, beaten		rolled oats
1	teaspoon vanilla	1	cup dried coconut
2	cups flour, sifted	2	cups Rice Krispies

1. Cream margarine and sugars. Add milk, eggs, and vanilla.

2. Sift flour with soda, baking powder, and salt; add to creamed mixture. Stir in oats, coconut, and Rice Krispies. Roll dough into balls between palms of hands and place on ungreased cookie sheets. Bake in a preheated 400 degree oven for about 10 minutes. Remove from pans to cool.

Birdseed

peanuts   M&M's
raisins

1. Mix equal amounts of peanuts, raisins, and M&M's.

May substitute mixed nuts for peanuts, carob chips for M&M's, or add sesame sticks to above mixture. Great for lunch box, traveling, or to fill party favor cups. Easy for children to make. May be prepared ahead.

Wheels of Steel

YIELDS: 24 snacks

Full of crunchy grains for a nutritious snack.

1 cup light brown sugar, packed	¾ cup whole wheat flour
½ cup butter or margarine, softened	½ cup nonfat dry milk (in dry form)
½ cup peanut butter	¼ cup wheat germ
1 large egg	¾ teaspoon salt
1 teaspoon vanilla extract	¼ teaspoon baking powder
1 cup old fashioned oats	¼ teaspoon baking soda
1 cup raisins	3 tablespoons milk
	3 tablespoons sesame seeds

1. In large bowl, beat sugar, butter, and peanut butter until smooth. Beat in egg and vanilla. When well blended, add remaining ingredients, except sesame seeds, and mix well.

2. Pat into circles on ungreased baking sheet. Sprinkle with sesame seeds. Bake in a preheated 375 degree oven for 10 minutes or until cookies are lightly brown around the edges. Cool 5 minutes on baking sheet.

Helpful Hints: Toothpaste will remove pencil, crayon and black marks on walls or doors. Rub on with fingers and wash off with damp cloth.

✙ KID'S KORNER

Caramel Crunch

Munch a bunch of crunch—it's great!

5	cups Rice Chex	¼	cup light corn syrup
5	cups Cheerios	½	teaspoon salt
½	cup margarine	¼	teaspoon baking soda
1	cup light brown sugar, packed		

1. Place Rice Chex and Cheerios in large metal bowl or pan.

2. Combine next three ingredients in heavy saucepan and bring to a boil, stirring constantly until margarine is melted. Boil 5 minutes. (Place pan on small burner of range. Large burner creates too much heat.) Remove from heat and add salt and baking soda. Stir well. Pour over cereal and mix well. Put mixture into a roaster. Bake in a preheated 200 degree oven for 30 minutes. Stir occasionally.

Variation: May be prepared with 10 cups popped corn replacing the Rice Chex and Cheerios.

Microwave S'mores

Don't let a rainy day or the lack of a campfire stop the fun of this world-renowned camping snack.

1	graham cracker (2 squares)	1	large marshmallow
¼	(1.45-ounce) Hershey chocolate bar		

1. Place graham cracker on a paper napkin to keep cracker crisp. Top with chocolate and marshmallow. Microwave on high until marshmallow puffs, about 20-30 seconds. Top with second half of cracker. Let stand 1 minute so chocolate melts. Easy for children to make.

Variation: Spread graham crackers with peanut butter in place of the chocolate.

Christmas Trees

Try topping this gelatin treat with a dollop of whipped cream and a candy star.

1	(3-ounce) box lime Jello	1	(16-ounce) can fruit cocktail
1	cup boiling water		
1	envelope unflavored gelatin	16	maraschino cherries, halved
½	cup cold water	9	Lily (cone shaped) paper cups

1. Dissolve lime Jello in boiling water. Dissolve gelatin in cold water. Combine and stir well. Add fruit cocktail, including juice, cherries, and stir. Cool at room temperature.

2. Rinse cups with water and place, pointed side down, in 6-ounce fruit juice cans or juice glasses. Pour cooled gelatin into cups and refrigerate. When ready to serve unwrap cup with care, especially at tip.

Children can make these.

Peanut Butter Haystacks

Fun and easy.

1	(12-ounce) package butterscotch chips	1	cup salted peanuts
1	cup creamy peanut butter	3	cups chow mein noodles

1. Place first 2 ingredients in 2 quart glass casserole dish or bowl. Cover with plastic wrap and microwave at medium power for 3-5 minutes to melt. Blend well using rubber spatula. Stir in last 2 ingredients. Drop by forkfuls onto wax paper. Let cool.

♆ KID'S KORNER

Double Delight Cones

YIELDS: 18 cones

The pudding center is a hidden surprise!

1 (3-ounce) package regular chocolate pudding	18 ice cream cone cups, wafer type chocolate frosting
1¾ cups milk	sprinkles (optional)
1 yellow cake mix	

1. Prepare pudding according to package directions, using 1¾ cups milk. Cool.

2. Prepare cake mix, substituting milk in place of water. Spoon 1 tablespoon cake batter into cones followed by 1 tablespoon cooled pudding. Spoon 2 tablespoons cake batter on top of pudding.

3. Set cones on baking sheet and bake in a preheated 350 degree oven for 25 minutes. Cool on wire rack.

4. Frost with chocolate frosting. May decorate with sprinkles.

Soft Pretzels

YIELDS: 16-18

Here's a good scout project.

1 package dry yeast	4 cups flour (or less)
1½ cups warm water	1 egg
¾ teaspoon salt	coarse salt (optional)
1½ teaspoons sugar	

1. Dissolve yeast in water. Add salt and sugar. Mix flour in with hands and knead to make a soft dough. Cut into 18 pieces and shape.

2. Cover a cookie sheet with foil and sprinkle with flour.

3. Beat whole egg and a little water. Brush pretzels with egg mixture. Sprinkle with coarse salt, if desired. Bake in a preheated 400 degree oven for 15 minutes. Serve with mustard.

Ice Cream and Pretzel Menagerie

Serve up the ice cream scoops and let your kid's imagination flow—bunnies, dragons, clowns...

ice cream scoops	**pretzel sticks**
pretzel nuggets	**pretzel rings**
raisins	

1. Cat: Place one scoop ice cream on a small plate. Use pretzel sticks as whiskers, eyes, nose, and ears.

2. Turtle: Place one scoop of ice cream on a small plate. Use pretzel nuggets for feet and face, use sticks for tail.

3. Porcupine: Place one scoop of ice cream on a small plate. Stud all over with pretzel sticks and use a nugget for the nose.

4. Funny Faces: Use pretzel sticks or pretzelettes as hair. Press into a scoop of ice cream placed on a flat bottom ice cream cone. Pretzel rings are ears and raisins are eyes. Use pretzel sticks for the mouth.

Bubbles

Just add some childhood giggles for an afternoon of outdoor fun!

1	**cup lemon Joy**	1	**cup light Karo syrup**
1	**teaspoon glycerin (available at your local drug store)**	5	**cups water**

1. Mix all ingredients well. Let set overnight. Try blowing bubbles through a funnel, a soda straw, or an old thread spool.

Note: The syrup warrants using these bubbles outdoors.

Witches Broomsticks

YIELDS: 100

For your favorite goblins.

1 **loaf Pepperidge Farm sandwich loaf**	1 **cup creamy peanut butter** ½ **cup peanut oil**

1. Trim crust from bread, putting heels and crusts on one baking sheet.

2. Cut each slice of bread into 6 strips and put on another baking sheet. Bake all the bread in a preheated 200 degree oven for 2 hours until dry. Put the dried crusts and heels in a blender until finely crumbed.

3. Over simmering water, on the top of a double boiler, heat the next 2 ingredients for 10 seconds until consistency of cream. Place 8 sticks of bread into the mixture turning to coat. Remove sticks to paper towels to absorb excess oil.

4. Roll coated sticks in coarse crumbs. Place on the paper towels 2 hours to dry. Store in airtight container.

Crystal Garden

The magic of turning coal (often found in hardware stores) into a frosty formation makes this a fascinating project.

4   **tablespoons salt**
 2   **tablespoons water**
 2   **tablespoons ammonia**
	2 **tablespoons laundry bluing**
	     lumps of coal
	     food coloring

1. Mix all ingredients.

2. Place coal pieces in flat glass bakeware. Pour solution over coal. If desired, sprinkle a few drops of food coloring over coal at this time.

3. Leave your project undisturbed for a few days and white crystals will begin to cover the coal in an interesting formation, growing, and spreading everyday.

4. For more color sprinkle several more drops of food color onto the formation.

Doggie Biscuits

A fun project for dog's best friend.

3½ cups flour	3 teaspoons salt
1 cup rye flour	1 envelope active dry yeast
2 cups whole wheat flour	¼ cup warm water
2 cups bulgur (cracked wheat)	3 cups chicken broth
1 teaspoon dry beef bouillon	2 eggs, slightly beaten with 1 teaspoon milk
1 cup cornmeal	
½ cup instant nonfat dry milk powder	

1. Mix dry ingredients with a wooden spoon in a large bowl.

2. Dissolve yeast thoroughly in warm water (110-115 degrees) in glass measuring cup. Add to dry ingredients.

3. Add chicken broth to flour mixture. Stir until dough forms. Roll out dough until it is ¼ inch thick. Using a large dog biscuit for model or a cardboard pattern, cut out bone shapes from dough. Place on prepared cookie sheets. Brush dough with egg glaze.

4. Bake bones for 45 minutes in a preheated 300 degree oven. Turn oven off. Biscuits should remain in oven overnight to harden.

Let's Color the Snow

Wouldn't Jack Frost be amazed?!

2 or 3 drops food coloring spray bottle	water

1. On a snowy day when there's nothing to do, pull out those empty spray bottles and fill them with water. Add a few drops of food coloring. You can spray the snow and make many colorful designs. You can spray one color on another to make new colors, and it is even safe to eat.

Finger Paint

Your child's teacher might enjoy these as a Christmas gift for her class. Accent with crayon colored ribbons.

¼	pound starch	¼	cup soap flakes
1	quart water	1	teaspoon glycerin
½	cup hot water		poster paint in your
¼	cup talcum		choice of colors

1. Mix ¼ pound starch and 1 quart water. Boil until thick.

2. In another pot, mix talcum, soap flakes, and hot water.

3. Combine the two mixtures, stir thoroughly. Add a teaspoon of glycerin. Divide the mixture into several small jars and add poster paint or vegetable coloring to produce the basic colors. Keep tightly closed.

Modeling Clay

2	cups salt	1⅓ cups water
1	cup cornstarch	

1. Combine salt and ⅔ cup water. Bring to a boil.

2. Mix cornstarch with ⅔ cup water and stir until smooth.

3. Combine the first 2 mixtures with a wooden spoon. The dough should be smooth, pliable, spongy, and snowy white. Store in an airtight container.

Variation: Add food coloring when mixing. When modeling, objects may be left to harden and may then be painted.

No Bake Bread Dough and Paint

Here's a great way for preschoolers to practice the math of measuring and the art of creating.

DOUGH
¼ **cup flour**   ¼ **cup cornstarch**
¼ **cup Elmer's glue**

1. Mix and knead until well blended. If mixture is too dry, add a drop or two of glue. If too moist, sprinkle with flour and cornstarch. After making the desired art project, allow to dry for 24 hours, turning several times. To paint, use the Elmer's glue paint recipe.

PAINT

1. Mix food coloring with Elmer's glue. This will produce a shiny sheen to your paint. This paint may also be used to paint on glass.

Play Dough

Alum is the secret ingredient that helps to preserve this dough from molding.

2 **cups water**   2 **tablespoons alum powder**
½ **cup salt**   2 **cups flour**
  choice of food coloring   2 **tablespoons oil**

1. Mix water and salt together and bring to boil until the salt is dissolved.

2. Remove from heat and add food coloring, to make desired color; add oil and mix together. Add flour and alum and mix again. Let it cool until you can handle.

3. Knead several minutes. Store in airtight container. This dough will last and last if kept in container after each use.

A few drops of peppermint, lemon, or orange extract may be added for a scented dough.

Silly Putty

Loads of fun! Keep on hand for your favorite little visitors.

3 tablespoons (plus a little more) liquid starch	¼ cup liquid white glue

1. Mix together for 5 minutes. Knead and squeeze out any excess moisture. It will be slippery at first. Add food coloring, if desired. Store in an airtight container in refrigerator.

Snow Ice Cream

A good project for a scout's winter camping trip.

1 pint creamy milk	1 egg
⅔ to ¾ cup sugar	6 cups very clean snow
1 teaspoon vanilla	

1. In bowl beat together milk, egg, sugar, and vanilla. Add clean fluffy snow. Stir well until mixture is thick. The more it is worked, the better it is.

Ideas for Parties

1. Give each child a large sheet of waxed paper, a large sugarcookie, a popsickle stick, and a dollop of canned frosting. Children ice their own cookie and then decorate with colored sugars and candies.

2. One way to get around the cupcake is to make a "Cake Cone." Fill a flat-bottom ice cream cone about half full of cake batter and place the cone in muffin tins. Bake as you would for cupcakes. The cake will rise out of the cone and form a nice "scoop" on top. Cool the cones and ice and decorate with orange icing and candy corn. This treat can be used for other holidays by changing the icing and decoration.

3. For Halloween, make a "Witches Brew" by adding dry ice to your punch bowl. Dry ice can be purchased at Baskin Robbins.

4. Make a "Ghost Cake." Make cake into the shape of a ghost and frost with creamy white icing. Take the halves from a broken egg and place on cake for the eyes. Saturate two sugar cubes in brandy, place in egg shells and light for a very special effect.

5. At Christmas make a Snowman Cake. Put two round cake layers together to shape snowman Cake. Frost with fluffy white icing. Add black gumdrops for eyes and buttons. Add orange gumdrop for nose. Red string licorice for mouth. Cut pieces of black construction paper to resemble branch sticks and use for arms.

6. Make Snowballs out of ice cream. Dry ice in cooler keeps ice cream very cold. These can be served with the snowman cake.

7. Make a Red Apple Santa. Push a toothpick into the top of an apple. Stick a marshmallow onto the toothpick for Santa's head. His legs and arms are toothpicks strung with raw cranberries. Make eyes, nose, and mouth from raisins and attach with toothpicks. Add a ribbon around the middle of the apple for Santa's belt.

Under the Big Top

This is a great party for getting children involved and interacting with one another. Don't we all have a bit of the clown in us? (Ages 4, 5, 6)

INVITATIONS
Blow up a balloon, but do not tie it. Using a ball point pen, write the invitation information on the balloon and let it dry! Place the balloon in the envelope and mail it. (Don't forget to send it with a note to blow up the balloon!)

DECORATIONS
Use bright primary colors! Of course attach balloons to the front light post or mailbox so no one will miss the house. Inside, attach streamers to the ceiling (or light fixture) to give a "Big Top" affect. Tie helium balloons to each chair with the child's name on it. Use a white sheet for a tablecloth and place 11 inch round cut out circles from multicolored construction paper to make place mats. The cake makes a wonderful centerpiece.

ACTIVITIES

1. On arrival, paint the guest's face to make them look like a clown.

2. Make a clown collar using a sheet of brightly colored tissue paper. Leave it folded and cut 6 inch strips. Using a needle, push a 20 inch piece of thread through the paper. Knot it at each end. Tie the collar around the guest's neck and work it around like a ruffle.

3. Make a clown hat from a piece of paper cut 24 inches in diameter. Cut a line from the edge to the center. The guest can decorate it with markers. After the guest is finished, staple the hat in cone shape and punch holes at the bottom on opposite sides. Attach yarn through the holes as straps.

4. Play carnival games! Make sure guests have a bag to put their prizes in.

Pin the nose on the clown
Bean bag toss into clown's mouth
Shoe race
Peanut relay (Carry a peanut on a spoon.)
Smash the balloon (Each team member must run to a chair, sit on a balloon and run back to his team.)

continued

484

Under the Big Top *continued*

FAVORS

Peanuts
Prizes from carnival
Balloons

Box of animal crackers
Fancy shoelaces (like a clown)

MENU

1. Funny Face Sandwiches: Provide guests with ready-made sandwiches cut in circle shapes. Let them decorate a clown's face with the following "face makers": peanuts, raisins, cheese triangles, meat cubes, pineapple rings, green peppers and carrot slices, etc. A thin coating of margarine will make the face stick better!

2. 3-Ring Circus Rings: See Apple Wheels in Kid's Korner.

3. Carrot and celery strips

4. Circus Soda: make your favorite ice cream soda.

5. Big Top Cake: Make a canopy cake. Frost a layer cake. Decorate the sides with gum drops and string licorice to look like balloons. To make the canopy, cut a circle 8 inches in diameter from colored paper. Scallop the edges and turn them down. Tape 6 inch straws at equal points around the circle and 7 inch straw in the center. Stand the canopy on the frosted cake.

 KID'S KORNER

Land of Make-Believe

Once long ago, in a land far away, there lived elves, fairies and pixies. Come join them for an enchanting afternoon! (Ages 4, 5, 6)

INVITATIONS
Tape a magic wand made from a toothpick with a gummed silver star on the front of a folded card. Under the wand, write, "Shhh, listen—the fairies and elves are having a special party for Sarah and you are invited!"

DECORATIONS
At the party entrance, stand a large arrow with the words, "To the Land of Make-Believe." Attach wispy streamers to the arrow. Scatter confetti in a path of "fairy footprints" for the guests to follow. Make a tunnel by opening a large box; this is the entrance to fairy land. As the guests crawl through, they are sprinkled with imaginary fairy dust. As they enter the Land, they will see paper moons, clouds and stars hanging from the ceiling. They can pick candy from a gumdrop tree made by hanging bags of gumdrops from a large branch.

ACTIVITIES

1. On arrival, each guest can make a fairy crown or elf hat.

2. Guests can play enchanted webs by following his web to the prize at the end. (Use different colored yarns and attach a prize to the end of each. Weave the yarn around a room spider-web fashion.)

3. Players take turns fishing in the Pot of Gold using a stick with a string and hook attached. The pot of gold might be a large foiled flower pot placed at the end of a rainbow. Gold covered chocolate coins or pennies might be in the pot.

FAVORS

Crowns or elf hats.
Prizes from enchanted webs.
Small books of favorite fairy tales.

Items that fairies might use (wands, gold glitter, wings, box of fairy dust, etc.).

continued

486

Land of Make-Believe *continued*

MENU SUGGESTIONS

1. Sandwiches: Cut sandwiches with cookie cutter into shapes of flowers, hearts, stars and butterflies.

2. Fairy Necklaces: String any of the following together with a needle and thread: strawberries, grapes, apple chunks, banana slices, pears, raisins, cheese cubes.

3. Vegetables cut in miniature slices served on flower leaves or in tulips (if in season).

4. Fairy Nectar: Any punch

5. Castle Cake: Cut a sheet cake into three sections. Use inverted ice cream cones as turrets and chocolate squares for windows and doors.

Who Dunnit?

This is a wonderful party for children with a good imagination. (Ages 7, 8, 9)

INVITATIONS
Use plain folded notecards. Cover the outside of the card with footprints made by dipping the side of your fist in poster paint and stamping the paper. Add toes with finger tips.

write backwards
EMOC ESAELP
Give Clue "Use a Mirror!"

DECORATIONS
Cut footprints of colored paper and tape them to the floor for kids to follow from the front door to the party room. Use a white sheet with footprints on it for the tablecloth. The birthday person can step in paint and walk on the sheet! The centerpiece could be a mobile of magnifying glass, clues, question marks.

ACTIVITIES

1. Arrival activity might be making an ID card from a 3 x 5 inch index card. The child fills in the information about himself. Have a stamp pad handy so the guest can put his thumb print in the corner and add a polaroid picture!

2. Make mystery boxes! Put something unusual in five different boxes (pickle, rubber band, macaroni, powder puff, etc.) With his eyes closed, the guest detective must figure out what is in each box. He records his guess on a paper and the detective with the most correct guesses is dubbed "Super Sleuth."

3. Police Sketch is fun. Read off a description of one guest's eye color, hair, weight, etc., and have detectives guess who.

4. Everyone loves the game CLUE! Prizes given to the best detective.

continued

Who Dunnit? *continued*

FAVORS

Badges
Plastic handcuffs
ID card

Magnifying glass
Notebook (to record clues!)

MENU

1. Guess What? Sandwich: Guests create their own sandwich!

2. What's Next? Salad: Fill paper cups ¼ full with strawberry gelatin. Chill until firm. Add a little vanilla yogurt and slice bananas to cover. Add another layer of flavored gelatin and chill. Top with more yogurt and sprinkle with nuts.

3. Puzzle Punch: Fill each glass with apple juice. Make each glass of juice a different color. The guest must figure out what they are drinking.

4. Cake: Decorate a sheet cake to look like the ID card of the birthday child!

 KID'S KORNER

Home on the Range—A Western Party!

Playing cowboys and Indians is a favorite child's pasttime. (Ages 5, 6, 7)

INVITATIONS
Use construction paper cards in shapes related to cowboy theme: Stetson hat, gun, Indian headdress, sheriff's badge.

DECORATIONS
Make the entrance of the party look like a wild west cemetery. Prop up tombstones labeled with names from the wild west (Calamity Jane, Buffalo Bill, Annie Oakley). Make a teepee by painting an old sheet with Indian designs and draping it over a card table.

The party table can be covered with brown paper or place mats made from grocery bags cut so the ends are fringed. Put an Indian teepee at each place at the table. To make the teepee, turn a pointed paper cup (or a sugar cone) upside down. Cut the point off and glue toothpicks in the top as tent poles. Write a guest's name on each. The centerpiece can be a covered wagon made from a basket with handles. The cover of the wagon is stiff paper tucked under the basket's handle. Glue black felt or paper circles for wheels. Fill the baskets with popcorn treats.

ACTIVITIES

1. On arrival, make wild west attire! Cowboys could choose bandanas. Indians make an Indian headband from a strip of paper 2 x 24 inches and 8 inch feathers. After guests color and decorate their feathers and headbands, staple feathers to headband, form a circle from it and staple ends to fit the Indian's head.

2. After all the guests have made their costume, decorate the Indians with "peace paint."

3. String colored macaroni to make Indian beads. Color uncooked salad macaroni by putting it in a jar, adding a few drops of food coloring and a splash of vinegar. Shake. Dry. String the macaroni on thread or yarn.

continued

Home on the Range—A Western Party! *continued*

4. Play Sutter's Mill. With pie tins, guests take turns panning for gold in a plastic wading pool. (Use pennies for the guests to take home.)

5. Smoke a peace pipe. (Bubble pipe)

6. Rent a horse for a real cowboy ride.

FAVORS

Pennies from Sutter's Mill
Headdresses
Bandanas
Bubble pipes

Lone Ranger masks/badges
Miniature cowboy and
Indian figures

MENU

1. Cowboy Joes—Sloppy Joes—See recipe in Kid's Korner.

2. Celery Wagons—See recipe in Kid's Korner.

3. Corn on the cob.

4. Chocolate milk served in camping mugs.

5. Cake: Totem Pole Cake. Bake one 9 x 13 inch layer cake. Cut to look like totem pole after cake has cooled. Frost each section with a different color and decorate with Indian symbols.

"Go for the Gold" Olympiad

Sports and competition are always popular with energetic childen. (Ages 7, 8, 9)

INVITATIONS
On a folded white paper, put the Olympiad insignia and the honoree's name and age. Put all the necessary party information on the inside.

DECORATIONS
Use the five colors of the Olympiad insignia (blue, yellow, black, green, red). Cover the table with white and make place cards with the olympic symbol and each child's name. Use paper streamers and balloons of the same colors. The centerpiece might be made using small flags of the countries represented attached to bamboo skewers and stuck together with skewered fruit, into a base made of half a head of cabbage.

ACTIVITIES

Backwards Run	Hopping
Ball Toss	Hop-Skip-Jump
Bean Bag Throw	Obstacle Course
Bonk on the Head	Pillow Case Race
Frisbee Throw	Sprints

The winner of each is given a gold medal!

FAVORS

Gold medals—purchase gold foiled covered chocolate coins and glue on ribbon necklaces.	Ribbons for runners-up Small balls, frisbees.

MENU

1. Tacos

2. Tropical fruit spears (centerpiece)

3. Gold Medal Chips (recipe is in Kid's Korner).

4. Juice Brenner (orange juice).

5. Olympiad Cake—sheet cake with olympiad symbol.

A Teddy Bear's Picnic

"When you go down in the woods today, be sure of a big surprise." (Ages 4, 5, 6)

INVITATIONS
Cut out paper bears as you would paper dolls. Put a part of the invitation on each of the connected bears. Ask them to bring their best loved bear to the party.

DECORATIONS
Have your biggest bear dressed to greet the guests at the front door. Hide bears all over your house or back yard to be counted during the party. Spread beach towels or large blankets on the floor or yard for guests to sit on. Cover your table with a plaid picnic cloth and set individual lunch baskets on the table. (Use mushroom baskets lined with print cloth.)

ACTIVITIES

1. Guests arrive with their favorite bear and each teddy gets a prize as the oldest, smallest, largest, most unusual, fattest, best dressed, best behaved!

2. Guests are challenged to count the hidden bears.

3. Pin the pink bow on the Teddy. (Like pin the tail on the donkey.)

4. Play the record "Teddy Bears Picnic."

FAVORS

The picnic basket makes a bed for the smaller teddies.
Gummy bears.

Bear stickers.
Jar of honey.

MENU

1. Chicken legs

2. Bread and butter sandwiches

3. Raisins, nuts, carrot sticks

4. Small cans of juice

5. Cake should be shaped like a bear, of course.

Formal Tea Party

Every little girl loves to dress up! (Ages 4, 5, 6)

INVITATIONS
Make the invitations formal using pink note cards.

Miss Sally Rhoades
Requests the Pleasure of Your Company
for a Birthday Luncheon
Saturday, November 5, at noon

DECORATIONS
Set a formal table with fresh flowers. Make place cards by rolling a napkin, tieing it with a ribbon, and attaching a card with the guest's name.

ACTIVITIES

1. Have lots of dresses, jewelry, gloves, scarves, high heels and hats for the ladies to put on.

2. Fill baskets with hair brushes, combs, ribbons, curlers and make up.

3. Have a style show.

4. Make a purse by cutting a round circle of fabric 10 inches in diameter. Using a hole puncher, punch holes one inch from the edges and one inch apart. Lace a 12 inch shoestring through the holes and draw together.

5. Make fancy dress hats using paper plates and paper bowls. Cut the center from a paper plate and staple a soup bowl to the plate. Decorate with straw flowers, ribbons, yarns, and bows.

FAVORS

barrettes	combs
ribbons	hats
brushes	

continued

Formal Tea Party *continued*

MENU

1. Tea Sandwiches: Cut bread rounds with cookie cutter. Fill with cream cheese, ham salad, peanut butter.

2. Colored mints/mixed nuts

3. Tea with lemon slices

4. Cake: A formal cake frosted in white with silver leaves and pink frosting.

KID'S KORNER

Blast Off or Beyond the Stars

Space fans will love this party! (Ages 5, 6, 7)

INVITATIONS

You'll have a BLAST
At a Spaceship Party
For Spaceship Commander _____

At Command Base _____

Lift Off Time _____

Blast Off Date _____

DECORATIONS

Set the stage by playing records from spaceship movies. Decorate the room with twinkling Christmas tree lights; paper moons, paper planets, white and silver balloons.

Cover the birthday table with aluminum foil and make place cards from cardboard tubes and paper stars.

Make a Space Robot for the centerpiece by using a box or large ice cream carton as the body. Use a cool whip carton for the head and cardboard cylinders for arms. Cover these with aluminum foil and decorate with spools, pipe cleaners, and buttons.

ACTIVITIES

1. Arrival activity - Make spaceship helmets either from white paper bags or from five gallon ice cream carton.

2. Make paper airplanes and have a contest to see who can fly the fastest, farthest and highest.

3. Make spaceships from toilet paper tubes with construction paper cones for the rocket nose. Attach streamers of yellow/red/orange to simulate flames.

FAVORS

Milky way candy bar
Space activity book
Helmets made at party

Paper airplanes
Little plastic space men

continued

Blast Off or Beyond the Stars *continued*

MENU:

1. Space burgers—small buns with large hamburgers.

2. Solar chips—potato chips.

3. Lunar discs—pickles.

4. Banana ships—See Banana Peanut Log recipe in Kid's Korner.

5. Moonshine—punch.

6. UFO birthday cake—3 layer cake (two 8 inch round and one 9 inch round). Frost and make windows in center of dish with colored lifesavers.

Pirate Party

"Yo, ho, ho and a bottle of...!" (Ages 5, 6, 7, 8)

INVITATIONS
Make invitations from brown wrapping paper torn to represent an old map. Print X and your address and this message.

> "X marks the spot for fun and pleasure.
> Join us in play and help find some treasure."

DECORATIONS
Decorate the table with a box filled with old costume jewelery and beads spilling out of it. Make "jolly roger" flags and use them as place mats for your pirate guests. Hang an old Halloween paper skeleton in the corner!

ACTIVITIES

1. Fill a box with fake mustaches, beards, hoop earrings, bandanas, sashs, pirate hats, and eye patches made from black felt. Let the pirates adorn themselves and a polaroid of each makes a great souvenir.

2. Follow the pirate's map! Each player receives a different map with pictures, dotted lines, and clues such as, "Walk three steps to the patio bench. Turn right. Walk five steps to the maple tree," etc. At the spot marked X on the map, each guest finds a treasure.

FAVORS
> pirates accessories
> little bag of foil wrapped coins
> polaroid pictures

continued

Pirate Party *continued*

MENU

1. Hamburgers with crossed bacon strips to represent crossbones.

2. Treasure chests: small boxes (animal cracker boxes) filled with raisins and peanuts.

3. Oranges (to prevent scurvy)

4. Pirate punch: 1 part orange juice to 1 part cranberry juice.

5. Cake: decorate a sheet cake. Put a treasure chest (fill a watch box with jelly beans) on the top.

# KID'S KORNER

Tramp's Supper

Don't worry about clothes for this party! (Ages 5, 6, 7, 8)

INVITATIONS
Write the invitation on a page from the "Jobs Wanted" section of the newspaper. Fold the paper, tie a string around it, and deliver. Tell guests to wear oldest, baggiest clothes.

DECORATIONS
Make a sign for the front door stating, "Tramps, back door please!" Decorate the table with a newspaper tablecloth; catsup bottles with weeds; and wooden crates for chairs. Centerpiece is an old hat inverted and filled with styrofoam. Arrange mini knapsacks filled with goodies on skewers.

ACTIVITIES

1.   Play "What's in the Hobo Bag?" Hobo guests reach into a large bag filled with "junk" and try to guess what they touch! (stick, can, rock, tin mug, bent spoon)

2.   Play police and conductor. Two players are the police officer and conductor. They try to catch the bums (as in tag) and put them in jail (a large cardboard box).

3.   Play "Gone Fishin." Attach string and paper clip to stick. Have guests fish for prizes.

FAVORS

Mini knapsacks filled with goodies.
Red bandana (from table decoration and lunch).

Bubble gum cigars.
Marbles.
Bubble pipes.

continued

Tramp's Supper *continued*

MENU

1. Lunch should be tied in a bandana and tied to a stick! Utencils should be old and jars or tin cups for drinks!

2. Hot dogs

3. Garbage pan lids (See Apple Wheels in Kid's Korner).

4. Trail mix.

5. Mud milk (chocolate milk).

6. Boxcar cake: Cut a sheet cake into boxcar shapes. Frost and decorate as railroad freight cars. Use lifesavors for wheels and thin black licorice for a track.

KID'S KORNER

Recommended Learning Materials

0-6 MONTHS

Flutter Ball
Cradle Gym
Teething Toys
Mirror
Puppets (to watch)
Soft Spongy Shapes

Rattle
Squeeze Toys
Balls
Busy Boxes
Soft Cloth Dolls
Familiar Sounds Tape

Chime Ball—Roly-Poly Apple Chime (Playskool)
Musical Mobile—Color Mobile
See & Say Animals (to listen)
Music Boxes or Radios

6-12 MONTHS

Flutter Ball
Clutch Ball
Chatter Phone
Music Boxes and Radios
Stuffed Animals
Fisher-Price Activity Box

Cloth Books
Plastic Mirror
Sponges for bath play
Pull-String Toys
Real Doll
Puppets

See'n Say (Farm Animals, Zoo Animals, etc.)—Mattel
Books with stiff cardboard pages
Bath Toys (Plastic and Rubber)
Plastic, Vinyl Building Blocks
Small, Soft Texture Balls

12-24 MONTHS

Stuffed Animals
Plastic Nesting Cups—Ambi
Telephones
Housekeeping Set
Record Player Music Box
Melody Mike

Dolls
Balls
Water Toys
Bristle Blocks
Blocks
Smack 'Em Bag

continued

Recommended Learning Materials *continued*

12-24 MONTHS *continued*

Stuffed Animals
Plastic Nesting Cups—Ambi
Telephones
Housekeeping Set
Record Player Music Box
Melody Mike
Shape Sorter Box
Jumbo Pegboard with Pegs
Animals-Farm and Zoo
Puppets

Dolls
Balls
Water Toys
Bristle Blocks
Blocks
Smack 'Em Bag
See Thru Beads
Pounding Bench
Familiar Sounds Tape
Large Knob Puzzles

Cars and Trains (Creative Playthings)
Wagon
Chubbie Stump Crayons for Scribbling
Blocks
Developmental Storybooks
Books—See-Feel-Look Books
(Richard Scarry's Best Word Book Ever)
Pound-A-Ball
(Child pounds a ball into hole, ball slides down ramp)

24-36 MONTHS

Music Box Record Player
Large Knob Puzzles
Stacking Toys
Plastic Mirror
Dolls
Bristle Blocks
Tricycle
Crayons
Paste
Chalk/Chalkboard

Rhythm Instruments
Jumbo Beads
Toy Telephone
Farm Pegs
Pounding Bench
Shape Sorting Box
Lego—Duplo
Wagon
Playdough
Magic Markers

continued

Recommended Learning Materials *continued*

24-36 MONTHS *continued*

Blunt Scissors
Waterfall Toys
Shopping Basket
Buttons with Laces

Kitchen Toys
Fingerpaint
Medical Kit

Creative Playthings (truck, bus, car, etc., some may be large enough to ride)
Simple Puzzles (3-4 pices)—Fisher Price
Pouring Toys (for water and sand play)
Books (Dr. Seuss, Children's Stories)
Peg Board with Plastic Jumbo Pegs

3-5 YEARS

Art Materials:

Crayons
Magic Markers
Chalk/Chalkboard
Playdough
Paste
Large Paintbrushes
Blunt Scissors
Clay
Fingerpaint
Blowing Bubbles
Pounding Toys
Creative Playthings Pulley
Wooden Play People
Playhouse Equipment
Children's Books
Magnets
Play Squares
Bristle Blocks
Animal House

Simple Games:

Candyland
Hungry Hippo
Chutes and Ladders
Forest Friends
Simon Says
Role Play with costumes, hats

Peg Boards and Pegs
Simple Tool Chest
Wooden Cars and Trucks
Dolls
Puppets
Records/Record Player
Lego—Preschool
Colors Things
Small Beads

continued

Recommended Learning Materials *continued*

3-5 YEARS *continued*

View Finders	Magna Doodle
Etch-A-Sketch	Attribute Blocks

Sewing Cards (sturdy cardboard)—Creative Playthings
Shape Box (square plastic box with shapes cutout)
Picture Puzzles (5-8 pices)—Fisher Price
Mini Bus and People—Fisher Price
Balls (various sizes and shapes)

5-7 YEARS

Puzzles	Barrel of Monkeys
Art Darts	Wipe Clean Cards
Lite Brite	Halve to Wholes
Puppets	Bean Bag Toss
Lego	Counting Box
Clay	Lincoln Logs
Paint	Crayons
Paste	Cut
Dolls	Housekeeping Toys
View Finder	Dress-up

Games:

Operation	Candyland
Blockhead	Blockhead
Cootie	Chutes and Ladders
Casper the Friendly Ghost	Bingo

Card Games:

Go Fish	Lotto Games:
Old Maid	Classification
	Picture, Zoo, Farm

continued

Recommended Learning Materials *continued*

7-12 YEARS

Tiddly Winks

Wipe Clean Cards

Etch-A-Sketch

Baking Activities

Arts & Crafts

Assorted Puzzles

Stamp Collecting

Games:

Checkers

Aggravation

Parcheesi

Cards

Clue

Deluxe Monopoly

Dominoes

Battleship

Lite Brite

Bean Bag Toss

Lincoln Logs

Bingo

Backgammon

Sorry

Uno

Barrel of Monkeys

The Un-Game

Operation

Yahtzee

13 YEARS AND UP

Bingo

Football

Air Hockey

Cards

Checkers

Yahtzee

Music

Reading

Un-Game

Pinball

Monopoly

Chess

Uno

Battleship

Password

Cooking

Arts & Crafts

CONTRIBUTORS

Dianne Abbott
Thelma Ackerman
Judy Albers
Sandy Alex
Madonna Allread
Joyce AmRhein
Trudy Amy
Geri Anderson
Kathy Anderson
Lana Apple
Sharon Archer
Harriet Argue
Geraldine Arndts
Cindy Arrico
Sherry Aselage
Pam Aukerman
Rachel Aumon
Kathy Bahns
Deb Baker
Joyce Baker
Kevin Baker
Norma Baker
Russell Baker
Zo Ball
Christina Barber
Frances Barber
Doris Barga
Susanne Barga
Eleanor Barry
Joan Barry
Carolyn Barthel
Julie Bartley
Maryann Bausman
Jane Behm
Michele Bendik
Maura Benseler
Rusty Bergman
Ellen Berry
Carol Berwager
Willetta Berwager
Amelia Bhatnager
Kathi Bigler
Lynne Binkley
Carlene Biron
Elaine Bishop
Enis Bissonnette

Linda Bledsoe
Patti Bobo
Marion Bodiker
Judy Bohardt
Nadelle Borst
Jackie Boyer
Pat Boyer
Maureen Bradly
Joanie Braisted
Cathy Brandt
Ann Braun
Bonnie Brenner
Cissy Brown
Mary Brown
Mary Beth Bruchs
Kathleen Brumbaugh
Marie Bucher
Valerie Bucher
Judy Bundenthal
Nancy Burnett
Ann Burshtan
Eileen Busch
Marilyn Calloway
Brenda Campbell
Mary Ellen Campbell
Carole Carlson
Gail Carlson
Rachel Carlson
Billie Carpenter
Donna Carpenter
Lynn Carr
Diane Case
Brenda Chodkowski
Harriet Christolear
Bonnie Clark
Gretchen Cleaves
Cheryl Clemmons
Jane Clum
Pam Clum
Jennifer Cole
Donna Conley
Dick Conner
Louise Conner
Pam Cook
Mary Cooney
Kathleen Cooper

Monica Cooper
Beverly Cowden
Nanci Crabtree
Shelly Crain
Cheryl Craver
Phyliss Crawford
Debbie Cress
Pat Crossley
Marti Culver
Dori Custer
Dean Davell
Michael Davell
Phyllis Davell
Karen Davis
Judy Dean
Jane Deem
Jessie Delater
Lee DeLauer
Karen Demeter
Louise Donahue
Martha Doody
Pat Doyle
Sandra Drain
Jeri Drew
Anita Drummond
Mary Drysdale
Anne Duff
Becky Dunbar
Shirley Duncan
Donna Duplain
Pamela Duran
Audrey DuVall
Marion Earman
Frannie Ely
Fayette Engstrom
Marge Erickson
Virginia Esken
Nancy Fancies
Kathy Fatzinger
Karen Feltz
Judy Fergus
Robin Fetter
Paula Fishman
Ellie Flaherty
Peggy Foley
Carolyn Fournier

Carol Fox
Laurie Franz
Edie Freytag
Mary Fries
Rosemarie Friz
Hannah Fry
Diana Frye
Jo Anne Frye
Gale Garrett
Sylvia Gayda
Judy Gayheart
Mary Ellen Geier
Nicole Genovesi
Mary Ann Gerlach
Renee Geyer
Bev Gillig
Stefanie Ginger
Vernie Glasgow
Mary Glesige
Rosie Goforth
Susan Gonzalez
Evelyn Good
Carol Gorsuch
Deb Gower
Jo Ann Graf
Evelyn Grant
Kristin Green
Susan Greene
Betsy Greenlee
Gwen Greenway
Debbie Gresham
Marge Griep
Rita Grier
Ruth Griffin
Kay Grissom
Kathi Gruner
Mary Ann Gulach
Nancy Hass
Erma Hagan
Linda Hageman
Judy Hahn
Barbara Hall
Sandy Hall
Chery Halteman
Linda Hamilton
Amy Hanes

♦ CONTRIBUTORS

Lorraine Harclerode
Mary Ann Harnun
Jan Harris
Julie Hauer
Mary Haught
Judy Hayes
Kathy Hayes
Bonnie Haying
Marcia Heben
Martha Heck
Christian Hedge
Sue Hedge
Barbara Hegele
Betty Hein
Ann Heller
Connie Henry
Peggy Henry
Sue Hiatt
Candy Hill
Graci Hill
Betty Hillgruber
Brenda Hinten
Terri Hoernemann
Mary Lou Holland
Ann Holt
Mary Houpis
Deborah Hunt
JoAnn Hunter
Kathy Hupman
Ann Huston
Cindy Huxtable
Shirley Jackson
Susan James
Lois Jamison
Janet Jared
Chris Jaynes
Susie Jones
Annette Jordan
Betty Jordan
Sue Kaloyanides
Marilyn Kaple
Stephanie Kaple
Helen Karn
Rita Kauffman
Dottie Kemmer
Alicia Kern

Jean Khrisner
Evie Evers King
Ann Kingston
Vicki Kinney
Jan Kish
Gwen Klemmer
Jean Kluesner
Barbara Knoth
Dianne Koehler
June Kogut
Susan Kolb
Rebecca Kraus
Clare Krinke
Phyllis Latham
Mary Jo Latkovic
Kathy Lawrence
Barbara Laymon
B. J. Lee
Erin Lee
Linda Lee
Nancy Lees
Marlene Leone
Sarah Leventhal
Shirley Leventhal
Bonnie Lewber
Linda Light
Anita Linck
Irene Lindner
Linda Link
Barbara Linn
Carol Litwinko
Gail Logan
Judy Logan
Barbara Long
Jennifer Long
JaNelle LoPresti
Amy Lunay-Miller
Mavis Lunsford
Irene Lusciano
Sandy Lutz
Marcy Mahle
Paula Malnar
Linda Maly
Denise Manley
Ruth Mantes
Marty Marcero

Katherine Mardas
Maureen Mariotti
Barbara Martin
Fran Martin
Ginny Martin
Jane May
Duff McAlpine
Helen McAlpine
Kathy McAlpine
Linda McBride
Joyce McCool
Linda McCune
Mary McDonald
Connie McEldowney
Charrie McFadden
Andrew McFall
Marianne McFall
Patrick McFall
Jill McHale
Nancy McHale
Carole McNeil
Cindy Meckstroth
Karen Medford
Mary Beth Melville
Karen Mercer
Susan Meyer
Kathy Miles
Pat Miles
Amy Miller
Betty Miller
Karen Miltko
Brad Mitchell
Bryan Mitchell
Jacquelyn Mitchell
Stephanie Mitchell
Gail Moore
Judy Moore
Shirley Moore
Susan Morgan
Sandra Kaye Morrison
Mary Jo Morrow
Ginny Morton
Cecily Mosier
Ellen Mowchan
Connie Moxley
Marsha Mullins

Joyce Murray
Barbara Murtaugh
Ellen Neidenthal
Bea Nekrosius
Fonda Newbauer
Lois Nisonger
Patty Noreikas
Penny Noyes
Judith Numbers
Kathy O'Bryan
Libby O'Bryan
Mary Ann O'Bryan
Mike O'Bryan
Marie Osbun
Ginny Ostberg
Kitty Owens
Stephanie Palmer
Shelia Parker
Karen Parnell
Glenda Parrillo
Pam Pasley
Marianne Patton
Barbara Peck
Cheri Pendley
Angie Pentenburg
Donna Peters
Claire Pfeiffer
Jean Plunkett
Nancy Poettinger
Connie Poland
Katie Poling
Garnet Pollard
Sharon Pomrink
Barbara Preddy
Ann Preonas
Janet Putney
Pat Rasnick
Lea Ravlin
Pam Readnower
Bonnie Reese
Lisa Reeves
Gesche Reuther
Carolyn Rice
Nathan Ridings
Pam Ridings
Debbie Rieman

CONTRIBUTORS

Janice Risko
Harriet Roberts
Connie Roe
Phyllis Rose
Shirley Rundell
Carol Ann Ryall
Babs Ryan
Dianne Ryan
Rita Saettel
Gloria Saintignon
Jan Sakada
Marianne Salter
Jenny Santurbane
Dorothy Sargent
Pam Sass
Nancye Schooley
Cat Schuman
Doris Scott
Cindy Seman
Mary Seman
Susan Serr
Mila Serve
Helen Shaffer
Cindy Shartle
Carla Shea
Norene Shelton
Nancy Shereda
Renee Shisman
Deborah Shiverdec
Dorothy Shoe
Sarah Sillin
Diane Simmons
Carol Sitton
Ann Smith
Georgia Smith
Libbey Smith
Sharon Smith
Jane Smithson
Judy Snell
Carol Snyder
Judy Snyders
Conni Soper
Sandy Spencer
Debbie Spitler
Cindy Spohn
Erica Sprenkel

Linda Sprenkel
Kathy St. Pierre
Kathy Stahl
Kay Stegner
Ingrid Stephan
Pat Steveley
Elaine Stewart
Kathy Striplin
Susan Strouse
Peggy Surdyk
Laurel Suttmiller
Linda Swartzel
Sue Tepper
Sandy Termuhlen
Judy Terrell
Paula Thalman
Rosemary Thesing
Lois Thomas
Kris Thurman
Ruth Tinnerman
Sue Tipper
Jackie Tippy
Jean Ann Tod
Christine Tokarz
Sudsy Torbeck
Jane Treiber
Sherri Tschudin
Vickie Turner
Kathy Tytko
Dianne van Ruiten
Mavis Verdoorn
Marla Vichich
Erika von Mohr
Linda von Mohr
Kae Wade
Colleen Wainwright
Lois Walker
Jan Walters
Vicki Ward
Linda Wegley
Carol Weiland
Peggy Welsh
Erin Wendrick
Kristi Wenrick
Peggy Wenrick
Kathy Weston

Mary Lou Whitacre
Aquila Wickline
Beverly Williams
Jeane Williams
Joan Wolf
Marcia Wood
Shirley Younkin
Ruth Zavaglia
Marilyn Zobrist
Nikki Zonars

INDEX

INDEX

INDEX

INDEX

INDEX

INDEX

INDEX

INDEX

INDEX

INDEX

INDEX

SIMPLY SENSATIONAL

The Children's Medical Center
One Children's Plaza
Dayton, Ohio 45404-1815

Please send _____ copies of Simply Sensational   @ 14.95 each $_____

Ohio residents add sales tax   @   .97 each $_____

Plus postage and handling ($1.00 extra copies to same address)   @ 2.50 each $_____

Please gift wrap   @ 1.00 each $_____

Make checks payable to SIMPLY SENSATIONAL   TOTAL $_____

Charge to Visa (   ) or MasterCard (   ) # _____ Exp. Date _____

   Signature _____

Mail to: Name _____

   Address _____

   City _____ State _____ Zip _____

SIMPLY SENSATIONAL

The Children's Medical Center
One Children's Plaza
Dayton, Ohio 45404-1815

Please send _____ copies of Simply Sensational   @ 14.95 each $_____

Ohio residents add sales tax   @   .97 each $_____

Plus postage and handling ($1.00 extra copies to same address)   @ 2.50 each $_____

Please gift wrap   @ 1.00 each $_____

Make checks payable to SIMPLY SENSATIONAL   TOTAL $_____

Charge to Visa (   ) or MasterCard (   ) # _____ Exp. Date _____

   Signature _____

Mail to: Name _____

   Address _____

   City _____ State _____ Zip _____

SIMPLY SENSATIONAL

The Children's Medical Center
One Children's Plaza
Dayton, Ohio 45404-1815

Please send _____ copies of Simply Sensational   @ 14.95 each $_____

Ohio residents add sales tax   @   .97 each $_____

Plus postage and handling ($1.00 extra copies to same address)   @ 2.50 each $_____

Please gift wrap   @ 1.00 each $_____

Make checks payable to SIMPLY SENSATIONAL   TOTAL $_____

Charge to Visa (   ) or MasterCard (   ) # _____ Exp. Date _____

   Signature _____

Mail to: Name _____

   Address _____

   City _____ State _____ Zip _____

Reorder Additional Copies

Gift wrap and send to the following:

Name _____

Address _____

City _____ State _____ Zip _____

Gift card to read: _____

- -

Gift wrap and send to the following:

Name _____

Address _____

City _____ State _____ Zip _____

Gift card to read: _____

- -

Gift wrap and send to the following:

Name _____

Address _____

City _____ State _____ Zip _____

Gift card to read: _____

- -

Gift wrap and send to the following:

Name _____

Address _____

City _____ State _____ Zip _____

Gift card to read: _____

- -

Gift wrap and send to the following:

Name _____

Address _____

City _____ State _____ Zip _____

Gift card to read: _____

- -

Gift wrap and send to the following:

Name _____

Address _____

City _____ State _____ Zip _____

Gift card to read: _____